2017

YORKSHIRE
DERBYSHIRE
STAFFORDSHIRE

N

TOWNS WITH 2 OR MORE GROUNDS	
BIRKENHEAD	PARK
	ST. MARY'S SCHOOL
BOWDON	BOWDON
	BOWDON VALE
BROMBOROUGH	BROMBOROUGH
	MARITIME
	PORT SUNLIGHT
CHEADLE HULME	CHEADLE HULME
	LADYBRIDGE
CHESTER	BOUGHTON HALL
	COUNTY OFFICERS
	WESTMINSTER PARK
CONGLETON	CONGLETON
	MOSSLEY
HYDE	FLOWERYFIELD
	HYDE
	NEWTON
MACCLESFIELD	MACCLESFIELD
	THE KING'S SCHOOL
MALPAS	MALPAS
	CHERRY HILL
MARPLE	HAWK GREEN
	MARPLE
OXTON	OXTON
	OLD PARKONIANS
SALE	SALE
	TRAFFORD MV
STALYBRIDGE	ST PAUL'S
	STAYLEY
STOCKPORT	STOCKPORT
	HEATON MERSEY
	" " + VILLAGE
	GEORGIANS
	OFFERTON
	TRINITY
WALLASEY	WALLASEY
	PARKFIELD
WARRINGTON	WARRINGTON
	RYLANDS
WIDNES	WIDNES
	BIRCHFIELD PARK
WILMSLOW	LINDOW
	WAYFARERS
	WILMSLOW

* DENOTES ABOVE TOWNS ON ADJACENT MAP

VENUE	CLUB TITLE
BEBINGTON	MERSEY S. & C
CLATTERBRIDGE	WIRRAL
ELLESMERE PORT	THE GROVES
LITTLE BUDWORTH	OULTON PARK
MERE	EUROPA EXILES

** DENOTES ABOVE VENUES ON ADJACENT MAP

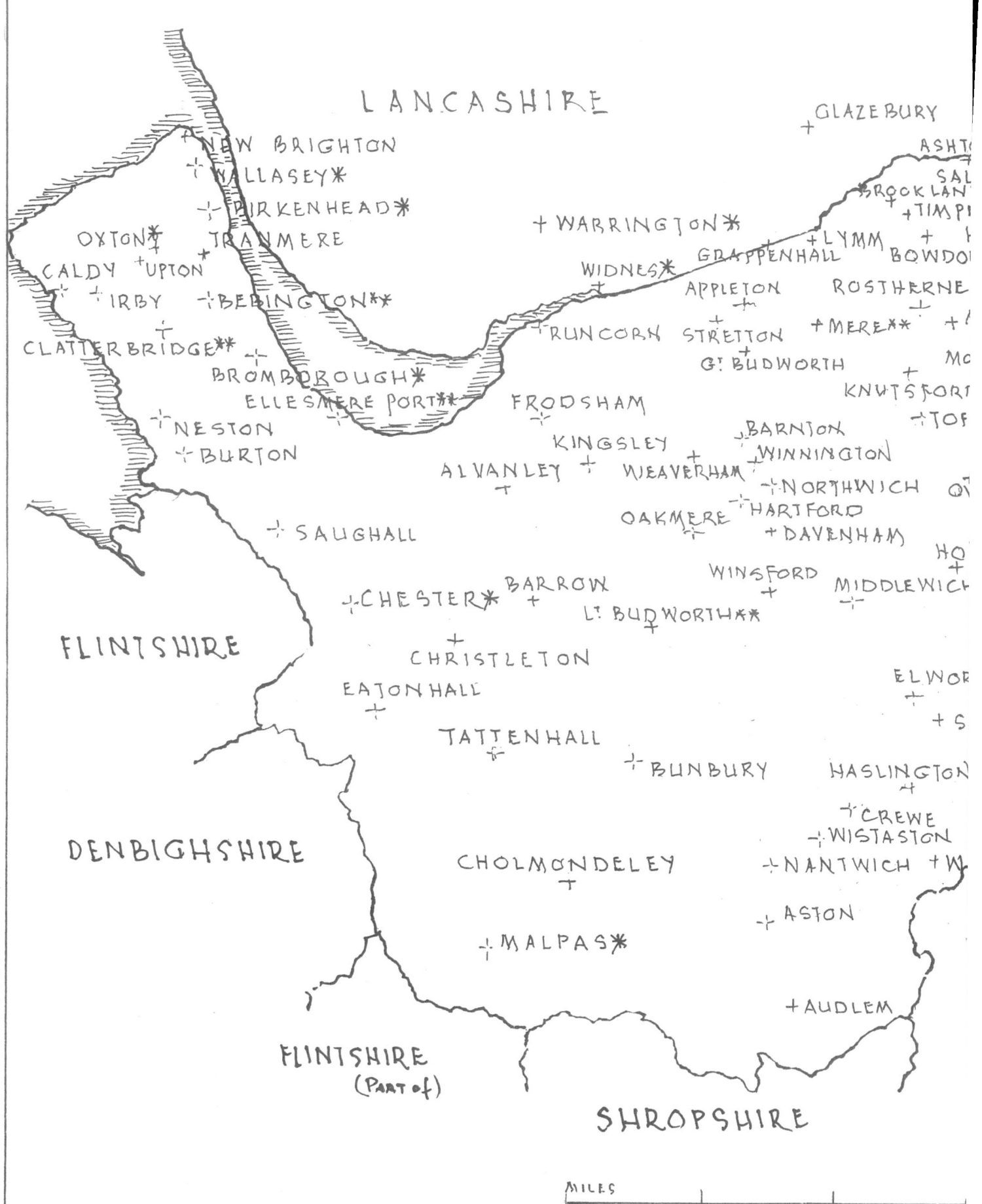

Pavilions in Splendour

THE CRICKET PAVILIONS AND GROUNDS OF CHESHIRE

Written and compiled by Geoff Wellsteed

To Matt,
Special thanks for all your help.
Regards,

MAX BOOKS

© Geoff Wellsteed 2018

First published in the UK in 2018 by Max Books

The right of Geoff Wellsteed to be identified as the Author of this work has been asserted by him in accordance with the Copyright, Designs and Patents Act 1988

All rights reserved. Apart from any use permitted under UK copyright law no part of this publication may be reproduced, stored in a retrieval system, or transmitted, in any form or by any means, without the prior written permission of the publisher, nor be otherwise circulated in any form of binding or cover other than that in which it is published and without a similar condition being imposed on the subsequent purchaser

A CIP catalogue record for this title is available from the British Library

ISBN: 978-0-9934872-4-8

Cover Design by Jane Mantel from Kreativ Ltd in Sale
Typeset and Design by Andrew Searle
Photography by Geoff Wellsteed
with additional material supplied by the clubs of Cheshire and Lancashire CCC

Printed and bound in India by Parksons Graphics Pvt.Ltd., Mumbai.

MAX BOOKS
Epworth House
34 Wellington Road
Nantwich, Cheshire CW5 7BX
Tel: 01270 625278
Email: maxcricket@btinternet.com
www.max-books.co.uk

Dedicated to all the Cheshire umpires, scorers, groundsmen and caterers who all play such a vital weekly role, but are rarely sufficiently appreciated.

The author officiating at Sir Paul Getty's ground at Wormsley in May 2017. On the left is Terry Wilkins. He has a Cheshire link, albeit a tenuous one, inasmuch as he umpired the National Village Cup Final at Lord's in 1997 when Caldy CC were victorious. Coincidentally, at the time the author was the Chairman of the successful Wirral side.

Contents

Forewords	
by Paul Allott, Neil Fairbrother & Bob Barber	7
Introduction	9
The County Boundary	10
Alderley Edge	11
Alsager	14
Alvanley	15
Appleton	16
Ashley	18
Ashton on Mersey	20
Aston	21
Audlem	22
Barnton	23
Barrow	25
Cheshire County Caps	26
Birchfield Park	27
Birkenhead Park	28
Birkenhead St Mary's	31
Birkenhead School	33
Bollington	35
Bowdon	37
Bowdon Vale	40
Bramhall	41
Bredbury St Marks	43
Early Cheshire references to cricket	44
Broadbottom	45
Bromborough	47
Brooklands	48
Finally a face – Reggie Wood	49
Bunbury	50
Burton	52
Caldy	53
Cheadle	55
Cheadle Hulme	57
Cheadle Hulme Ladybridge	59
Chelford	60
Cherry Hill	61
Chester Boughton Hall	62
Cheshire County Officers	65
Cheshire CCC Honorary officials 1908-2017	66
Cholmondeley	67
Christleton	69
Compstall	71
Congleton	73
Crewe Vagrants	74
Davenham	75
Didsbury	77
Disley	79
Dukinfield	80
Eaton Hall	82
Elworth	83
Europa Exiles	86
Flowery Field	87
Frodsham	89
Glazebury	90
Grappenhall	91
Great Budworth	94
(The) Groves	95
Hale Barns	96
Hartford	98
Haslington	100
Hawk Green	101
Hazel Grove	102
Heaton Mersey	103
Heaton Mersey Village	105
High Lane	106
Hollingworth	107
Holmes Chapel	108
Hyde	109
Irby	112
Kerridge	114
(The) King's School, Macclesfield	115
Kingsley	117
Knutsford	119
Langley	120
Lindow	122
Lymm Oughtrington Park	123
Macclesfield	125
Three Cestrians opening up for England	127
Malpas	128
David Bailey	129
Maritime	130
Marple	131
Mellor	133
Merseyside Sports & Cultural	134
Middlewich	135
Mobberley	137
Mossley	138
Mottram	139
Nantwich	141
Once a Dabber, then a Lion – Liam Livingstone	142
Neston	143
New Brighton	145
Newton	148
Northwich	150
Oakmere	153
Offerton	155
Old Parkonians	156
Oulton Park	157
Over Peover	159
From Alvanley CC to England	
– Sophie Ecclestone	160

Oxton	161	Cheshire CCC – the last four captains	206
Parkfield Liscard	163	Trafford MV	207
Port Sunlight	165	Tranmere Victoria	208
Pott Shrigley	167	Upton	209
Poynton	169	Urmston	211
Prestbury	171	Wallasey	213
Cheshire's Finest – Arthur Sutton	172	Warrington	215
Rode Park & Lawton	173	Weaverham	218
Romiley	174	Westminster Park	220
Rostherne	176	Weston	221
Runcorn	177	Widnes	222
Rylands	178	Cheshire CCC	
Sale	179	– Championship records 1909-2017	224
From Heswall to Hollywood		Wilmslow	226
– Ian Botham and Birtles Bowl	180	Wilmslow Wayfarers	227
Sandbach	181	Winnington Park	229
Saughall	183	Winsford	231
Stalybridge St Paul's	184	Wirral	232
Stayley	186	Wistaston	233
Stockport	188	Woodford	234
Stockport Georgians	190	Woodley	235
Stockport Trinity	193	Cheshire Pyramid	237
Stretton	195	14 England cricketers born in Cheshire	238
Styal	196	Grateful thanks	239
Tattenhall	198	Bibliography	240
Timperley	200	List of subscribers	242
Tintwistle	202	Glorious Bygone Days	245
Toft	204		

The Oulton Park flypast in 2016
(permission of Janet Emmett)

Forewords

AS A BOY I regarded the Pavilion as a perfunctory item; as purely functional, as a place to get changed and prepare for the critical events ahead such as taking wickets, scoring the odd run or two and generally looking forward to the thrills of the game.

I gave little thought to their architecture, appearance, facilities or social role, they were nothing more than a means to an end, sometimes a sanctuary, a nuisance occasionally, when those splinters in your socks formed an injury hazard before you even got onto the pitch. Pavilions were an irrelevance to me in my pursuit of glory.

They were a decent place to watch from, a bench in front of the dressing room gives a sense of status to an aspiring fifteen year-old, but that was about it as far as I was concerned.

It was only as I got a little older that I began to realise their relevance and importance, not only to me as a player but to the ground as a whole, the scene setting, the framing of the picture and the focus they demanded that all went towards creating atmosphere, character and the spirit of the venue.

Perhaps this was no better illustrated for me than when I first played in front of that magnificent Victorian facade of the pavilion at Old Trafford, still thankfully preserved despite the modernisation around it.

The domination of the ground by the grand pavilion, almost acts as a distraction to the inexperienced performer, especially at the great grounds of the world.

It is the pavilion that defines Lord's, the Sydney Cricket Ground, Trent Bridge, and the Oval, over and above the modern multi-sport stadia that are beginning to litter the cricketing canvas. There is something eminently soulless about a cricket ground without the definition of a pavilion, where players emerge from the bowels of some multi-tiered stand.

Nowhere is this better illustrated perhaps than in India, where the concrete bowl now dominates. Pre-fabricated circles bereft of character seem to spring up at will and all the while I think back to my first tour of the sub-continent and my initial practice in Mumbai. There was something incredibly beguiling about the Brabourne Stadium, its pavilion encompassing everything and more that an aspiring cricketer could need, spacious changing rooms, with attendants bearing towels and water, a marble terrace in the shade for viewing and relaxing and a swimming pool and squash courts in case you got out early, but above all it is the overwhelming presence of the building that sticks in the mind.

But let's begin this trip around the cricket clubs of Cheshire with a nod to the past and my earliest memories of club cricket, the pavilion at Ashley (it was more a collection of raw timber huts, with the smell of a paraffin stove and, curiously, grass cuttings), and the glorious Victorian facade at Bowdon. They could hardly have been more contrasting; one totally rustic and purely functional, the other a testament to architectural glory. They both did their jobs in their own way and should be recognised and lauded for such but there can be few more imposing cricket club pavilions in the country, let alone the county, than that at South Downs Road. It is my favourite still.

Paul Allott
(Bowdon, Cheshire, Lancashire & England)

THE COUNTY of Cheshire is blessed with some of the most beautiful and picturesque cricket grounds in the country. I may, of course, be slightly biased, but sitting on top of the list in my eyes is the ground at Broad Lane, the home of Grappenhall CC.

From the moment I joined the club as a junior at the age of 11, it has always been a very special place to me. Maybe this is because it has always been a batsman-friendly wicket or, perhaps, for the 40-odd intervening years, the place has always been kept in the rudest of condition, both on and off the field. The views from the pavilion towards the bottom end of the ground are stunning on a nice day and even when the rain is coming you can see it from miles away!

Although the club has now hosted Minor County games it has managed to keep its wonderful charm - an amazing village club.

My selection could be a lengthy one if I listed all my favourite Cheshire grounds, but looking from South Downs Road into the facilities at Bowdon CC takes some beating, as does the view from the pavilion at Alderley Edge. 'The Edge' is a splendid backdrop.

All the cricketers of Cheshire are blessed with an array of superb cricket grounds and all are to be greatly enjoyed.

Neil Fairbrother
(Grappenhall, Lancashire & England)

Neil's County and England caps and shirts in the Grappenhall clubhouse

SADLY MY schoolboy memories of cricket matches have largely receded leaving me with, no doubt, only rather selective remnants. However, I certainly played schoolboy games, kindly organised by two cricket-loving gentlemen, a Mr Frank Callaghan and a Mr 'oh dear' on Wirral grounds, perhaps Birkenhead Park, even before I first played at the age of 14 for Chester Boughton Hall, or as it was then, just Boughton Hall. The latter played in the Liverpool Competition so our experience of Cheshire grounds was confined to those on the Wirral - Neston, New Brighton, Oxton, Wallasey and Birkenhead Park. My experience of the grounds in the rest of the county is inevitably limited, so although I cannot propose the most beautiful ground or the best cricketing wickets I can disclose that records show my first match for Cheshire was in 1952 when I was just 16 years old. It was against Northumberland at Neston CC. I batted only once and ended up with a rather modest score of 5 alongside my name. Less than a month later I played my second county match, this time against Staffordshire at Macclesfield. I did no better, scoring 0 and 8. Of course, I was still a schoolboy at the time and between those two matches I played at Lord's for the Public Schools against the Combined Services. The opposition included Colin Ingleby-Mackenzie, Micky Stewart, Freddie Titmus, Keith Andrew and Jim Parks. I was bowled by the latter, who, of course, later became the England stumper.

130 plus grounds, my goodness. Have I still got time to visit them all? Good luck with this splendidly researched book.

Bob Barber
(Boughton Hall, Cheshire, Lancashire, Warwickshire & England)

Introduction

LIKE EVERYTHING else in life cricket is changing.

The big burly blacksmith is no longer a regular member of his village team, the smell of linseed oil has long disappeared and a bowl of curry or pasta is now as popular as a traditional cricket tea sandwich, but cricket remains an essential part of quintessential England.

Pavilions of yonder years with primitive facilities have made way for modern structures with top of the range gadgetry. Elaborate two-tier clubhouses are now commonplace. In Cheshire we have a wide and splendid array of pavilions. This book purports to be a comprehensive record of Cheshire clubs *active* in 2017, plus a few worthies, along with a photograph of their current pavilion, some historical notes, club records, pen pictures, anecdotes and reminiscences.

Ask a representative group of cricketing enthusiasts to nominate the three most successful, best-known and influential counties and there is a very good chance that the majority would nominate Lancashire, Surrey and Yorkshire (in cowardly alphabetical order!). Extend the list to twelve and a further nine first-class counties would emerge. A further extension to twenty-four might see Cheshire appear in the bottom quartile, but if the criteria were changed to base the judgement purely on the beauty of its club grounds surely Cheshire would justify a much higher rating?

If a picturesque setting and a quaint pavilion are established as the determining factors, Cheshire has a host of both and these sporting theatres deserve to be collectively recorded for posterity and joyously shared with the wider cricketing world. Heritage is important to cricketing folk and Cestrians can be justifiably proud of their monuments to the summer game.

There is bound to be some contention as to what constitutes the Cheshire county border, but a liberal interpretation has been used based on pre-1974 boundaries and, primarily, the inclusion of all the clubs participating in the 2017 'Cheshire pyramid' (and therefore the inclusion of Lancashire-based Urmston and Didsbury) plus clubs competing in neighbouring leagues. Clubs from the Liverpool Competition, the Derbyshire & Cheshire League, the North Staffordshire & South Cheshire League as well as the Greater Manchester League and the Pennine League all feature. Two pre-eminent educational institutes with a strong cricketing pedigree have been selected, as has Eaton Hall on the Duke of Westminster's estate. And are you aware of Cherry Hill?

'Lost' grounds and disbanded clubs get no more than a very occasional passing mention. Regrettably, over the last century many clubs have folded and by their sheer volume the inclusion of a worthwhile list is impractical.

Having established the two fundamentals of mapping and exclusions I hope you will enjoy meandering around the cricketing landmarks of Cheshire.

Over!

Geoff Wellsteed
Caldy, Wirral
2018

The Cheshire county boundary

Does the boundary fence at the bottom of your garden belong to you or your neighbour? Is Todmorden in Yorkshire or Lancashire or both! Do you still regard London as being in Middlesex? For centuries international borders have been argued over, indeed a good number of issues have led to eventual conflict. County boundaries also lead to confusion, the more so since the 1974 re-organisation and the creation of Metropolitan boroughs. It is hardly surprising therefore that the Cheshire boundary shimmers depending upon your interpretation or preference. Various experts have persuasively argued their case to me but each has provided a rather different outcome.

For the purposes of this particular project I decided to avoid protracted intellectual debate or reasoning and opted for a very straightforward assessment. My solution has been to include any cricket club in what is now indisputably Cheshire, what was Cheshire (at some point) and, maybe, some contentious marginals! This blissfully simple solution allows me to maximise the number of entries and, unashamedly, indulge some personal preferences and whims.

Of course, I recognise that such a liberal interpretation will offend some, but as the author I have also taken the liberty to appoint myself as the umpire and the man in the white coat is never wrong. His decision is final, incontrovertible and binding - look in the book!!

Alderley Edge

Moss Lane, Alderley Edge, SK9 7HN

IN 1882 GEORGE Ormerod, in his book the *History of Cheshire,* described Alderley Edge as 'an abrupt and elevated ridge which bears the appearance of having been detached by some great convulsion of nature. The entire mass presents a striking object to the surrounding district, over which it commands a most extensive prospect'.

At the foot of a sandstone outcrop is the ground, which was originally held on lease from the De Trafford Estate which owned and developed most of Alderley Edge. In 1960 the club did, however, manage to acquire the freehold (7.5 acres) for the princely sum of £3500. The splendid pavilion dates from 1900 and despite an extension in the 1970s, and the subsequent addition of four squash courts, the building has maintained its Victorian character.

Sport has been played on the field at Moss Lane since 1870. Originally there were two cricket pitches and at least two croquet lawns. Lawn tennis followed (now 14 courts) and then hockey and squash. With the exception of croquet all the sports sections are thriving, although all the hockey matches are now played off-site.

Folklore has it that in the very early days players were chauffeur-driven to the ground. Cars were parked on Mottram Road and trolleys used to take the players' kit to the pavilion. The opposition changed in a hut located to the east of the pavilion. As now, the scorers enjoyed a unique view of the match through a hatch above the front door. Matches finished promptly so that the chauffeurs could take the players home in good time for them to dress for dinner.

Members still here to tell the tale confirm that in the years after WW2 the club employed a steward, and a groundsman providing accommodation for them and their families in properties owned by the club on Moss Lane. The groundsman, Pickstock, maintained all the tennis courts - all grass in those days - as well as the cricket table. The grass nets complete with poles and guy ropes were laid out in the current car park. The steward, George Wood, always dressed in a white jacket and black tie and called everyone 'Sir' (very few women in the clubhouse in those days) and pulled a good half (no pints!) of Robinson's Mild. Mrs Pickstock, helped by Mrs Wood, prepared the teas – egg & cress and speciality banana & jam sandwiches along with a selection of cakes and chocolate biscuits.

In the early days membership was restricted to the business and professional classes, and they played similar teams like Bowdon, Hale and Didsbury, which reflected the extreme polarisation of Victorian society at the time. Indeed, any locals wishing to watch could only look through the slats of a fence on Mottram Road, but were then graciously allowed up to an old oak tree. However, for those who were allowed in, the club was the main centre of social activity in the village.

After WW2 all day matches were played against visiting 'Gentlemen' teams. The team was 'self-selected'. The club umpire at that time, Tomlinson, was very popular and seemed to be around forever. He was a teacher and coach at Ryleys, the local preparatory school. Later a 2nd XI was added, but it was essentially a completely different set of players from the 1st XI with no movement up or down.

The club has seen many fine cricketers and a good number have played first-class and minor county cricket. Jim McConnon played two Test matches in 1954 and Noel Darrah was a post war big-hitting all-rounder, but David Sharp particularly recalled Roger Pearman in the 1970s, as good a batsman and captain as any in the game, and Patrick Kelly – the quintessential AECC member of his day.

> Patrick Arthur Charles Kelly died in June 2002 aged 73. 'PACK', an MCC member, had been a leading light at Alderley Edge since 1958, having two spells as captain from 1961-63 and 1970-73, followed by two terms as chairman from 1976-79 and 1982-87. He continued his involvement with the club as the scorer and he also wrote colourful match reports for the local press. Earlier he had played some cricket for Middlesex 2nds and Hornsey and for London Irish at rugby. Moving north, he played 124 times for Cheshire between 1958 and 1977, scoring 3218 runs. He was a member of the team that won the championship in 1969. He served as the Cheshire County Club President from 1986-88 and was a Committee member for many years. His other sporting love was hockey. He represented Essex, then later Bowdon and Cheshire and the North of England. In 1994 he oversaw the formation of the Alderley Edge women's hockey section, becoming its founder chairman. His ashes were scattered on the Alderley Edge ground at a moving ceremony during Cheshire's match against Cornwall in July 2002.

In 1975 the club joined eleven others as founder members of the Cheshire County League and won the top division in the inaugural season. Since then with the help of overseas players and a wealth of home-grown talent the club has maintained its status as a leading club in Cheshire, winning the top division again in 1983, (jointly with old rivals Bowdon) and more recently in 2008 and 2016. The development of juniors is paramount and the club has been rewarded with significant success at all age levels.

The club has hosted many high profile matches. Cheshire CCC play matches here and in particular a Cheltenham & Gloucester Trophy match against Hampshire in 2004 stands out. The south-coast side fielded seven international cricketers (including two Australian captains) - Warne, Clarke,

Mascarenhas, Pothas, Tremlett, Udal, and Mullally. A bat signed by all players is mounted in the pavilion. Although Cheshire lost, Jason Whittaker received the Man of the Match Award. The MCC plays regional matches here and the club regularly host MCC dinners.

Since the 1970s, overseen by a series of dedicated and experienced committee members, the club has continued to prosper on and off the field. Professional house and ground staff provide excellent catering and sporting facilities for all members and visitors. Open daily, the clubhouse is used for a wide range of social activities for members and the community.

I am greatly indebted to David Sharp for all the information he has provided about the club of which he has been a member since 1964. David is, of course, Secretary to the Cheshire Cricket Board and the current President of the Cheshire County Cricket Club. Is there any wonder that the Alderley Edge ambience still retains a certain magic for him even after a fifty year association?

> Mike Roff, the most senior AECC member, recalled that in the 1960s Dudley Bailey took two hat-tricks during the same innings. Beat that! Surely as rare as a golfer getting two holes in one in the same round?

Shane Warne addresses the crowd at the conclusion of the match. On Warne's left shoulder is Robin Fisher of Chester Boughton Hall. Warne scored 1 batting at '3' and Fisher 22 coming in at '10'. Both were wicketless.

SURREY V LANCASHIRE, County Championship match at The Oval, 23-26 August 2016

Lancashire took a squad of 13 to the Oval. FIVE of that party had played in the Cheshire Premier League in 2016

FOUR played against Surrey –
Nathan Buck (Cheadle)
Jordan Clark (Alderley Edge)
Rob Jones (Toft)...............on debut
Liam Livingstone (Nantwich)
Danny Lamb (Bramhall) was 13th man (drinks waiter).

Other CCCL links -
Glen Chappell (Bowdon) = Coach
Steve O'Shaughnessy (ex-Alderley Edge) was one of the umpires.

Alsager

Fairview Avenue, Alsager ST7 2NW

THERE ARE 1874 papers which record a match played between Alsager and Kidsgrove, but it was George Skene, an Old Etonian and a local rector, who is credited with its proper establishment in 1882.

1904 - The club moved to Parsonage Field and by now were playing in the North Staffordshire Combination League.

WW1 - Cricket was halted at the start of the war and not re-established until 1930.

1950s - The club was nicely settled at Parsonage Field with a thriving membership and with two teams playing at weekends, but in 1953 the council purchased the land from the church and asked the club to find a new home. Donations were sought from members and two fields were purchased incorporating an orchard, an open ditch and a number of very large trees. The trees had to be removed with explosives and the wet land was drained at great expense.

1956 - The first match was played at Fairview Avenue and as part of the Cheshire Conference. The new pavilion was opened in 1957.

1972 - Bert Flack, the Lancashire groundsman, was engaged to formulate a plan to improve the square which was generally recognised as 'challenging' with scores above 150 relatively uncommon.

1990s - The Cheshire League championship was secured in 1992 under the captaincy of Eddie Gilhooley with huge input from the influential Mike Tudor and ex-Stoke City goalkeeper Ken South. They joined the expanded Cheshire County League in 1993 and were 1st XI Cup winners in both 1995 and 1997.

2008 - The club decided to join the North Staffs & South Cheshire League and entered its Third Division. Within four years they were in Division 1.

2013 - An Olympic legacy grant was received which enabled major refurbishment. The pavilion is now very well appointed.

When you next visit a ground try plonking yourself on a bench alongside a mature-looking citizen. I did just that at Alsager and had a fascinating chat with Peter Hancock, who played for the club in the 1960s. His father, Harry (b 1908, d 1987) played alongside Jack Ikin for Staffordshire. When Jack went on to play for England, Harry continued to represent his minor county (1935-53). Peter proudly recalled his Dad had once taken seven wickets for no runs against Knypersley. Just behind our seat was a plaque on the pavilion wall which informed that Sergeant JF McNamara, aged 21, was killed in 1942 when his Spitfire crashed near 'this spot'. Apparently the wing of the plane clipped the chimney of the local school in a training accident. The scoreboard, dedicated to Matthew Nixon (1988-2010), revealed another disaster. He was a young Alsager player who worked as a gas fitter and was fatally overcome by fumes. RIP 'Nico'.

Alvanley

Frodsham Road, Alvanley, Frodsham WA6 9DB

ALVANLEY CC WERE reaping the advantages of recycling long before local councils persuaded householders it was a trendy and fashionable thing to do. In 1956 they had the wisdom to replace the original pavilion with a structure which had previously served as the village hall at Cuddington, and in the early 1980s they acquired a Shropshire-located army building. Members looked on in trepidation as 'Building 69' arrived on the back of a very large flat-bed lorry. Its construction looked like a very daunting task, but after sterling and arduous work by dedicated club members over a period of years, it was ready in time for the centenary celebrations in 1984. It is still in place to this day, albeit extensively refurbished.

At one time the ground was so small that a boundary hit only counted as two runs and there were no six hits, but in 1961 more land was acquired which literally doubled its size.

Although there is a record of a match between a team from Alvanley and one from Frodsham played in 1874, it is generally accepted the club was not established until 1884. An early match recorded in the archives of the *Chester Chronicle* was on 20 June 1885 when a game was played against Norley Hall. The opposition batted twice but could not reach the single Alvanley innings score of 49.

The club originally played on a field behind Alvanley church but moved to the present ground in 1900. One of the original items of equipment transferred to the new ground was a stone pitch roller made from a cheese press. This roller, although no longer in use, is still at the club. The horse was fitted with specially made leather shoes so that it could pull the roller without damaging the pitch!

The club's centenary in 1984 was a real opportunity to celebrate the 'new' pavilion and a nine day programme of fixtures was arranged. The opposition was provided by Hale Barns, Tattenhall, Northern Nomads, Pakistan International XI, Cheshire League XI, The Spasmodics, a Local XI, Christleton and Cavaliers. On the Saturday evening the entertainment was provided by the Blue Magnolia jazz band.

> **Incredibly, Fred Noden served the Club as Secretary for 51 years. When he gave up the position in 2001 he became President, a position he held when he tragically died in a farming accident in 2006, aged 81. He joined Alvanley in 1946 and was absolutely dedicated to the club as a player, a groundsman, a coach and an administrator. His services to the club were recognised by an OSCA (Outstanding Services to Cricket Award) presentation at Lord's.**

Appleton

Lyons Lane, Appleton, Warrington WA4 5JG

THE FIRST meeting of Appleton CC took place on 17 November 1976, so the club have yet to doff its cap and raise its bat to acknowledge 50 not out years, but its relative juniority disguises the fact that cricket has been played at Lyons Lane for over a hundred years.

In his splendid little book *The History of the Lyons Lane Cricket Ground*, Graham Whibley quotes the late Henry Collin, who was a one-time Stockton Heath player, as saying the ground was first used by that club in 1908. At the time, the Lyons family, entrepreneurs and landowners, were in residence at Appleton Hall (demolished in the 1960s) and described in the *Cheshire Gazetteer* of 1860 as 'a beautiful modern mansion, stuccoed, surrounded by fine undulating parkland interspersed with shrubberies and plantations.'

> By 1957 the maintenance of the ground had become an issue. The Radiation company were prepared to pay rent and rates but not for the groundsman. The matter was resolved by a fund-raising initiative which involved raffling '20 cigs' at each home match with 60% of the takings going to the groundsman!

There is no evidence that Stockton Heath CC existed after 1939 and during WW2 personnel from the local US military hospital played baseball at the ground, but by the early 1950s it is clear that the Radiation group of companies were playing at Lyons Lane as recorded at an inaugural meeting held on 13 November 1952 '...to be known as Radiation (Warrington) Cricket Section with ground and headquarters at Lyons Lane'.

The eventual emergence of Appleton CC in 1976 is an interesting one and in reality arose from a merger of Radiation CC, a works team who only played friendly matches, and Winwick CC. The original players of the latter club, who played their home fixtures at Winwick hospital, were staff from

The old pavilion

The new pavilion

Winwick and Newchurch hospitals. That particular player source dried up over the years and the membership was far more widely based when they were accepted to play league cricket in the Cheshire Cricket Association from 1976. That arrangement lasted just one year as at the end of that first season Winwick Hospital management wrote to the club advising them that a new hospital team was to be formed and that they had been accepted into the West Lancs League. An urgent dialogue with Radiation CC followed and, despite reservations from some Radiation members who did not wish to play league cricket, an amalgamation proposal was unanimously agreed, but the new club would be known as Appleton CC.

The new club took over the tenancy of the Lyons Lane ground from Warrington New Town Development Corporation, but by 1996 the new club was able to purchase the ground with assistance from the National Lottery Grant Scheme. A new pavilion was also proudly opened in 2006.

The club currently field four Saturday teams, a Sunday social side, a midweek team, a 1st XI women's team and a thriving mixed junior section.

If you plan to visit picturesque Appleton CC don't over-shoot the entrance! It's very neatly tucked between the houses numbered 8 and 10.

APPLETON ACHIEVEMENTS

1981 PJ Dean recorded the first club hat-trick.
1984 Gordon Woods scored 160 not out v Old Wirralians
1989 Mike Arnold recorded 9-41 v Barrow
2010 Emma Barlow led the ladies to the triple crown – Div 1 champs, KO Cup and T20 winners. The team won the Warrington Sports Personality 'Team of the year' and Sue Barlow collected the 'Unsung hero' award.

Ashley

The Railway Field, Ashley Road, Ashley WA14 3QE

1880 - MR NORBURY reported that his field would not be available and as an alternative the Railway Field - the present ground - was eventually rented from a Mr Erlam. Initially an annual ground rent of £6 with the option of cattle grazing was suggested, but the cricketers clearly did not relish scraping up cow-pats before a match and offered £8 for exclusive use!

1892 - Eleven Gentlemen of Ashley took on eleven ladies in a two innings match. The gentlemen batted with broomsticks and were further restricted by fielding and bowling left handed. Gentlemen 35 and 38. Ladies 19 and 18.

1896 - Robert Hall, a leading player and founder member, headed the batting averages with 11.2 from 19 innings. Mr Barwell described the pitch as 'pretty fiery'.

In Elliot Smith the vice-captain
we have a man of strength,
He sends balls with lightning speed
and keeps a decent length;
Whilst little Freddie Davenport,
who stands behind the stumps,
Finds spite of all his pads and gloves
he gets some ugly bumps.

1902 - The club set in motion possibly the most ambitious fundraising activity in its entire history. The concert was deemed to be a huge success, but it clearly required significant effort from the members as 2500 handbills were delivered to houses in Altrincham and Hale. Additionally many more were distributed in the streets, posters were placed on ten railway stations and fifty bills placed in shop windows.

The efforts of Robert Hall tower above all the others in the early years. He had an insatiable love of the game and served on the Committee for many years, ten of those as Secretary. A heavy scoring and aggressive batsman, he was noted for the correctness of his style. He captained the 1st Xl for eight years and the 2nd Xl for three years towards the end of his playing career. A man of equable temperament, he shaped the education of many Ashley villagers who spoke of him with great respect. A public-spirited man, he devoted himself to numerous good works in the village and was the local Assistant Overseer of the Poor. He died in 1934.

1921 - Red (blue?) letter day. Major Hamilton, the Conservative MP for Altrincham, consented to be a Vice-President and actually paid a subscription!

1929 - The first mention of a petrol mower, evidence that the horse had been pensioned off or had dropped down dead?

1949-52 - The provision of piped water and the purchase of a pavilion from Garswood Tennis Club large enough to accommodate two teams to sit down for tea.

1952 - John Allott, for many years a member of the club and its Secretary between 1943 and 1956, took six wickets for no runs against Prestbury. The honours board displayed in the pavilion also shows he had match figures of 8-23 against Mobberley in 1956. His son is the former Lancashire and England bowler Paul Allott, who played here for

> **KM Dunsmuir** - to those who did not know him well he seemed aloof and laconic and he gave short shrift to those he didn't think took the game seriously enough. When dismissed by what was probably a debatable decision, he'd say nothing but on at least one occasion he made an erasure in the scorebook against his name and substituted 'umpired out' accompanied by the initials KMD!

JN Allott (right)

one season as a junior before moving on to Bowdon.

1957 - Ashley become founder members of the Cheshire Cricket Club Conference. Its main purpose was not to encourage competitive league cricket but to form an association of clubs who wished to preserve traditional friendly cricket.

1962 - Calor gas lighting was installed in both the main pavilion and tearoom.

1963 - The 75th anniversary year was celebrated with a dinner in April at the Unicorn Hotel in Altrincham. The principal guest speaker was Lancashire and England cricketer, Cyril Washbrook. In June, a President's match was held. Included in that side was David Millner of Derbyshire CCC who scored a century. The happy day was enlivened by the Knutsford Silver Prize Band.

1969 - The death occurred of EA Coupes, a Vice President, who for many years had been the 1st XI umpire. He bequeathed £2000 to the club. His umpiring abilities were often called into question, particularly as he grew older, and in the end, with much reluctance, he was asked to stand aside. Typical of him, he accepted the judgement in a very dignified way, merely making some remark about his eyesight not being altogether what it was. He walked to the ground all the way from his home in Sale and back again when in his seventies and did the same in the opposite direction when Lancashire were playing at Old Trafford.

1970-78 - League cricket was played as a member of the Cheshire Cricket Association and from 1978 in the Cheshire Cricket League. In 1975 electric lighting was provided as well as a bar.

1986 - At an Extraordinary Meeting it was resolved to merge with Old Altrinchamians CC and for the club to be known as Ashley CC (incorporating Old Altrinchamians). The Old Boys had found it difficult to carry on because of the high rent they were paying for the use of the Air Force ground on Clay Lane, Hale.

For the cricket enthusiast who is also a plane and train spotter a visit to Ashley CC is a 'must do'. Why not start your adventure with a pub lunch at 'The Greyhound' in the heart of the village?

Ashton on Mersey

The Beets, Little Ees Lane, Sale M33 5GT

ASHTON ON MERSEY Cricket and Tennis Club was founded in 1897. Early matches were played on a ground in Atkinson Road, Sale, which was the sports ground of Lancashire Dynamo. In 1911 the club relocated to a site at Carrington Moss before moving again in 1919 to its present facility at Little Ees Lane. Six years later in 1925 the land was bought for £500.

1926 - Two army huts were brought in as changing rooms and these were the beginnings of the first pavilion. For 12 years the club operated with water brought up from a nearby well. Power services were installed in 1938.

1946 - Joined the Manchester Association Cricket League.

1947-50s - A magazine article reports the Golden Jubilee of the club was celebrated with a match in Victorian costume and at much the same time, there were lawn mower races around the boundary. The Club also hosted benefit matches for Cyril Washbrook (1948) and Frank Worrell in the fifties. At the time the former West Indian captain was studying at Manchester University (BA in 1959).

1958-60 - The pavilion just about survived a freak whirlwind in 1958, although part of the roof ended up on the golf course more than 50 yards away. The club clock was found in a bunker! Perhaps the unfortunate incident had a motivating effect as the prestigious Stockton Trophy was won in 1959. Within another year the building was completely destroyed by fire.

1971 - Although the car was popular by this time, the Manchester Association handbook still included bus directions; 63 from Piccadilly or 64 from Deansgate to Glebelands Road or 222/223 from Piccadilly to Ashton Park.

1985 - A second wooden pavilion was burnt to the ground just six weeks prior to the start of the season. This prompted the building of the present brick pavilion which left the club with a large debt.

1990s - In 1995 Bill Lowes led the 2nd Xl to the Manchester Association title (Edward Barton Trophy) while 1st Xl titles followed in 1996 (Stockton Trophy) and 1997 (President's Trophy). In 1999 AOM left the Manchester Association to join the Cheshire Pyramid.

2000s - After a period of instability Mark Timms led AOM to the Cheshire League Division 2 Championship in 2006 and in 2009 they won the top division with a team mostly made up of players who had come up through the junior ranks.

Roll-on covers were introduced for the first time in 2005 and a brand new purpose-built score-box followed in 2007. By 2009 a three-lane net facility had been provided. That year also saw the installation of a Solar Thermal and Solar Photo Voltaic system, a major development towards the club energy plan.

> Two Ashton on Mersey players have worn the Cheshire shirt. Ernest Nicholls (b 1925) played 22 matches between 1952-57. Alan Barratt (b 1936, d 2010) played one match in 1956 against Yorkshire 2nds. The Tykes declared on 287 for 1 when Barratt dismissed Frank Lowson for 118. Brian Bolus remained undefeated with 160. Barratt took 1-72 off 21.2 overs and scored 10 batting at 10. Additionally, the Manchester Association Centenary (1892-1992) book reports that Graham Atkinson, formerly of Somerset (1954-66) and Lancashire (1967-69), played here after his first-class career finished.

Aston

Sheppenhall Lane, Aston, Nantwich CW5 8DE

ASTON CC MOVED to their current location in 1953. At that time residential properties only occupied one side of the ground, now there are houses on three and developers would relish the opportunity to build more. Of course there are associated health and safety issues resulting from hefty-hitting batters. The club lives with that ongoing building threat. The club purchased the field for £500. Local farmer, Raymond Sheen of Woodcott Hill Farm, a lifelong supporter of the club, provided a loan to be repaid whenever funds allowed. An old black and white wooden cricket pavilion was brought from Four Lane End, their previous home, and erected at the new ground but there was no running water or electricity. Water was carried in a milk churn. A new pavilion was built by members in 1970. Cyril Chesters, chairman (1967-1981) and president (1982-2001) was at the forefront of that initiative. His father had played against AN 'Monkey' Hornby (b 1847, d 1925), the famous Lancashire and England captain who is buried at St Mary's Church, Acton, Nantwich.

Aston & District Cricket Club was actually formed soon after the Great War by merging the playing resources of three local teams – Combermere, Broomhall and Wrenbury - who had played in their own villages from the late 1800s until the outbreak of WW1.

An early photograph of the Combermere team in 1894 has survived. Tom Young, a farmer, was the captain and two of his brothers were also in the team, as was William James George who was the landlord of the Bhurtpore Inn. The umpire was the local shoemaker, Samuel Edgeley. A fixture card for 1895 included matches against Wistaston, Cholmondeley and Audlem. A total of 14 matches were played, of which nine were won, two drawn, two lost and one tied.

The only record of Broomhall Cricket Club is a photograph taken in 1908 which contains several players who also featured on the Combermere photograph. Broomhall played in a field at Oak Farm, opposite Broomhall School (Sound School) and later in a field close to Pritch Farm. Wrenbury played on parkland at Wrenbury Hall.

For a good number of years Aston regularly entered the Whitchurch Knock-out Cup. That trophy was lifted in 1955 when local footballing favourite Johnny King scored 83 not out to ensure a 14-run victory against Prees. Wrenbury-born King (b 1932) played most of his 543 Football League appearances for Stoke City and Crewe Alexandra, scoring 172 goals.

In later years league cricket became a reality. In 2008 Aston were promoted alongside Sandbach, who had pipped the villagers by one point, from the Cheshire Alliance Division 1. More success followed in 2009 when they were runners-up to Lindow in Division 3 of the Cheshire League. Elevated to Division 2 they maintained that level, their highest-ever league status, until 2013, since when they have competed in Division 3.

Audlem

Gorse Croft Farm, Bunsley Bank, Audlem CW3 0HS

I DIDN'T ACTUALLY see a badger when I visited Cheshire's most southerly ground, but that adopted nickname is highly appropriate given the delightful rural setting. On my arrival I overshot the entrance and ended-up in the farmyard, and when I found my way into the ground I watched the match with one other spectator and fifty plus inquisitive cows. As I got out of the car I was reminded of a story Roy Ramsbottom (see Oulton Park) used to tell about the Audlem 'Test' - not so much a match but more of an orienteering exercise! Talking of tales it is said that a good number of decades ago when Audlem crossed the county border into Shropshire to play Market Drayton they were dismissed for 20, but the visitors had the Shuker brothers, who were blacksmiths by trade and red-hot fast bowlers. Suffice to say Market Drayton were all out for 12, but anxious for revenge they wanted to play a second innings. Audlem refused and went home. The hosts were not happy, especially when they realised the victors had not paid for their tea!

The club cap badge reveals Audlem CC was established in 1965, but there is a conflicting sign on the side of the pavilion, 'founded 1878'. Both are misleading as there is evidence to suggest the club played at Parks Farm, Monks Lane in the 1850s. However, by 1880 they had moved to Woore Road, Mount Pleasant until WW2 when the club disbanded. A new start was eventually made at Bunsley Bank.

In 2017 Callum Mcilveen might lay claim to be star player? He aggregated the most league runs (304) and clocked up more wickets than anybody else (52). Audlem finished third in Division 4 of the Cheshire League.

Barnton

Broomsedge, Townfield Lane, Barnton CW8 4QL

NOTHING IN CRICKET is more coveted than a century and Barnton clocked up that particular milestone in 1980 when they marked the occasion with a July Cricket Week. The highlight was a centenary match against a side badged as a combined XL & All Star XI. The most prominent names in the celebratory side were Mike Bissex (Gloucestershire, played 212 first-class matches, 1961-72, and Cheshire 1977-8), David Millner (Derbyshire, played 31 first-class matches, 1960-63), Ramesh Sethi (played one first-class match for East Africa in 1975), Richard Cragg (see Bramhall entry) and Brian Jackson (Derbyshire, played 148 first-class matches, 1963-68 and Cheshire 1956-70). The match was played at Broomsedge, which has been HQ since 1957.

1862 - There is documented evidence of a game being played in the village from this early date and the local newspaper of Wednesday, 6 August, as well as recording that 'the Houses of Parliament will reassemble at noon tomorrow for the purpose of being prorogued' also reports on a match between Frodsham and Barnton & Anderton. 'The return match was played on the ground of AH Smith-Barry Esq., of Marlbury Hall and finished in favour of the former. Frodsham scored 80 and Barnton & Anderton 18 and 15'.

1880 - It was 18 years later when the club was properly established, its origins being attributed to the Reverend Samuel Lancaster Laidman who at the time was Vicar of Christ Church, Barnton. His venture was actively supported and encouraged by the aforementioned local squire. The team was largely drawn from the church congregation.

1885 - Over the decades a number of sites in the village have played host to the cricketers. In 1885 they played at 'Clover Croft', but by 1901 home matches were played at the 'Watercress Beds'.

1904 - The first pavilion was acquired, a second-hand pigeon cote. The facilities were described as basic!

1912-13 - A new pavilion was urgently required and the Committee set about raising funds. Draws were organised, loans accepted and house to house appeals were made. Eventually, with a substantial gift from the directors of Brunner Mond & Company, a splendid new pavilion with a verandah was opened at a cost of £75. The old pigeon cote was sold for £1 5s.

> The game was becoming more popular but participation was, for the most part, limited to those who could spare the time away from their business or profession. By 1880 many Barnton inhabitants were employed by Brunner Mond (producers of soda ash) and were working 56.5 hours per week as a dayman or an 84 hour week as a shiftman. They were entitled to only one day off per fortnight and were not granted any holidays until 1884.

1914-18 - Cricket was played throughout WW1, even to the extent of paying the opposition's travelling expenses.

1923 - The club moved to the 'Meadows'. The square at the Watercress Beds had been beautifully cultivated and not wishing to lose this valuable turf it was lifted and re-laid at the new ground. The pavilion was also re-sited.

1931 - Until this time the outfield was cut with hand scythes. Albert Sandbach became the first Barnton player to score a century.

1939-45 - Hostilities caused the club to cease activities. The ground was taken to support the 'grow more' food campaign. The pavilion, which at the time was being used as a Home Guard hut, was disposed of for £60. After the war friendly matches were played but not at home.

> During their nomadic existence after WW2 players went to matches on bicycles, in Dudley's Rolls Royce, in Bill Capper's bus, and most enjoyable of all, on the back of Les Charlton's coal lorry.

1951-53 - After many frustrations a new home was eventually found at the 'Pickups'. A hut was purchased from the Radio Society for £35. A mower was donated and a roller purchased for 15 shillings and much hard work ensued. The ground was officially opened on 30 May 1953 when the club played the President's XI.

1954 - Yet another site was identified and a bid of £250 was accepted by ICI Alkali for the purchase of land off Townfield Lane. During the negotiations the package of land was increased to 4.8 acres without a further charge. The ground was levelled and made ready for seeding. Within months a letter was received from the Cheshire Education Authority expressing their intention to purchase the club's newly levelled ground as they intended to build a new school on the site. A deal was done which allowed the club to purchase adjoining land and suitable compensation was secured. Clearly time was lost while yet more levelling and seeding was undertaken but Mr Pickup again came to the rescue, granting the club a rent-free extension with matches played on a concrete strip.

1957 - Some matches were played at Broomsedge despite the absence of a pavilion which was eventually finished in October. The construction was carried out by Joe Hayes, whose father had built the 1913 pavilion. The new wooden building cost £1800.

1977 - The iconic Broomsedge slope was levelled.

> Not renowned for his batting prowess, Frank Richardson would often light a cigarette before walking to the wicket and would just as often return, on completing his innings, to pick up the still burning butt!

1980s - The most successful time in the history of the club both on and off the field. The senior teams regularly won their respective divisions in the Cheshire Cricket League. Under the guidance of the then Chairman, George Haspell, the club embarked on an expansion of the pavilion, including the building of state of the art squash courts and a crown green bowling area.

2005 - The club celebrated its 150th year with an exhibition game against the Lashings World Cricket XI watched by over 300 people.

2016 - Little acorns and great oaks – more improvements saw new changing rooms built at the squash courts and the lounge was completely refurbished, considerably increasing the capacity. The club membership is now substantially over one thousand and as well as cricket the club offers facilities for bowls and squash plus the gentler pursuits of dominoes, darts and quizzes and plays an important role in the community life of the village. The excellent ground and pavilion are now a very far cry from the basic facilities of yesteryear.

Barrow

The Croft, Station Lane, Great Barrow, Chester CH3 7HN

THE OLD English village names of Bearu or Barue, variously construed as meaning a wood, grove, hill or mound, had long since been confined to history when Barrow CC came to be established in 1890. The first ground was situated near to the centre of the village but the cricketers subsequently moved to 'The Croft' where the first pavilion was erected in 1923.

The ground is rented from the Okell family, who have had village connections since the 1730s. The late David Okell (d 2007), who lived at 'The Croft', was very supportive of the club. He acted as President and helped to develop both the ground and the pavilion and that sympathetic family link has continued through John, his son, to this day.

Like Topsy the pavilion has just 'growed'. The original, modest in size and facility, has had a number of expansions and refurbishments over the years, but, importantly, it has maintained an appearance sympathetic with its lovely rural setting.

A number of key surnames transcend the club's history. These include Arnold, Ruscoe, Woodcock, Blackburn, Law and Barnett. In fact Vere Arbuthnot Arnold (b 1902, d 1994) was both the son and grandson of former Rectors of Barrow. He was educated at Haileybury and Cambridge University and appeared for Cheshire on five occasions in 1937-38. He was a wicketkeeper who claimed six victims but only made a modest contribution with the bat, scoring 12 runs in three completed innings. He was a prominent Liverpool businessman, Chairman of the Runcorn Development Corporation (which supervised the creation of the New Town) and was High Sheriff of Cheshire in 1958. Like his forefathers he served the local church of St Bartholomew. He was the Churchwarden for 30 years and then appointed Warden Emeritus in 1989. Barrow was both his place of nativity and his death.

The ancient church depicts in the east window, in the roundels at the foot of the outer panes, David and Goliath, and when Cheshire A took on the might of the Yorkshire Academy the minor county team might have felt akin to David. In the event, the match, which was played in July 2005, was won by Yorkshire, but only by one run and only after Cheshire

> **Another Cheshire player was Harry Beech (b 1894, d 1981). He played three matches in 1927, contributing a total of 48 runs, one wicket and two catches. Like VA Arnold he died in the village where he had been born.**

lost their last three wickets without adding to their total. Three future England players appeared in the White Rose team: Jonny Bairstow (36 runs), Adil Rashid (25) and Ajmal Shahzad (7) all played but all were out-scored by Nick Cantello (83), the Cheshire A captain on the day. If the visitors found the dressing rooms a touch cramped they had no reason to complain about the idyllic surroundings or the pitch, which provided for such an exciting match.

Barrow lifted the Cheshire League T20 Cup in 2014 and won a hat-trick of promotions in 2013/14/15 to ensure a place in the top section of the Cheshire pyramid, a position they consolidated in 2016. Another promotion followed in 2017. They regularly host Cheshire age-group representative sides and provide a home venue for the Cheshire disabled team. In addition to their weekend cricket they participate in the Chester & District Midweek Cricket League. Gratifyingly, former junior players are the backbone of the club, but that should come as no surprise recognising the camaraderie and community spirit which exists at this friendly and picturesque little ground.

Cheshire County Caps
131 Caps have been awarded since records began

Year	Name	Year	Name	Year	Name
1926	E.H. Steventon	1957	R. Fox	1987	J.J. Hitchmough
1928	S.M.H. Spearing		K.F. Holding		K. Teasdale
1929	H. Eyre		M.J.B. Riley	1988	J.F.M. O'Brien
1932	J.K. Edmundson	1958	B.S. Jones	1989	M.G. Boocock
	L.J. Pearson		A.B. Jackson		G.J. Blackburn
1933	F.C. Shreeve	1959	P.A.C. Kelly	1990	S.T. Crawley
	W.E. Bates		J.A. Sutton		P.H. De Prez
	T.J. Bartley	1960	S.D. Cooke		N.D. Peel
1934	T.W. Jefferson	1961	C.D.R. Barker		S. Bramhall
1935	J.A. McEntyre		S. Davies	1991	G. Miller
	F. Dennis		A.L. Shillinglaw		D.W. Varey
	W.H. Barber	1962	D.F. Cox	1992	J.D. Bean
1936	A.M. Wolstenholme		G.C. Hardstaff	1994	J.D. Gray
1937	G.A. Hosking	1964	R. Collins	1995	R.G. Hignett
	J.D. Canevali	1965	P.D. Briggs	1996	P.J.R. Bryson
1938	R.D. Fairbairn		R.A. Richardson		T.J. Bostock
	H.E. Prescott	1966	N.R. Halsall		A.D. Greasley
	L. Parkinson	1967	S.L. Wood	1997	N.D. Cross
1939	G. Bull	1968	W. Blackburn	1998	C.S. Lamb
1947	K. Dean	1969	M.S.R. Byrne		S.A. Stoneman
	A.D. Lord	1970	R.M.O. Cooke	2000	E.S. Garnett
	H.N. Nuttall		J.R.A. Cragg	2001	A.J. Hall
	S.G. Shepherd		C.R.V. Taylor		M.R. Currie
	L. Wilson	1972	N.T. O'Brien	2002	S.J. Renshaw
1948	W. Winstanley		T. Hodson	2003	R.W. Fisher
	D.E. Mount	1973	D. Bailey		J. Whittaker
1949	J.R.L. Davies		M. Riley	2005	S.J. Ogilby
	B.M. Lowe		A.J. Mumford		D.B. Pennant
	H.W. Hall	1975	I. Cowap	2006	D.N. Leech
1950	C.R. Barker	1976	R.G. Rodger		N.R.C. Dumelow
	A.G. Liggins	1979	N.D. Barker	2007	C.C. Finegan
	A. Vickery		I.J. Gemmell	2008	M.R. Dawson
	L. Blunt	1980	K.J. McCullagh		A.J. Syddall
1951	F.W. Millett		T.J. Taylor		B.J. Spendlove
	B.E. Jones	1981	Mudassar Nazar	2010	J.A. Duffy
1952	J.A.H. Barrett	1982	J.K. Pickup	2011	W.M. Goodwin
	G.H. Wigglesworth	1983	J.S. Hitchmough		R.J. Logan
1953	W.G. Allen		P.A. Tipton	2012	D.A. Woods
	G. Harding	1984	S.C. Yates	2013	J.P. Kettle
	W. Wood		I. Cockbain	2014	R.A.L. Moore
1954	E.C. Nicholls		I.P. Davies	2015	D.O. Berry
	D.J. Smith		A.J. Murphy		L.F. Dixon
1956	R.J. Digman		I.J. Tansley	2016	J.J. Williams
				2017	C. Rowe
					W.A. White

Birchfield Park

Birchfield Road, Widnes WA8 9ES

WERE THEY, like the rugby section, founded in 1968 or rather later? Probably the latter according to Steve Shuttleworth, the Birchfield man who wears the 'Jack of all trades' hat. Steve's Dad was the landlord of the Prince of Wales and his footballing customers were keen for some summer exercise so a cricket team was entered into the Halton Midweek T20 league. They subsequently migrated to weekend cricket and became a full member of the Liverpool Competition in 1997. They play at the Birchfield Park Sports & Social Club alongside the footballers and Birchfield Rugby Union club.

The cricket square is a good distance from the clubhouse and beyond the rugby pitch so when at the crease it is advisable to score big so as to prolong the passage of applause on the very long walk back.

In mid June 2016, occasional wicketkeeper Dan Oliver hit the batting jackpot by scoring 133 not out against Caldy. He proudly sat at the top of the play-cricket Lancashire Honours Board, but if there was a downside he recorded his century on the Wirral, denying himself all that extended adulation!

In 2016 both their 1st and 2nd XIs played in the Saturday 3rd XI, Division 1. They respectively finished 2nd and 10th and so as runners-up in 2017 the 1st XI will play in the 3rd XI Premier Division.

A good number of clubs revolve around a couple of families and this one is a good example. Steve and his two sons are regularly in the same side and 'Mr Cricket', Peter Findlater, is still opening the batting despite his advancing years. His brother, Mike, is another veteran. As a team with pub roots they put a heavy emphasis on enjoying their cricket, not winning at all costs, and we should all drink to that.

Widnes CC are near neighbours and the two clubs often work in a partnership to their mutual advantage. The club colours are gold and green.

Birkenhead Park

Park Drive, Lower Park, Birkenhead CH43 4TS

OF ALL THE clubs featured in this book there can be no doubt that Birkenhead Park has the most illustrious history. When the club was formed in 1846 it had a very exclusive membership made up of Old Boys from the top Public Schools.

The oldest club on Wirral has only ever had one home and the current pavilion dates from 1849 (now Grade ll listed). *Early Club & Village Cricket* by John Goulson (1972) records an 1846 match against Seacombe CC in the park. FL Olmstead, architect of Central Park, New York, (the laying out of Central Park was influenced by the design of Birkenhead Park) in his 1852 published book entitled *Walks and talks of an American Farmer in England*, describes walking in Birkenhead Park 'and, coming to an open field of clean, bright, greensward, closely mown, on which a large tent was pitched, and a party of boys in one part and a party of gentlemen in another, were playing cricket'.

Park was one of the top sides in the country and in their first thirty years they played MCC at Lord's, Surrey at the Oval and both Oxford and Cambridge Universities. They also played six matches against the professional All-England Eleven.

1870 - In their fourth match against the All England XI, Park won by 126 runs. A newspaper report of the day said 'the weather was glorious and here and there the tall masts of some big ships pierced the sky deeper than the highest trees'. The band of the 4th Dragoon Guards played warlike music during the intervals.

1872 - Notable for a 'fourth wicket' experiment.

1873 - a crowd of 10,000 watch Park play the All England XI again.

1892 - Cheshire County CC held successful negotiations with BPCC with regard to their ground becoming Cheshire's county ground. The club's oldest surviving minute book records the club's attempts to secure a telephone. This was for the *Daily Post* reporter so that he could telephone the score through instead of having to take the ferry to Liverpool and back.

> In 1858 Robert Carpenter was the club professional and at the time was one of the most famous cricketers in the country. Only a wealthy club could have afforded his wages. Carpenter was a fine and powerful hitter and a useful change bowler. He later became a first-class umpire.

1893 - The wealth of the club was revealed by the way it paid rail fares and £1 a head hotel expenses for members who undertook the Scottish tour. The tour caused quite a furore among cricket followers north of the border because of the ease of the touring club's victories over the local sides. Letters were sent to the newspapers by irate readers complaining about the efforts of their teams and especially of the influential Grange (Edinburgh) side.

1894 - Cheshire County CC, based at Birkenhead Park since 1892, folded.

1896 - A sensational innings by Cecil Holden set a Liverpool Competition record. Holden opened the batting but wickets fell quickly until the last man joined him. At that stage the score was 83-9 and Holden had 43. By the time he was out they had added 178 runs in 58 minutes. Holden, batting like a 'galvanic battery', cut and drove in masterly fashion, eventually reaching 202 out of 261.

1900 - For the match against Sefton Park on 19 May the scoresheet was endorsed 'Mafeking Relieved'.

1904 - Cecil Holden was censored by the committee for removing a list of unpaid subs from the noticeboard. His brother was on the list.

1904 - In *Cricket Memories of the Far East* by EIM Barret, he writes: 'I accompanied the Straits of Settlements side to take part in a triangular tournament against Hong Kong CC and Shanghai CC and TR Hubback a game warden and mighty hunter was in our side. He played for Birkenhead Park and six matches for Lancashire in 1892. (*Cricket Archive* reveals he was an engineer on the Malayan railway, a plantation owner and a game warden in Pahang from 1920 who became an expert on large fauna and a pioneer of conservation. He was killed after being on the run in the jungle from the Japanese Army for two years in 1942).

1906 - The beginnings of a row between Park and Oxton CC over fixtures started up? Park wouldn't offer any Saturday dates and Oxton wouldn't agree to any midweek fixtures.

1908 - The simmering row between Park and Oxton broke out into open warfare when the Park secretary sent a letter to their neighbours in these terms... *The committee direct me to say that the evening matches which were formerly*

played were ultimately made a farce by the direct action of Oxton CC and following the last game played your then captain informed Mr Holden that no matches would be played in the future except on Saturdays. Park CC viewed this as being dictatorial and insulting to them and unless Oxton withdraws from that position and from the action thus adopted by them, I am directed to inform you that the consideration of fresh fixtures with Oxton cannot be further considered.

1912 - A circular letter was received from Liverpool CC with regard to the formation of a local league. The committee replied: 'Birkenhead Park CC wish to place on record their total and complete disapproval of the suggestion, and refuse to have anything to do therewith'.

1933 - The club, once again, applied to the council for permission to enclose the ground with railings due to vandalism. Permission was eventually given, but only after a bitter debate in the Chamber with Labour councillors accusing the club of trying to make the public pay to watch the cricket in what was a public park. The club decided to erect the railings in instalments to prevent any further outcry.

1940-46 During the war the railings encircling the ground, for which the club had fought so bitterly to erect, were removed by the council for

> At some considerable financial cost to the club the services of Jack Bartley were secured for 1931, 1932, 1935 and 1936. With his penetrating bowling he helped Park win the Liverpool Competition in 1931 and 1935. In all matches in 1935 he gained 158 wickets at 6.12. Against New Brighton he took 10-37 and the following week he dismissed nine Neston batsmen and then denied himself a rather special double by catching the tenth! He played for Cheshire between 1931 and 1939. He also played for New Brighton in 1940 and Oxton in 1947. He later became a first-class umpire and officiated in 321 matches (1948-1960) including six Test matches (1954-6). He died in 1964.

the war effort. Ironically, they were never used as they contained an unsuitable metal content. To this day the railings have never been completely replaced.

1951 - Ben Wright, who became Secretary in 1951 and a future club President, remembered speaking to Dapper Danson about the refusal of the club to grant him membership. Although Dapper himself was a Latin classics teacher, it was because his father had been in trade. Ben also thought that the nature and exclusiveness of the club had started to gradually change after WW1. Slowly divisions had broken down and a wider spectrum of candidates were allowed to become members in order to keep the club from closing. This had taken such a long time that it was almost imperceptible but WW2 did accelerate this change. When Danson died in 1965 the club sent a three guinea contribution towards a seat in his memory to be placed at Oxton CC.

1964 - Noel Overend retired as 1st XI captain having won the Liverpool Competition each year between 1960 and 1964. Tony Shillinglaw, Park's youngest ever captain, took over and won it again in 1966 having failed to do so in his first season by one point. In 1973 Tony took 10-28 against Neston. He played for Cheshire (1959-1971) and subsequently wrote an acclaimed book, *Bradman Revisited*, in 2003 which examined Sir Donald's batting technique.

1966 - Burglaries were occurring at the club premises at frequent intervals. For well over a hundred years the club records do not record one single break-in but from the start of the 1960s they occur with monotonous regularity.

1993 - Having originally mooted the idea of an indoor cricket facility in 1966, Tony Shillinglaw's dream became a reality in the autumn of 1993. Clive Lloyd, the former West Indies and Lancashire captain, officially opened the new indoor school and the refurbished clubhouse. The total cost of the project was £750,000, which was funded through Wirral Citylands, the Foundation for Sports & Arts, the Sports Council and the Peter Johnson (one-time chairman of Everton FC) Foundation. Graham Smith, player and former captain, was instrumental in seeking the funding and without his devoted work it is doubtful if the project would have succeeded.

Cheshire county players and first-class cricketers who have played for Birkenhead Park are just too numerous to list, but the club has had an impressive list of International cricketers within its membership:

1879	SS Schultz	England v Australia, Melbourne
1887	R Wood	England v Australia, Sydney
1892 & 1896	TW Routledge	South Africa v England (four appearances in South Africa)
1909	JH King	England v Australia, Lord's
1939	N Oldfield	England v West Indies, Oval

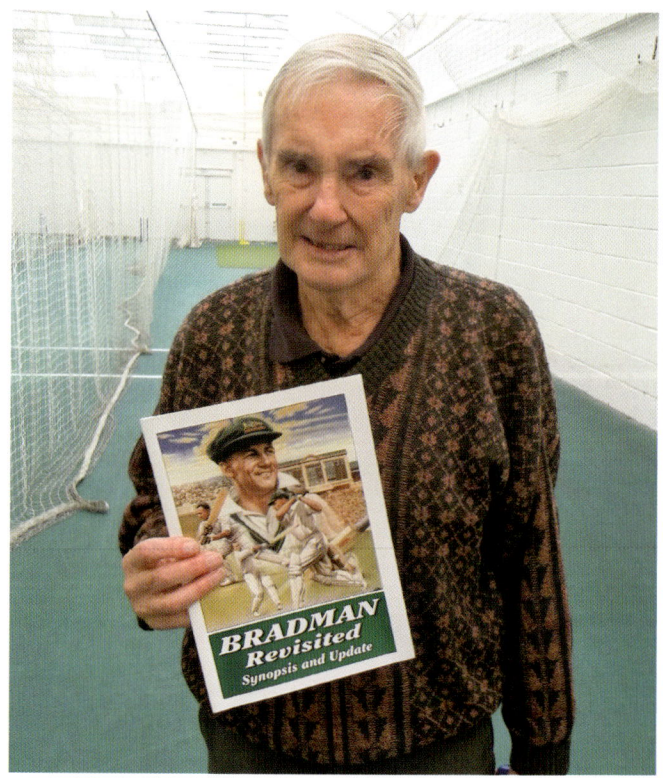

Octogenarian Tony Shillinglaw - Birkenhead Park through and through

Birkenhead St Mary's

Ashville Road, Birkenhead CH41 8AU

IF YOU HAVE been to BSMCC in the last thirty odd years you must know that larger than life character Bill McGenity. Mr Birkenhead St Mary's by reputation and, indisputably, its most enthusiastic ambassador. He is rightly proud of his club and describes it as 'a beautiful little cricket club that only the almighty powers of nature could construct'.

Of course, he is not the only star turn at the club. Ralph Dodd and Bob Davies, who still attend to the square, are both octogenarians and long-serving. Bob started scoring as a youngster in the late 1930s, captained the side for six seasons between 1955 and 1979 and has now gone full circle having taken over the scorebook again. He has been a member for 77 years and is in his ninth decade with the club. He is very grateful to the Sunday school teachers of the parish church of Birkenhead who had the vision to start a cricket team in 1878 and quick to praise the band of unpaid workers who work for the good of the club. He also points out they have their share of guys who 'bat, bowl and bu**er off!'

Writing at the time of the club's centenary in 1978, the late Tom Jones, the Merseyside Competition Secretary between 1963 and 1996,

Billy McGenity

> The late Bert Bushell, who achieved a ten wicket haul in 1952, told a story about a plaque which was commissioned to commemorate the official opening of the current pavilion in 1971 by the Mayor of Birkenhead. Unfortunately the Cammell Laird worker who made it spelt cricket with two t's! Bert asked his brother to take it back into the factory and arrange for the superfluous 't' to be removed. This proved to be rather embarrassing as it transpired the tradesman he approached was the one who had done the original engraving!

recalls his visits to this 'compact and homely ground noted for its warm and friendly hospitality'. He recalls the time when the modest boundaries only brought the reward of a four, no sixes, and when there was a huge elm tree inside the boundary at fine leg. It had been there since before the club was founded but had to be felled in 1976 because it was suffering from the dreaded Dutch Elm disease.

Ken Ingman (b 1927, d 2000), a former wicketkeeper/batsman, played here in the 1950s and represented Cheshire between 1958 and 1964. He did much to promote schoolboy and youth cricket. In this pursuit he became well-known throughout the country. He was Chairman of

1895 fixture card

> **Fred Gillmore, Club Secretary 1971-1986, once recalled the day a when a rat appeared out of a manhole on the bank near the pavilion and with great presence of mind, Bob Davies, who was fielding in the vicinity, threw the ball at it with unerring accuracy and killed it stone dead. Surely not! He also told a tale about the day the team set out to play at Helsby. They all travelled by train from Woodside but the train divided at Hooton. Four of the side ended up in Helsby but the other seven, including Bob Lambert, who worked for British Rail and should have known better, finished up in Chester. They had to travel from Chester to Helsby by bus and arrived an hour and a half later!**

Wirral Schools Cricket Association for 25 years and while holding that office he managed England Schools tours to India in 1978-79, to Zimbabwe in 1983-84 and coached many England U19 teams. A teacher by profession, he became Chairman of the NCA Coaching Committee and represented that body on the MCC Committee and the Cricket Council. Michael Atherton, in the company of other England players, spoke glowingly of his achievements at an Oxton wake after his funeral.

St Mary's are, of course, near neighbours of Birkenhead Park CC. The boundaries are barely 400 yards apart. If you have never been to the Park add it to your bucket list. The 226 acre park was the first in the country to be provided from public funds.

When it opened in 1847 over 56,000 people attended the ribbon-cutting ceremony. Many of the fine large properties built at the time for the wealthy merchants still survive in the surrounding roads.

The last word goes to writer and sports commentator, the late Bill Bothwell. In 1978, when he was President of Upton CC, he wrote: 'When those of us who live by our pens and write about cricket from time to time, seek an apposite but elusive phrase, we turn, almost inevitably to the writings of the late Sir Neville Cardus. And there the search ends. So it is on this occasion, for, looking again at his *Days in the Sun*, I came across the opening paragraph which says almost all there is to say about the abode St Mary's have made for themselves. "There is surely," wrote Cardus, "some interaction between a cricket team and the ground it mainly lives on. Does not the play of the side assume tone and colour from the scene?"

The old pavilion at Birkenhead St Mary's

Birkenhead School

58 Beresford Road, Oxton CH43 2JD

BIRKENHEAD SCHOOL moved to its present site in 1871, but it was not until 1899 that the ground alongside Beresford Road was levelled to create the school's playing field. The original wooden pavilion was replaced in 1910 with the lovely black and white structure that substantially enhances the view across the ground to this very day.

The pavilion steps at the time of their opening in 1910.

In 1948 the LC McAllester Memorial ground, opposite Oxton CC, was presented to the school and, after all the preparatory work, was officially opened in 1952. This is used for junior cricket as is a third field on Nocturum Road. The Sports Hall within the school complex was completed in 1992 and is equipped with three cricket nets.

The school has produced a good number of first-class cricketers and others that have represented Cheshire (see table).

1982 - When Oxford met Cambridge in the Varsity match at Lord's the Varey twins found themselves on opposite sides. Jonathan might have concluded he had the better of the family rivalry given that he recorded two not out scores of 32 and 12 and, most notably, he also dismissed his twin brother (c Cowan b Varey) for 22. David will argue he had the last laugh as Cambridge won the match.

2006 - To coincide with the centenary of the Old Birkonians' Society, a Birkenhead School XI hosted a match against a Lashings World XI. A star-studded side, which included Gordon Greenidge, Richie Richardson, Aravinda de Silva and Chris Cairns, was led by Alvin Kallicharran. Chasing 260-4d the School side replied with 170ao. The current

Birkenhead School cricket ground in winter (from the Ian Boumphrey collection)

Neston pairing of David Hurst and Simon Stokes top scored with 55 and 36 respectively. I recall the match in some detail as I was one of the umpires.

When Richie Richardson was at the non-striker's end he asked me the name of the spin bowler at my end whom he immediately confessed he could not read. I told him it was Simon Marshall, who was playing with Lancashire. 'Should be playing with England' was his reply. An over or two later he whacked Simon way over the boundary rope and I observed to him that he was reading him now. With a huge grin he said, 'No mon. I don't need to pick him to thrash him!'

BIRKENHEAD SCHOOL PUPILS WHO HAVE PLAYED FIRST-CLASS CRICKET AND/OR FOR CHESHIRE

Name	Birth/Death	First-class	Cheshire
Birley, Andrew B	1976	x	1999-2012
Carpenter, James R	1975	Sussex 1997-2000	1996
Clarke, Andrew D	1991	x	2014-15
Cooper, Jason	1972	x	2000
Crawley, Stephen T	1962	x	1982-94
Cross, Neil D	1972	x	1995-2005
Davies, Andrew G	1962	Camb U 1982-89	x
Davies, John RL	1926	x	1946-58
Davis, Ashley J	1994	x	2014-16
Ewing, David A	1950	x	1975
Hodgson, Joseph P	1893/1979	x	1921-32
Goodwin, Warren	1986	x	2005-16
Jefferson, Thomas W	1905/1960	x	1928-36
Marshall, Simon J	1982	Camb U 2002-04 Brit Univs. 2004 Lancashire 2005-08	2001-03
McEntyre, Kenneth B	1944	Surrey 1965-66	1962-68
Renshaw, Simon J	1974	Hampshire 1996-2000	1994
Rogers, Basil J	1917/1992	x	1938-47
Rogers, John H	1910/1968	Oxford U 1932	1930-34
Taylor, Chilton RV	1951	Warwickshire 1970 Camb U 1971-73 Middlesex 1981	1969-72
Varey, David W	1961	Camb U 1981-83 Lancashire 1982-92	1982-92
Varey, Jonathan G	1961	Oxford U 1982-83	1982
Willmer, Arthur F	1890/1916	Oxford U 1912	1914

Bollington

The Recreation Ground, Adlington Road, Bollington SK10 5JT

IN THE SAME way that a fierce rivalry exists between the footballing blues and reds in Manchester and Liverpool so, over the decades, a competitive spirit was developed between the cricketers of Bollington and Macclesfield.

1896 - An Athletics Meet was organised at Whitsun and grew in importance as a money-spinner for the cricket club. By the early 20th century it had gained the reputation for being one of the best annual amateur sports gatherings in the North of England.

1901 - The history of the cricket club and the town's recreation ground are closely linked. The history of the recreational facility started to unfold in 1901 when Francis Greg died. He left the cricket ground, as it then was, to the people of Bollington to be administered by Bollington Urban District Council. It was one of a long line of gifts given to the town by the Greg family. The club based on Gnat Hole, as Greg's ground was then known, had started around 1885 by bringing together smaller clubs in Shrigley Vale and Bollington Cross. Greg generously provided a pavilion, a bandstand and paid £20 for a roller to make sure the pitches were properly prepared. The footballers were not so well accommodated. They wished to play on the ground but for many years the cricket club prevailed and footballers were excluded. The political influence of the cricketers on the Urban District Council was a decisive factor.

The cricketing glory days of the club were, mostly, before the WW1. In 1905 the *Macclesfield Courier* carried a report of a local journalist: 'Fancy a village of 6000 challenging and playing a city like

Manchester with a population of over 60 times that.' There can be no doubt about its prominence given The club hosted nine Cheshire matches between 1909 and 1923. Of course, given its public designation, the recreation ground was used for other things and two of the earliest events were celebrations for the respective Coronations of King Edward VII in 1902 and King George V in 1911. There are local photographs showing huge crowds dressed in their Sunday best, with men in three-piece suits and women in long dresses and splendid hats crowding the grounds. During WW1 it was used as a parade ground and during WW2 part of it was dug over and planted as part of the 'Dig for Victory' campaign as well as being used to train the Home Guard.

1958 - Sweeping aside the years the Pakistan Eaglets visited in 1958 and their captain, Mohammad Ramzan, scored a quickfire 66. In the same year Bollington won the Lancashire & Cheshire League and were also winners of the Saville Whittle Trophy. The local council refused permission for a Sunday match.

> The Cook brothers, Jack (1920-24) and James (1925-28) played for Cheshire. Two other brothers, William and Lawrence, played for Lancashire. Bill Goodwin, educated at King's, Macclesfield, also played for Cheshire between 1954 and 1959.

2010 - There were many successful events in the Club's 125th anniversary year. They included the Chairman's Anniversary Ball, the Cricket Week festival in July and The Bollington Ashes when the Over 40's entertained an Australian Veterans touring team.

Under the chairmanship of Colin Rowe the club has made real progress. Why not have a morning stroll around this picturesque area and watch some cricket in the afternoon? Close your eyes and imagine the scene a century before.

BOLLINGTON AND MACCLESFIELD RIVALRY

1890 - The *Courier* reports that Macclesfield (151) travelled to Bollington (40) and won very comfortably. Macclesfield made the most of their victory - and had need to - for they were not to beat Bolly again until 1900, and not to beat them at Victoria Road for eighteen years!

1901 - Sanford departed to Bollington in the footsteps of Hope. The Bollington fixture was discontinued and not revived for five years. The *Courier* hoped that the unpleasantness which caused it to be dropped had been resolved. The alleged poaching of players was a clear factor.

1906 - A crowd of 500, paying a total of £10, saw a rather one-sided match. Bollington (204) beat Macclesfield (75). There was an unfortunate incident when Heath was given out by the Bollington umpire, who was unsighted, ignoring the 'not out' decision of the other official. Play was resumed after a five minute delay, to the accompaniment of loud and unruly barracking. Appeals for order from both teams were ineffective in quelling the noise.

1908 - Jack Milward defected to Bollington after seven years and 250 wickets in the 1st XI. He had been vice captain and, perhaps, thought he should have been given the captaincy but was overlooked.

1908 - Macclesfield (159) beat Bollington (73). At 7pm 'a mighty shout, penetrating and prolonged', the waving of hats and parasols greeted the first defeat of Bollington in eighteen years.

1919 - Before a crowd of 5000 Macclesfield beat Bollington. As they had also won the earlier match in the season it was the first time in the history of matches between the two that they had done the double over their opponents from 'Happy Valley'.

Bowdon

South Downs Road, Bowdon WA14 3DT

BOWDON EXPANDED rapidly in the 1850s from a rural village to a suburban town as the construction of the Manchester to Chester railway allowed easier access to Manchester. The location of the railway line combined with the prevailing wind took the smoke from Manchester's factories to the North East and meant that North Cheshire quickly became a desirable residence for the wealthy of Manchester's cotton boom. Large houses were built to accommodate these families and their retinue of servants.

Bowdon Cricket Club was formed in 1856 by a group of about a dozen individuals who practised on a piece of waste ground on Rose Hill (near East Downs Road). Shortly afterwards sufficient funds were raised to establish a ground which is now the site of the Lawn Tennis Club in Stamford Road, Bowdon. In 1865 they finally moved to their present ground.

Saturday, 18 April 1874 was gloomy but fine, with just a few drops of rain in the afternoon. A match between the married and unmarried members took place to celebrate the opening of the pavilion and was attended by a large and gay (sic) assemblage of friends. The game was won by the married members (116 against the bachelors' total of 90) though two single gentlemen had to be included in the Married XI! The

> **The opposition, by the necessity of transport in those days, were all close to the railway lines and included Urmston, Northwich, Trafford, Broughton Park, Rusholme and Cheetham Hill. There were many games against the Manchester Cricket Club, whose home ground was Old Trafford. Many features of the club remain to this day; the club crest was established at this time, as well as the motto 'Semper Paratus' (always ready). The club colours of Oxford blue, Cambridge blue and Cheshire Regiment cerise are also still used.**

Altrincham Borough Band was present throughout the afternoon and in the evening there was a dinner in the pavilion for 60 people.

The menu for the evening consisted of:

Potages: oyster spring
Poissons: salmon tarbot
Entrees: sweetbreads kidneys calves head
Reives: lamb saddle of mutton beef
Rotis: ducklings turkey poulets
Entremets: ice pudding jellies creams

There was an abundant supply of wines of the best quality.

Mr HK Balstone, the vice chairman, stated in his speech that "England had the best cricketers, the best shots, the best riders and the best sailors and so long as they had, it might still be said 'This England never did, and never shall kneel at the proud foot of a conqueror'".

At the end of the dinner Mr Maw, the treasurer, was presented with a silver claret jug, two goblets and a salver.

The main room of the pavilion at that time measured 50 feet by 14 feet, the home changing room 18 feet by 14 feet. The visitors changing room was rather smaller. There were separate lavatories together with sundry out-offices and underneath a small wine cellar. The total cost of the pavilion was £400. The pavilion was situated in Victorian fashion facing the North East away from the sun to prevent the gentleman receiving a sun-tan that might suggest they had been labouring in the fields.

Late additions to the pavilion include a stable for the horse (underneath where the kitchen is now). After WW2 the Hockey Club used the stable as a changing room for certain of their teams and this arrangement continued well into the 1970s.

In 1939 Helen Bickham bought the South Downs Road ground from Lord Stamford and gave

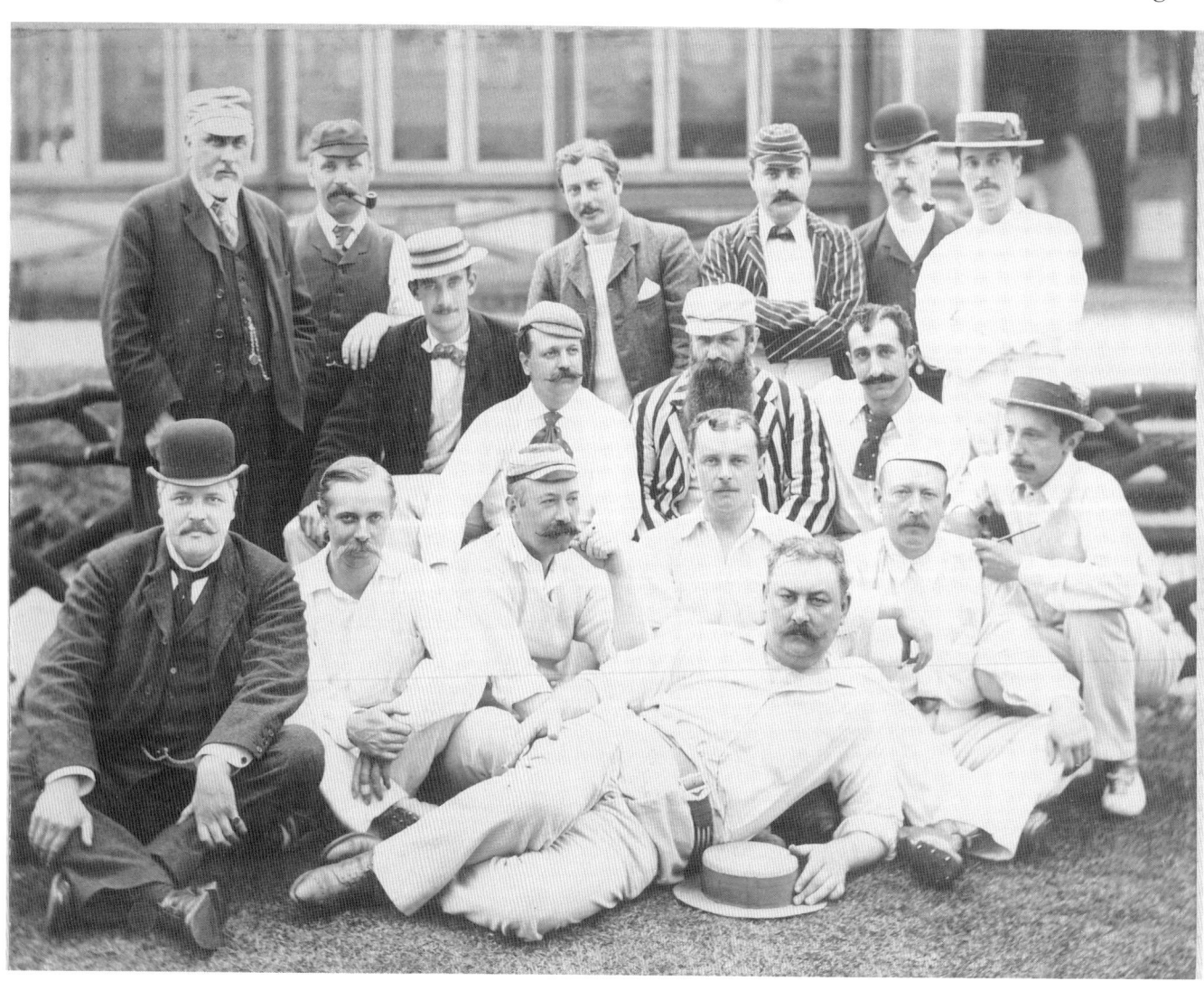

Edwardian Bowdon

it to the club in memory of her brother Earnest Bickham. The club remain eternally grateful for this act of generosity.

Ladies were not allowed in the pavilion until 1957. One young lady was reprimanded for pushing a pram in front of the pavilion. The person who reprimanded her was her sister's father-in-law! The ladies had a separate pavilion (actually a small shed with a corrugated roof) in the drive leading down to the club. Here they served teas to visitors to the ground. There was also a primitive toilet for the ladies.

There is an entry in the club's minute books for February 1957 stating that the club will expend £310 by screening off a portion of the east end of the pavilion installing heating and lighting AND a ladies' lavatory (where the trophy cabinet is now). This ladies' section would be available for use on all match days.

Bowdon Cricket Club is rightly proud of its history and its position in the Cheshire County Cricket League, being one the original founding clubs in 1975. The club has finished 1st XI champions a record eleven times (including one shared).

Bowdon quickly took a shine to the new League by winning the title in its second year in 1976. This showed the strength of the side that would take the club to probably its finest hour by stepping out at Lord's for the final of the National KO in 1977. Sadly events conspired against John Riley's side as the weather intervened, and then, in the rearranged match at Edgbaston, the opponents, Southgate, proved too strong. Amongst the Bowdon team was a young Paul Allott, who would go on to have an illustrious career with Lancashire and England.

The club won the Cheshire Cup for the first time in 1980 by overcoming the dominant Cheadle Hulme team of that era. The league title was shared in 1983 with Alderley Edge, and in 1989 it was won outright by an excellent side led by Tony Dawson. This team was described by Neville Walton, a stalwart member of the club for 70 years from the 1930s onwards, as the finest Bowdon team he had seen.

A young Manchester Grammar School boy, David Green, made his debut for the club in 1956 and continued to play for Bowdon until he entered the first-class scene playing for Lancashire and Gloucestershire. In more recent times Bowdon captains Steve Bramhall, Gareth Edwards and Simon Marshall, and also Bowdon's leading bowler of the last few years, Chris Ashling, have all appeared in the first-class game.

The modern era for Bowdon cricket began with Alan Farrow becoming chairman in the early 1990s, and combining with Jon Gray as captain. The club recorded a hat-trick of league titles in 1996, 1997 and 1998, with the Cheshire Cup won in 1997. Steve Bramhall replaced Jon Gray in 1999 and additional league titles were secured in 2000, 2002, 2003 and 2004. Further Cheshire Cup titles were gained in 2003 and 2004.

A visit to Bowdon could not be regarded as complete without a chat to David Young, who is a former chairman and the club historian. He has prepared a *History of Bowdon Cricket Club* and has been a great help to me in producing this piece.

BOWDON C.C. FIRST ELEVEN: 1974

This photograph, taken at Northwich C.C., shows the Bowdon team in 1974. It includes the 17-years-old Paul Allott.

Back row (left to right): Albert Brown (Umpire); David Webb; Paul Strzelecki; David Parker; Simon Milner; Paul Allott; Tony Dawson; Bill Tootill; Tony Beasley (Scorer).
Front row (left to right): Tony Ham; John Savin; Steve Murrills; John Riley.

Bowdon Vale

Priory Street, Bowdon, WA14 3BH

IN 1871, AS Vicar of Bowdon, the Archdeacon Pollock laid a plan for the formation of the Bowdon Vale Church Institute and at much the same time was responsible for establishing the cricket club. The first record of any match involving Bowdon Vale is a report in the *Altrincham Guardian* of 26 July 1873. The match was played at Lymm and was won by Bowdon Vale.

1920s - At this time the club were playing in the Altrincham & District League. The detail is sketchy but it seems they were champions on at least one occasion around this period.

1930s - The club's original ground had been close to the present one on the opposite side of the bowling green on what is now a school playing-field. The move to the present ground happened in the early 1930s. In the early days of WW2 the club's ground was given over to agriculture.

After the war, cricket quickly got back to normal. The club returned to its own ground in 1946 and for a number of years played friendly cricket.

1950 - Alan Emery took ten wickets for no runs against Heaton Mersey Parish CC. When their opponents were dismissed for 30 odd it was agreed to play another game. Vale won the toss and Alan took a further 3-0 in the second match before being withdrawn from the attack. Quite some performance!

In 1957, nine Cheshire clubs, including Bowdon Vale, were responsible for forming the Cheshire Cricket Association. The other founder members were Barnton, Sale Moor, Weaverham, Stretford, Winton, Lostock, Toft and Wythenshawe. A steering committee was formed and it was subsequently agreed that competitive games should commence in April 1959. The club's one championship success was achieved in 1966.

1964 - The new pavilion was completed.

Why not split your Saturday cricket-watching programme with a match at Bowdon Vale before making the short journey to their more illustrious neighbours in South Downs Road?

> Long-serving player and official John Brocklebank died in 2017, aged 85. After sterling service at Bowdon Vale he served the Cheshire League as secretary and later president.

Bramhall

Church Lane, Woodford SK7 1PQ

THE 125TH ANNIVERSARY (1886-2011) booklet summarises the history of the club and a few pages into the book is a sub-head, 'The 1990s to Present Day'. The opening sentence reads: 'To state that Bramhall CC nearly died in 1996 is no exaggeration'. Such a profound statement needs justification and the following is a direct lift:

The Bramhall Queensgate Sports Club, comprising five sections – bowls, tennis, hockey, squash and cricket – fell into a financial downward spiral which resulted in even basic repairs remaining unremedied. The club premises looked woe-begone and fourth rate. Regrettably, the only escape was to sell the cricket field which had stood for 110 years and move the other sections elsewhere in the neighbourhood. To cut a tortuous story short, after planning permission problems and wranglings between the five sections over the distribution of money made from the sale of the cricket field, the cricketers received £246k to purchase land and create a new ground out of an undulating farmer's field.

How quickly things can change! Within five years they were resident at Church Lane and crowned National Club Champions when they defeated Bath CC at Lord's in September 2001. Bramhall scored 175-6 (45 overs) before the strong Bath outfit subsided to 128-8, but then rallied and needed a mere 11 off the final over with the last two batsmen at the wicket. In the event Charlie Lamb bowled the Bath number 11 with the last ball of the match and the men from the West Country ended up five runs short of victory. Charlie Lamb finished with bowling figures of 9-2-23-3. *Wisden* reported the Bramhall total owed much to Lamb and Mike Bolger, who added 40 in the last four overs. In the circumstances Lamb might have felt hard done by when the Man of the Match award was given to Andrew Hall, who contributed the only half-century of the game. (Known to everybody as 'Albert', Hall celebrated by scoring a century for Cheshire against Lincolnshire at Grantham in the Minor Counties Play-off Final just three days later).

> Occasionally clubs are blessed with great men, truly outstanding leaders, long remembered after their careers are over.
>
> Richard Cragg is one and still going strong. It's a very fair bet that whenever you visit Church Lane you are bound to see him, but he may not spot you because he will be busy rolling the pitch or chugging round the outfield on the tractor. He has served the club since 1957 as a player, groundsman and administrator. As a Cambridge University student he made his first-class debut in 1970. In that match against Warwickshire he played on the same side as Majid Khan, who had already played ten Test matches for Pakistan. Majid got a pair. Richard did rather better scoring 31 and 9. In common with England captains, Alastair Cook (2005), Michael Vaughan (1993) and Michael Atherton (1987), Richard (1966) was nominated by The Cricket Society as their Most Promising Young Cricketer of the Year. In 2016, during the Edgbaston Test match, Richard was a guest in the TMS commentary box and met another winner, Henry Blofeld (1956).
>
> And what about Peter Babbage? What a contribution! He was Chairman for 13 years and, crucially, at the time of the migration from Queensgate, it was his absolute commitment to the task that spearheaded the development of the new ground. On the field, as 1st XI captain, he led Bramhall for 11 years and in 1988 oversaw the winning of the Cheshire County League championship for the first time. The anniversary brochure selects a playing squad for each decade and, notably, Peter is included in three of them - 1970s, 80s and 90s.
>
> Richard Cragg also featured in the 1960s, 70s and 80s nominations. The only other members to warrant three entries were Bob Lees and Mike Bolger.

2016 - Another successful year in the history of the club. In June, after a very wet few days the weather just about relented long enough for the PCA England Masters match to be hosted, raising £23000 for the '1000 Hearts For Harry' charity. In September they participated in the National T20 Finals Day held at Derbyshire CCC. Having won

ENGLAND-BORN FIRST-CLASS CRICKETERS WHO HAVE REPRESENTED BRAMHALL CC

	M	Rs	HS	Ave	100/50	Ct/St	Wts	B/B
Bob Cooke	42	1450	139	22.30	2/4	25	4	2-55
Richard Cragg	7	149	55	11.46	0/1	2		
Peter Gooch	4	0	0no			3	6	4-52
Tony Good	8	10	6	1.66		1	17	5-62
Matt Hughes	3	391	116	65.16	2/1	2	2	1-16
Ewan McCray	2	68	37	34		1		0-12
Paddy McKeown	19	679	75	26.11	0/3	14		
Jim Pickup	3	19	14	3.16		1		
Nick Ross	8	224	68	28	0/1	5		
Neil Smith	187	3336	126	17.93	2/8	395/51		

the Cheshire County League competition they subsequently beat Menai Bridge, Barnards Green and Norden to reach the last four before losing to Sandiacre Town CC. Sky Sports covered the event at Derby. In the qualifying round against Menai Bridge, Iftikhar Naseer contributed the most spectacular display of big hitting, biffing 160 not out from only 58 deliveries. His memorable innings included 18 sixes and 9 fours.

Bramhall's strong junior section continues to produce many youngsters playing representative cricket for Lancashire and Cheshire. A fine all-rounder, Danny Lamb is on the Lancashire staff and in 2016 his sister Emma broke into the England Women's squad. Additionally home-grown batsman Matt Hughes captained Oxford University in 2016.

On the extreme right is the late Ken Thomas.
He was chairman of the Lancashire & Cheshire Cricket Society for 49 years (1968-2017).

Bredbury St Marks

Hillside Road, Woodley, SK6 1HS

JUST ONE year before the start of WW1 the footballers of Bredbury St Mark's FC decided they needed some summer sporting activity and formed a cricket team. The club is still resident at its original home, although at that time access to the ground was via a stile and fields on Werneth Road. Patriotically the wooden pavilion was painted blue and white, the original club colours. At the outset the ground was rented, but eventually they purchased it in 1940 for £500.

1948 - Whaley Bridge were dismissed for 112 and when Bredbury had reached 108-2 victory looked to be a formality. At this point a bowling change proved to be a very shrewd move as five wickets were snared in seven balls for no runs. Another two runs were added before the last three wickets were lost without further addition. All out 110!

1959 - Fred Bonsall recorded match figures of 9-26 against Hazel Grove. He was denied a 'full set' by his brother who took a catch off the bowling of Eric Mays. The following season Fred went one better. Having to chase only 136, Hayfield set off purposefully and at 35-1 looked to have made a good start, but from thereon things started to go rapidly downhill. Fred struck with a wicket in his fifth over, two more in the sixth and another in the seventh. 41-5 quickly became 41-9 as Fred took a wicket with each of the first four balls of his eighth over. Three more dot balls and then another wicket. (Note: Eight ball overs in the Derbyshire & Cheshire League at that stage). All out 41! Fred had match figures of 8-2-16-10 and six batsmen were clean bowled. Just for good measure, club records show he had scored a 118 against Romiley the previous week. A supporter who obviously had very high standards suggested if he could get ten catches in a match they'd need to acknowledge he was an all-rounder! After two decades with the club he left to take up professional appointments at Denton West and Flowery Field.

> A declaration by the Bredbury skipper left Norman Wood stranded on 98 not out. Not to be outdone, and very many years later, Norman recorded a century of a different type when he became a centenarian in 2012. He had a life-long association with the club. His father, Bob, had been the club wicketkeeper in the very first Bredbury fixture in 1913. Norman died in November 2016, aged 104.

1967 - A young David Wilde, having been told by Glossop CC to come back when he was a bit older, arrived at Bredbury. In 1967 he played for the 2nd XI and the U17s and commendably finished the season with 53 wickets and won the Les Wyatt memorial prize as the most promising junior. He played the opening match of the 1968 season in the 1st XI but was never seen again. He had been snapped up by Glossop! By 1970 he was playing for Derbyshire. He played 13 first-class matches and 10 List A matches over three seasons and shared the new ball with England cricketers Fred Trueman, Fred Rumsey and Mike Hendrick.

1972 - The *Stockport Advertiser* covered the Bredbury St Mark's Ladies visit to Compstall Ladies for a challenge match. The visitors won convincingly, Ros Mountford scoring 113. Ros is the sister-in-law of Geoff Mountford, who has served the club with distinction on and off the pitch for in excess of 40 years. The next highest scorer was Jan Noble (now Amison). Jan is currently the Bredbury Secretary and the wife of Steve, who is well known across the county for his management and coaching work. He was awarded an OSCA (Outstanding Services to Cricket Award) in both 2005 and 2015.

Steve Amison (right) receives his OSCA from Andrew Strauss.

> How times change. A modern irritation at meetings is the distracting use of mobile phones, but in bygone days it was the noise of a very different type which annoyed the Chairman of the Tea Ladies group. He complained about the constant 'clacking' of knitting needles!

Long service and family connections abound. There have been four generations of the Barlow clan. Graham captained the Club 1995-2001 and is still a first team regular, while his father, Harry, is still attending committee meetings in his nineties! Dave Downes has served variously as captain of the 2nd and 3rd XIs as well as the Over 40s. He was also the Secretary for a period of fourteen years before taking the Chair in 2011. The Wood family have been associated with the club for many years and there is a nice story that links Dave with Daisy Wood. When DD was captain in the 1980s he planned to cancel a match as the outfield was plainly unfit after heavy rain, but the tea lady, was having none of it. She had boiled the eggs! Tactfully he deferred the abandonment until after the tea had been taken. The Wood dynasty were active in the 1940s when the aforementioned Daisy and her husband Tom were keen committee members. Tom had a leather bag and would strut the boundary selling raffle tickets. Tom had a nephew called Bill who played some useful cricket for the club after a semi-professional football career, but it was his three sons, Ian, Chris and Paul, who made a massive contribution to the fortunes of the club through the 1990s and into the 21st century. Chris was voted as Cheshire County League 'Player of the Year' (Division 2) in 2006 and Paul in 2011. Between them they have scored more than 20,000 runs and taken more than a 1,000 wickets for Bredbury.

2013 - The centenary year was celebrated by the 1st XI winning the Cheshire County League's Fairplay award, the 2nd XI winning their division and the Over 40s lifting the South East Division trophy.

2018 - The prospect of a new ground?

Early Cheshire references to cricket

The first mention of cricket being played in Cheshire was in 1781 when a combined Haughton (Lancashire) and Bredbury (Cheshire) team met eleven gentlemen in the printing business on Brinnington Moor. The first reference to a County match was on 7 October 1818 when the *Salopian Journal* reported 'a few days ago at Oswestry, the gentlemen of Cheshire beat those of Shropshire'. In the same year on 14 August the *Chester Chronicle* reported a match had been played at Eaton Hall, the seat of the Earl of Grosvenor, on 7 August. Several gentlemen of the Cheshire County beat Lord Belgrave, Earl Wilton etc. A great number of people from Chester were spectators.

Broadbottom

Hill End, Mottram Road, Broadbottom SK14 6BB

BROADBOTTOM SITS right on the Cheshire/Derbyshire border. At this point the River Etherow forms the border.

The earliest reference to cricket being played in Broadbottom is to be found in the 1848 accounts of Glossop Cricket Club. The note states 'June 16th 1848: Paid expenses going to Broadbottom to make a match, one shilling'. We might assume this was the return rail fare for eleven players and an umpire at a penny each. The match consisted of two innings per team and 'the contest was commenced about half-past ten, and continued until after three in the afternoon'. W Green secured the first seven-wicket haul by a Broadbottom cricketer.

No official club records have survived before 1938 and so the historical notes have been gleaned from the newspapers of the time. The *North Cheshire Herald* of August 1863 reported that four teams from the village played matches in the same week - Broadbottom Juveniles, Broadbottom Alma, Broadbottom United and New York - against local opposition. Further reports were sporadic, but in 1866 a team called Broadbottom Crescent United appeared. Intermittent reporting continued into the 1870s and only from 1881 do we gain a more complete picture of the embryonic cricket club when the name Hill End was seen for the first time. This would be the club's name until 1949.

The first match in Hill End's history was against the Bankfield Sunday School of Broadbottom, which was won by 40 runs to 34. The frequency of matches increased throughout the 1880s and a committee was formed. End-of-season presentation evenings became the norm. The star of the team was Wright Cooper. He could bat a bit and, of the first dozen 'seven-fers', he claimed six of them.

1889 saw the cessation of cricket in the village as four houses, a school and a church were built on the outfield, but the club was back playing in 1893. In 1894 it joined the North Cheshire Cricket Combination, where it remained until it transferred allegiance to the Glossop & District League in 1897. Success avoided Broadbottom and their two teams were generally considered to be the whipping boys of the league.

> In the 1860s the American Civil War had a severe impact on the village when UK cotton imports dried up and the Broadbottom mills closed. The cotton famine lasted until 1865 when the weaving looms started to clatter again. During the 1860s many villagers were starving and it is said some survived on turnip tops. The mills were a key employer until the industry finally withered away in the 1930s.

In 1919 the Glossop League decided to operate with only one division following the ravages of war upon the cricket-playing youth of the district. When the Hill-Enders turned up for their fourth pre-season practice night they discovered, to their horror that the ground had been ploughed up by the local tenant farmer. All home games were played away and the team finished the season in rock bottom position, although a collection by the rest of the league clubs, amounting to £17 10s 2d, went some way to making amends for lost gate money. Local rivals Mottram made the largest contribution with £3 2s 6d. In March 1920 the farmer paid for his sins at Hyde court, ordered as he was to pay £45 in damages plus costs. He offered no defence and freely admitted that he only wished to prevent cricket being played on the field!

1927 - The first silverware was secured: the 1927 G&DCL championship (and runners-up in the Rhodes Bowl knock-out cup). This signalled the start of the club's golden age; 1930 championship (shared with Tintwistle), 1932 Rhodes Bowl winners and 1934 league champions. The Ball brothers - Harold, Edwin and Sid – played pivotal roles, as did the marvellous all-rounder Harry Braddock, to this day Broadbottom's most decorated cricketer.

Following WW2 a spat between club and league meant that Hill End did not resume league cricket until 1947, but in 1951 they again won the league, this time under Gordon Mellor, but Harry Braddock was still on the scene. The name on the trophy now read 'Broadbottom Sports Club' following a merger with the football club. In 1958 Broadbottom Cricket Club came into being.

The next significant chapter was in 1962 when the exaggerated slope on the ground was levelled - a massive effort by the members. Another protracted period in the doldrums was broken in 1966 when the second team won their knockout cup. In 1967 victory in the Rhodes Bowl again suggested that more success was on the near horizon but was not quite achieved until back-to-back Rhodes Bowl wins in 1974 and 1975, following the first Second Division championship win. One of the unassuming stars of the 1950s and 60s was Jack Heywood, a deadly bowler feared around the league. Jack collapsed on the field in August 1968 and died six days later. The G&DCL trophy for the league's leading bowler was named in his honour.

1975 saw changes off the field with a 'new' pavilion, at a cost of £2,200, overseen by Chairman Eric Potter. Sadly it brought no further success on the field but a re-model of the buildings in 1991, including a new tackle shed and scorebox, coincided with a second Division 2 title and a Rhodes Bowl win in 1995.

The Glossop & District League disbanded in 1999 and, along with a several member clubs, Broadbottom opted to join the Derbyshire & Cheshire Cricket League. Although the second team twice won the Division 4 title in the early 21st century, success in the top flight did not come to Harryfields until 2016 when the first team finally lifted the first division championship with a squad of which 22 of the 24 players used had grown up through the club's own youth cricket system.

> There have been three known ten wicket hauls. When Hollingworth entertained Broadbottom in July 1967 Graham Fox recorded figures of 21.2-7-28-10 for the visitors. Hollingworth were dismissed for 104 but as they were 68-9 'Foxy' must have wondered whether it was going to happen for him before he eventually dismissed the top scorer. Twenty-two seasons later Richard Margave wrote himself into the record book when he claimed his full bag on a visit to Hadfield St Andrew's. The hosts were dismissed for 147. His final figures were 17.5-2-58-10. Mick Mills is the lone player to have achieved a ten-fer on his home turf. Playing for Broadbottom 2nd XI against Mellor 2nd XI in July 1972 he recorded figures of 13.4-5-21-10.

The pavilion in 1975.

Bromborough

Leverhulme Fields, Bromborough CH62 3PU

STORK MARGARINE was launched in 1920. It was produced in Bromborough by Planters, at the time a part of William Lever's group, later Unilever. After food rationing ended in 1954, and advertising campaigns dispelled thoughts that margarine was unhealthy, the production burgeoned. By 1956 the factory as regarded as the largest refinery of edible oils in Europe.

Post WW2 factory football and cricket teams emerged. At the outset the cricketers of Stork CC played on a field which is now the Croft Retail Park and at nearby Woodslee School. Post-match jugs were consumed at the Stork Social Club. In the 1960s they moved to their existing ground where they play alongside Port Sunlight CC.

They re-badged themselves as Bromborough Hotel CC at the very end of the 1990s and then subsequently became plain, Bromborough CC. They have only ever fielded one team. After a period in the Flintshire League, they played in the Merseyside Competition but they now participate in the Cheshire pyramid.

> Former Tranmere Rovers favourite Ken Beamish played for Stork CC in the 1960s. He had a reputation as a sharp-shooting forward, scoring 159 goals in 555 Football League matches, but I'm reliably informed his bowling was less accurate than his shooting. 'Fast, but very erratic' was how it was described to me!

> We are all prone to exaggeration and sceptical about big hits claimed by others but a good number of people have told me about a huge whack by Dave Devlin, who played here in the 1990s. It is claimed during a local midweek league evening fixture he launched the ball out of the ground, across the New Chester Road and onto the frontage of Robert's garage. It's a very long way!

Brooklands

Brooklands Sports Club, Georges Road, Sale M33 2RP

ON 20 JUNE 1883 seven young men met at a house in Sale to draw up the rules for a new club - Brooklands Cricket and Lawn Tennis Club. A plot of land was rented from the Brooks' family estate, the area's largest landowners, and work began to get the club up and running.

1888 - It was proposed that when the professional, Clay, made 50 runs in a match he should receive half a guinea.

1890 - Charged 6d per person for admittance to the ground on match days.

1893 - Joined the Manchester & District Cricket Association.

1897 - The Association wanted neutral umpires. Brooklands said it was unnecessary.

1906 - Taylor, the groundsman who was also in charge of the bar, was relieved of his duties because of deficiencies in the bar receipts.

1910 - Proposed by the Reverend C Jones that the price of whisky and soda should be reduced to 5d but it was decided to keep it at 6d!

1917 - Sale CC were allowed the use of the Brooklands horse for one day per week.

1924 - Special meeting held re Sunday play – split decision just in favour.

1930 - Joe Allured was thought in the opinion of most opposing skippers to be the best bowler in Cheshire. In 1931 he played 18 matches and took 50 wickets, average 7.82. In 1932 he captured 83 wickets, average 8.73 (44 clean bowled).

1937 - Most of the club's present thirteen acres of land was finally purchased from the Brooks' estate.

1940 - In August Joe Allured took his 1000th wicket for Brooklands in twenty playing seasons. At the AGM he received a suitably inscribed, mounted ball.

> **Undoubtedly Nigel Howard is the most eminent cricketer to play for Brooklands. He captained England in four Test matches against India in 1951-52. He played 198 matches for Lancashire between 1946 and 1954. He was the county captain, 1949-53. His younger brother, Barry, played for Brooklands for an even longer period. He also played 35 first-class matches for Lancashire and was Club President 1977-78. Both played hockey for Cheshire.**

1951 - As part of the Borough's programme for the Festival of Britain, a team was picked from five neighbouring clubs to play Nigel Howard's XI.

1959 - Harold Bailey, the groundsman, died having been with the club for 35 years. He had turned the ground into a first class playing area said to be second-to-none. Cheshire matches were hosted.

1968 - MT Thorburn wins the John Riley shield after scoring a century in an hour. (MJB Riley had died earlier in the decade and the shield was

Brooklands' pavilion in 1930.

1980 - It was around this time that the club decided to trade under the name of Brooklands Sports Club in order to embrace all sports.

1999 - The old pavilion was beginning to look tired and a lease was granted to a fitness company to build a new centre which would include changing and bar facilities for Brooklands Sports Club members. The new building opened in January 2000.

Brooklands' pavilion in 1998.

awarded in his memory. He was a fine servant to Brooklands and played for Cheshire).

1975 - Founder members of the Cheshire County League. Cheshire Cup winners.

1979 - Cheshire County League champions. Only 15 players were used during the whole season.

Ten years without missing a game!

Brooklands claim a League record for David Madden, who had not missed a 1st XI game between 26 May 2007, when he was taking his finals at Cambridge University, and his absence from the final fixture of the 2016 season. Before then, ever-present David had played in 220 consecutive league and cup games for the club without ever crying off, going on holiday, being injured – or dropped. Says Treasurer David Garnett: "This is a remarkable record for a good player, nice guy and superb club man".

Finally a Face... (and born on the Wirral)

Reggie Wood was born at West Kirby on the Wirral in 1860. He was the tenth of twelve children. He played cricket for Birkenhead Park, Lancashire (1880-84), Victoria (Australia) and one Test match for England (1887). Until well after the millennium he was last England cricketer for which there was no known photograph. *Finally a Face*, researched by Philip Paine and published in 2007, is the story of how a photograph was eventually found at Charterhouse School and then another at Birkenhead Park Rugby Club.

Bunbury

School Lane, Bunbury CW6 9NR

MY RESEARCH has taken me in so many different directions and on this occasion it led to a winter afternoon meet-up in the pavilion with three stalwarts of the club. Nick Swinbank, the hard-working groundsman, Jerry Tweddle, one-time leading batsman and father of Olympic bronze medal gymnast, Beth Tweddle MBE, and Bob Harris, who added to his cricketing exploits by being an extra in a Bunbury-filmed cricketing scene which featured in the very popular ITV drama, 'Home Fires'.

My attention was drawn to a period framed photograph of the village team entitled 'Undefeated, 1909' and in a glass-fronted case was a splendid worsted-type cricket cap with BCC delightfully embroidered on the front panel. Underneath was an engraving which revealed the cap had belonged to Reginald Alfred Parker. He was too young to go to war but nine of his teammates joined up and tragically all died together in the same battle. It had been donated by local resident, Paul Wilgose, a former umpiring colleague of mine, who had been given the cap by his grandfather.

After WW1, although there is evidence to suggest some informal matches were played in the mid-1960s, remarkably the club did not substantively reform until 1993. Initially a few matches were played at Tarporley School but the local parish magazine reports that 'on 16 July 1994 the Church bells rang to mark the first ball bowled on the ground for some 27 years'. The opposition for this inaugural game were the patrons of the Bunbury Aldersey Primary School, the Worshipful Company of Haberdashers. At the time the field was generously rented to the cricketers by a local land-owner, Simon Sherrard, for an annual rent of £50. He became the club President and once a season he raised a side to play against the club and paid £50 for the privilege! A souvenir bat kept in the pavilion records that Jerry Tweddle scored the first century on the ground in 1994. He could vividly recall changing in an army tent before the

Undefeated, 1909

The cap belonging to Reginald Alfred Parker

current pavilion arrived in readiness for the 1996 season. Alongside the Army tent was a toilet tent and the job of emptying it fell to the batsman who recorded the first duck of the innings!

In the early days a number of high profile matches were organised. In 1995 David English, he of Bunbury Festival fame, was keen to bring along a side given the name association. Heavyweight boxer Gary Mason was in the visiting side, as were Liam Botham and Miss England! Garry Sobers was a spectator. Some years later the fixture was repeated.

When the club was re-formed the constitution directed that 90% of the membership must live in the catchment area of the primary school which is opposite to the ground. Later the rule was relaxed, but this is still very much a community club with a high percentage of locals in the side. That community spirit is demonstrated by an annual match played against the congregarians of St Boniface. A pre-match service is conducted on the outfield and local residents are invited to bring along their pets for a blessing. No ducks allowed?!

It's a delightful ground in a delightful village. The ground slopes gently away from the car park down towards the distant wooden pavilion clad with its colourful hanging baskets. If you visit out of season, there is a good chance you will see sheep grazing on the outfield to this very day.

Heaven forbid but if the cricket were to get a touch tedious how about a nice stroll? A brisk walk to the Dysart Arms opposite the impressive church of St Boniface, or for the more energetic a slightly longer walk to the impressive staircase locks on the Shropshire Union canal.

An aerial view of Bunbury CC

Burton

Gladstone Hall Ground, Dunstan Lane, Burton CH64 5TH

IN THE DELIGHTFUL conservation village of Burton, just a short distance from Ness Gardens, the local cricketers played a combination of T20 in the Chester & District Midweek League and friendly fixtures, but from 2017 they joined the Cheshire pyramid.

The cricket club forms part of the wider Gladstone Village Hall social club, which offers a number of other sporting and recreational pursuits and facilities, including tennis, crown green bowls, snooker, walking and painting.

The cricket club's formation can be traced back to the year of the Queen's silver jubilee, 1977, when a group of locals wanted to enjoy competitive cricketing contests with like-minded teams, played in an idyllic setting. The view across the Dee estuary has always proved popular with the visiting teams.

As reported by Mollington CC (September 2012)

The tactic seemed to be to get Burton's Guy Tilby into bat as soon as possible. Nicholson duly obliged by bowling their opener with the very first ball of the match and in he came. The opposition may as well have just boarded up one end for the remainder of the innings as Tilby brought all his usual qualities to the crease; an immovable beast full of obduracy, determination and endurance. One has to admire his defiance as both the Mollington bowling attack and the home team heckling left him unfazed. He remained in the middle for the entire innings.

Mrs Tilby is always troubled by her husband playing cricket on a Sunday. She sought assurance from the local vicar asking whether it is indeed a sin to play on a Sunday. "It's not a sin," replied the vicar. "The way he plays, it's a crime!"

Caldy

Paton Field, Telegraph Road, Caldy CH48 1NZ

CALDY CC IS the most westerly of all the clubs in the county.

Members of the rugby section will argue that it is by far and away the largest and most successful part of the Sports Club, and there is much evidence to support this viewpoint. Indeed, they won promotion to National Division 1 as recently as April 2017, but when did they last play at Twickenham cry the cricketers!? In both 1996 and 1997 Caldy CC won the National Village Cup on the hallowed turf at Lord's in what, indisputably, have been the twin high-points in the history of the cricket club.

In 1996 Langleybury from Hertfordshire were defeated and the following year it was the turn of Shipton-under-Wychwood, whose side included theatre/film producer and talented cricketer Sam Mendes, to collect the runner-up medals. As a matter of fact the game was almost cancelled as it was played on the day Princess Diana died and there were frantic morning telephone calls between Lord's, the Football Association, Downing Street and Buckingham Palace observing protocols before the game was given the green light. The following week *OK* magazine included a photograph of the two teams lined up at the pavilion steps for two minutes of respectful silence. I am bound to ask what other Cheshire cricket team has appeared in such a best-selling magazine! In the clubhouse is a lovely showcase displaying the stumps and other souvenirs from the two games.

The victorious Caldy Village Cup team of 1997. Two of the players on the middle row, Keith Findlay (second from left) and Jason Cooper (fourth from left) both went on to play for Cheshire. Findlay played two Trophy matches in 1998 and Cooper represented his county in four Championship games in 2000. The author is on the extreme left.

Having mentioned those two momentous occasions, the scales must be balanced and a stupendous low-point occurred on 19 April 2015. Ill-advisedly, as a mere Liverpool Competition Division 2 side, they entered the perennially strong National Club KO Cup and were drawn away to a powerful Nantwich side. A young and inexperienced team turned up and after their 45 overs the home team had racked up 579. Liam Livingstone, who has subsequently played with considerable success for Lancashire, had 350 against

his name, scored off 138 balls. When Caldy were dismissed for 79 and lost by 500 runs the news went viral and the club chairman, Dave Brown, spent the next two days fielding worldwide requests for telephone interviews! Manchester brewer Joseph Holt commissioned a new brew - Livvy's 350!

By the way, it is not a good idea to record a duck at Paton Field as the pavilion is a very long way from the cricket square via the 1st XV rugby field, which forms a part of the cricketing outfield, and then up a steep flight of steps. Plenty of time for thoughtful reflection!

The wooden pavilion, a pre-requisite given its location on National Trust land, sits prominently on the highest part of the ground and affords splendid views across the River Dee towards North Wales. Moel Famau shyly peeps over the Clwydian hills.

The club was originally entitled West Wirral and based in Hoylake but moved to Caldy in 1953. The club celebrates its centenary in 2021.

Mark Gillespie on tour with Caldy CC in 1999 having scored centuries on three consecutive days. He spent two seasons with Caldy and subsequently represented New Zealand, primarily as a bowler. He played five Tests (best bowling 6-113), thirty-two ODIs (4-58) and eleven T20s (4-7).

Cheadle

225 Kingsway, Cheadle, SK8 1LA

FOR SEVERAL years the village of Cheadle has been without a cricket organisation, but at length effort has been made which promises to result in the establishment of a really good club, the proposal being to throw the membership open to all grades of society able and willing to pay a subscription of 15s per annum. A ground has been secured from Mr Oswald Lowe, of Gatley, situate on the Gatley Road, the entrance being from High Grove Lane. Already Mr Walter Field, of Cheadle, is engaged in laying a large pitch and the appearances are decidedly favourable to the success of the organisation. Between 40 and 50 members have up to the present been enrolled, and at a meeting of the committee on Wednesday night the body placed the contract with Mr Jonathan Alcock, joiner and builder, of Cheadle, for the erection of a commodious tent. The pitch will not, however, be ready for play until June or July, so that the fixtures of the club will be required to be played away from home. The managing body includes some of the most energetic spirits in the local athletic world, and if they are supported, as they ought to be and as we believe they will be, the Cheadle Cricket Club

> I am told by my mother that one summer's day in 1930 my father returned home after a day watching cricket at Cheadle cricket ground without an important member of the family, namely me. Whether he had not yet become used to parenthood or had been toasting too exuberantly a century is not recorded. Nevertheless, I was apparently left in my pram on the boundary edge to be later retrieved by my no doubt out of breath sire!
>
> **Recalled by Basil Garratt in 1996.**

will very shortly take a prominent position among the organisations of the district.

The above is an extract from the *Stockport Advertiser* of 12 April 1895 and is repeated in *150 Not Out*, the impressive 412 page tome produced in 2013 by Andrew Taylor and Paul Sperring. That title and its year of publication suggest a founding date of 1863 and the early pages tell of at least two grounds before the existing site was acquired. It also refers to an entwinement with the lacrosse club going back to 1880. So far as records allow the book plots the history of the club. It celebrates the triumphs, the characters and the challenges that have shaped it over the period. The story is told through scorecards and reminiscences and the inclusion of numerous quality photographs help to provide a unique insight into the social history of the club.

The book concludes by selecting an All Time (Post WW1) XI. Garry Cash, Tom Mather, Tony Murphy, Ian Tansley and Jack Holt are nominated as automatic picks. There is debate around the remainder, but as there were surprisingly few candidates for the spinning berth a place was found for the 2016 captain, Paul Sperring ('who also adds to the batting and can drop any number of chances at first slip!'). Tony Murphy is identified as the Cheadle player who went on to achieve most in the game, playing first-class cricket for both Lancashire (1985-88) and Surrey (1989-94). He also represented Cheshire (1984-99).

> **Gary Cash played for Cheadle between 1977 and 1995 and scored a club record 11016 runs. He was just 18 when he joined from High Lane CC having attended Stockport Grammar School and played for the English Schools Cricket Association. He was a virtual ever-present during his stay, a young tyro through the initial tough early years, a brilliant match-winner as the Cheadle team grew into a trophy-winning prospect, an assured batsman and accomplished leader in one of the club's finest periods in the mid-to-late 1980s and the stand-out player afterwards in a team that was clearly in decline. He moved to Marple and remarkably he is still playing. No one has scored more runs in the history of the Cheshire County Cricket League.**

Photograph from the Iain Taylor collection

> **After playing some Minor County cricket with Cheshire and receiving his Cheshire cap in 1984, Tony Murphy played 84 first-class matches and bagged 208 wickets with a best bowling analysis of 6-97. Additionally, he played in 99 List A fixtures and captured another 121 victims. Best bowling 6-26. On six occasions he played for Surrey against Lancashire, his former county. Included in that half-dozen was 'Fairbrother's match' at the Oval in May 1990. This was the occasion when 'Harvey' recorded 366 in a Lancashire all out total of 863. Tony, rather more modestly, had 44-6-160-2 against his name in the bowling column. It was a flat deck and most will have forgotten that Mike Atherton scored 191, Gehan Mendis 102 and Ian Greig, captaining Surrey, 291. One of the umpires in that match was Cheshire-born, Barry Dudleston. After Tony's Surrey playing days were over he returned north to play for Cheshire until 1999. Latterly he has played Over 50s cricket for Surrey.**

Cheadle Hulme

Grove Park, Cheadle Hulme SK8 7NB

IT IS DIFFICULT to picture Cheadle Hulme as a tiny village with only a couple of hundred inhabitants but that was the reality in 1881 when a handful of enthusiasts decided to form a cricket team. A farm field belonging to Mr Leather was the original home and, better known as Ladybridge Road, it remained home until the move to Grove Park in 1970.

By 1894 membership of the Manchester & District Cricket Association had been gained and sections for tennis and bowls had been formed.

Just before WW2 the ground was purchased but a new pavilion worthy of the sporting amenities was a priority. The dream of more than half a century eventually came to fruition in May 1939 when a £3000 two-storey clubhouse was opened. In that same year, as the shadows of war gathered, the coveted Manchester Association trophy was secured by a team which was abruptly broken up by the impending conflict, but the names of Connolly, Sanderson, Scarborough, Chadwick and Collinge were as respected amongst their contemporaries as

> **Cheadle Hulme on tour. Recollections penned by Howard Marston in 1981...** To begin with the tour must have a 'Mr Fixit', who, whatever other qualities he possesses, must be cunning, conniving and devious. These personality defects are absolutely essential to secure fixtures with good clubs who have never heard of Cheadle Hulme. More importantly, hotel personnel need to be convinced that all the members of the touring party, while enjoying an odd glass or two of 'lotion', are thoroughly reliable, stable and well-mannered young men interested only in upholding the true traditions of the sport of gentlemen. My favourite incident involves my first tour when I was persuaded to take my car plus a young gentleman, who has since become one of the club's best known captains. He was roused from his slumber with difficulty, only to discover that his kit and the tour bag had been safely locked away in the clubhouse. A flash of inspiration produced a note of apology wrapped around half a brick which was hurled through a large window pane in the main lounge. The kit was retrieved and a lightning departure made! ...Bert, the proprietor of a certain Bournemouth hotel, drank brandy like most landladies drink tea and his wife had the unwanted reputation for providing the nastiest toilets and serving the greasiest breakfasts! ...The tour organiser must ensure that the bar hardly ever closes and that the breakfast waitresses are suffering from advanced stages of nymphomania! ...Our sporting activities on tour are not confined solely to cricket and on one of the most memorable indulgences in other pastimes must be the occasion when one of our number, after a heavy lunchtime session, decided along with other brethren to attend an aqua show. Temptation overcame him and, fully clothed, he joined the lovely ladies in the water, much to their consternation and that of the management. The audience, however, were delighted and, I suspect, believed it to be all part of the show. Happy days! Long live the tour!!

the names of Howarth, O'Brien, Beckett, Locke and Thompson were in the 1980s. Disaster struck on 8 May 1946 when the clubhouse was burnt to a shell. It was re-occupied some years later but was never quite the same.

During the late fifties a modest young student, who was living locally, arrived at the club. His name was Abbas Ali Baig and he transformed the batting strength of the team. He went to Oxford University and was, very soon, playing for India against England at Old Trafford, scoring a century on debut. He played in ten Tests for India with a top score of 112. At the first-class level he played 235 matches and amassed 12,367 runs with 21 centuries and a best score of 224 not out. While at Oxford University he collected four Blues, 1959-62.

A major post-war event having more significance than anticipated was the incorporation of Didsbury Rugby Union Club, but then in 1967 the club were faced with a difficult decision when it became clear that Manchester RFU (the oldest rugby club in the world) were selling their Salford base and moving to Cheadle Hulme. The rest is history but suffice to say that by 1970 the ground was shared with them at Grove Park. A new clubhouse typical of the era's architecture, low-rise and functional, was built. Now in the Cheshire County League, initially under the inspired leadership of Eddie Pimlott and then John Howarth, Neil O'Brien, Dave Hancock and Neil Smith, the club went from strength to strength, winning the top division in 1977, 1978, 1980, 1981, 1982 , 1984 and 1990. Additionally the Cheshire Cup was won in 1978 and 1990.

> Neil O'Brien had such a glittering playing career it is tricky to know where to start. He played more than 200 matches for Cheshire between 1965 and 1991. He was captain between 1987 and 1990. Commendably, he played two first-class matches for the Minor Counties, against the Indians in 1979 and the Sri Lankans in 1981, plus another 34 List A matches. In two of the one day matches he won Man of the Match awards - one of these was for Minor Counties East against Leicestershire in 1978. He top scored with 31 and captured 4-15 off his 11 overs. His very notable scalps were Brian Davison, Roger Tolchard, Jack Birkenshaw and Paddy Clift. The other was at the Oval in 1981 against Surrey. He scored 51 out of his side's modest total 98. Coincidentally, his Cheshire colleague, David Bailey, was his captain in both those matches as well as in his two first-class appearances.
>
> In addition to his distinguished record at that level he was the Cheadle Hulme captain when they became 1st XI champions in 1981 and 1982 having joined the club in 1978. In 1990 he starred in the Cheshire Cup final when Heaton Mersey provided the opposition. In a closely-fought match Neil received the Man of the Match trophy from Freddie Millett for his all-round performance – 33 not out, 2-14 and a fine catch. Oh, and by the way, when he turned out for Minor Counties East at Jesmond in May 1977 he dismissed Geoffrey Boycott.

In more recent times Ewan McCray has given over a decade of dedicated service helping to bring on some promising youngsters prior to hanging up his boots in 2014. He played for Cheshire between 1989 and 2002 and with Derbyshire CCC in 1991 (two first-class matches and four classified as List A).

THE CHESHIRE HEARTLAND

The Manchester conurbation properly ceases to the south of the River Bollin; from there onwards for many a mile there is spread out before one a beautiful rural landscape barely altered for over a century. We are now in Cheshire proper, well described as 'the greenest county in England'.

GF Turton, 1988

Cheadle Hulme Ladybridge

Meadway Road, Cheadle Hulme, Stockport SK8 5NZ

THE NAME Cheadle Hulme Ladybridge was not adopted until 1980. Originally they played as Christ Church CC and later as Moorfield CC.

1948 - The original members of Christ Church CC were either from the church youth club in Heaton Norris or from the local scout group. Maurice Levy was the captain and it was his mother who had organised some fund-raising events to buy the first bag of shared equipment. At the outset, matches were played on local school pitches in the Youth Organisation Council League.

1951 - Many of the founder members were now too old to play in youth cricket and the club joined Division 2 of the Stockport & District League. Regular opponents were Heaviley Sunday School, Woodlands Methodists, Old Stocconians and Stockport Sunday School. In 1957 they were promoted and to coincide with playing in the top division they also changed their name to Moorfield CC as most of the players lived in that particular area.

1960s/70s/80s - All change! By 1968 they were playing in the North Cheshire Federation and a year later in the South Manchester League. In 1971 they moved to the Ladybridge Road ground after it was vacated by Cheadle Hulme. By 1972 they were playing in the High Peak League and in the Cheshire Cricket Conference by 1976. Club records show that in 1977 Clairmonte Depeiaza played for the club and scored 40 without being dismissed. It appears to have been a one-off appearance against Kerridge, but very few clubs at this level can boast a Test player.

1990s - An EGM was held in April as the club had lost up to ten senior players, but the club rallied and only a year later the Bardsley Trophy was won when Hawk Green were defeated in the final (196 for 7 v 167 all out). 1996 proved to be another good year, undefeated in the league and runners-up to Mottram in the Rhodes Bowl final. Neil Worthington starred with the ball (50 wickets) and Simon Clarke with the bat (700 runs).

2000 - Joined the Cheshire Cricket League. They were relegated in the first season. Promotion followed in 2002 when ably assisted by their first Overseas acquisition – Steven Howells from Barbados - who collected 70 wickets during the season. 2005 was, arguably, Ladybridge's highest ever league finish; fourth in Division 2. Jim Stuart and Ryan Lindsay starred with the bat and Matt Bishop and Anton Roach with the ball. Another relegation followed in 2006.

2008 - One of the founder members, Norman Haskell, attended the sixtieth anniversary dinner.

2015 – The first team gained promotion from the Cheshire League Division 3, finishing as runners-up to Port Sunlight. Matthew Bishop became the first Ladybridge player to score 500 runs and take 50 wickets in one season.

Chelford

Peover Lane, Chelford SK11 9AJ

CHELFORD CC CELEBRATED their Silver Jubilee in 1973 and AS Potts penned an interesting article for the Cheshire Club Cricket Conference handbook in that same year. Mrs Evans, the wife of the local doctor, was reported to be the 1948 catalyst for the establishment of the village team, encouraged by the equally enthusiastic Colonel Fox. She had persuaded Fred Hope, who occupied Abbey Farm, to allocate a field behind the post office. The author describes the enormity of the task of converting an overgrown, uneven field complete with a large hump and a substantial ridge and suggested the cleaning of the Augean Stables by Hercules was a half hour of light entertainment by comparison!

A very mixed Alderley Edge team provided some early opposition. Given the extremely rudimentary facilities on offer it must be assumed that their Fixture Secretary had been unable to refuse the wily charms of Mrs Evans? At the time the ground had no pavilion and the visitors were shocked when they were invited to change in the vicarage garage! It must be presumed they never recovered from this experience as they lost the match. Eventually a shed was purchased from Siddington Tennis Club and used as the first pavilion.

As was often the case, cattle continued to graze the cricket field, but the small square was pegged off and protected by an electric fence. The Colonel was anxious to try out the newly-acquired gadgetry, "Does it work, old boy?" Sensing an opportunity for some fun, one of the working party got the Colonel to grasp the wire and switched on the power. Hardened troopers though the lads were they could not but help admire the full-throated flow of army invective language that followed! Fortunately Mrs Evans and the Reverend Gamon were away making drinks for the workers and safely out of earshot!

Also recalled were regular visits from occasional player, Professor Sir Bernard Lovell, who would sometimes bring along an overseas visitor from Jodrell Bank. The writer suspected that a mystified Russian delegation went home firmly convinced the British were quite mad.

As the years rolled by, so the facilities improved. The pitches were turned round, a new pavilion was built in 1965 and a new scorebox was added in 1990. One of the great successes for the club was the Junior Festival, which was inaugurated in 1983 by Mike Shenton, groundsman for more than twenty years, Derek Higgins and Paul Heath, and quickly became an important competition for local junior cricketers.

A foundation date of 1948 might suggest Chelford were late starters, but the opposite is true. The first village associations with the game go back to at least 1861 when the County team played in the village, close to the railway station. When the County Club moved out in 1882, the ground was used by the Gentlemen of Cheshire.

Cherry Hill

Chorlton Lane, Malpas SY14 7EP

A DELIGHTFUL, privately-owned ground a couple of miles distant from the impressive Grade 1 listed parish church of St Oswald's in the centre of Malpas. It is set in beautiful rolling countryside with lovely views across the surrounding landscape to the Welsh Hills beyond. It has a charming pavilion and a large playing area complete with a very substantial tree within the field of play, or overhanging the boundary if preferred. A 'local law' allows a batsman to be caught off the tree, but it has yet to happen!

The owner established the ground in 1987 and unusually(!) commissioned his local postman, the late Terry Winter, to lay the square. The facility is superbly maintained and as well as hosting friendly cricket - in 2017 the Laconics, the Spasmodics, Malpas CC and the Young Salopians were amongst the invited clubs - it provides a highly desirable venue for weddings and other celebratory events. A 1990 fixture card confirmed the Gentlemen of Cheshire, the Free Foresters, Rydal Dolphins, Cholmondeley CC and the Pink Elephants were all visitors.

Over the years the Gentlemen of Cheshire have played a good number of matches here. The Gents are a club with a very rich history that dates back to 1805 when they first played the Gentlemen of Staffordshire. It is reputed they played for a purse of 50 guineas and a hogshead of beer, and the losers had to buy dinner at the Myrtle & Mermaid in Shrewsbury. Former Neston, Lancashire and England cricketer Ken Cranston (b 1917, d 2007) was a leading player in the ranks of the Cheshire Gents as well as a good friend of the Cherry Hill owner, Miles Clarke and was one of many distinguished guests to frequent this cricketing idyll.

The Cherry Hill tree

There is much to admire in the superbly appointed pavilion, but I was particularly intrigued with the pavilion's downpipes which are actually rain chains with ornamental cricket balls positioned just above the soakaway. They don't have these at Lord's!

If you are not planning an imminent family wedding here, watching a bit of cricket on the ground would be a pleasant experience and a good opportunity to dust off your old club cravat and panama hat.

Chester Boughton Hall

Boughton Hall Avenue, Filkins Lane, Chester CH3 5EL

UNTIL THE emergence of Boughton Hall CC, a Chester club had played cricket on the Roodee and had been regarded as the leading local side, but they fell on hard times and eventually went out of existence in 1899.

In the 1870s Boughton Hall was a large private house standing in spacious grounds. Its owner and occupant was John Thompson, a wealthy businessman. His enthusiasm for the game was established while he was educated at Rossall School and Trinity College, Cambridge and it prompted him to convert part of his land into a cricket ground and invite his friends to play under his captaincy.

1874-85 - The fixture list included matches against quality opposition. Resounding defeats were inflicted on both Liverpool and Warrington. The top of the Warrington scoresheet was appended, 'who batted shamefully'.

1884 - Liverpool, the senior side in the area, were extremely strong at this time and were able to regularly include the Steel brothers, AG, DQ and HB (all played for Lancashire and AG for England), but they were defeated thanks to the efforts of Harry Hack, who took 8-24. The Hack family had club connections for many years; indeed, Frank Hack, another fine player, was President of the club in their (1973) centenary year.

> In the 1880s, Dr Archer, a GP in Chester, was unsure whether his patients would approve of his sporting activity so he played under the unsubtle pseudonym of AM Bowman!

1910 - Cheshire hosted Northumberland in the first County match played at Boughton Hall.

1911 - *Cricket Archive* records that Cheshire played Staffordshire at Boughton Hall in a Cricket Week that featured the opening of the new pavilion. Sydney Barnes rather spoilt the local celebration with match figures of 12-50.

1913 - Chester Nomads football club, founded in 1904, started to play at Boughton Hall.

1922 - After WW1 the Liverpool *Daily Post* compiled a table of matches of the area's leading clubs, which it called the Liverpool Competition. Boughton Hall had fixtures with most of the teams involved and sought recognition as a member. The newspaper replied to the Secretary as follows... *I think I may assure you that if you are able to arrange home and away fixtures with at least 8 clubs already in the table you will find that the press will include the club in next year's table automatically, and without any formal application to any authority – because none is constituted, the Championship being, as I have frequently said, only a notional one. I will go a step further and will add that the local cricketing public would most heartily welcome the accession of Boughton Hall to the list of the clubs competing for our District Championship. They will prove foeman worthy of the steel of the best of our clubs.*

1923 - First year as a Liverpool Competition member, but as the club declined to drop traditional fixtures against the likes of Llandudno, Winnington Park and Newton-le-Willows they were never able to accumulate enough points to feature near the top of the table but performed well on an 'average points per game basis'. The ownership of the ground had changed hands in 1899 and the current owner made it known he proposed to dispose of land situated between the club and Filkins Lane. After protracted discussion a General Meeting held in 1925 resulted in the club becoming a Limited Liability Company with capital of £1000 divided into 1000 shares of £1, each with all club members taking up one or more shares. The land previously used as allotments was then used to extend the cricket ground, lay tennis courts and re-organise the access.

1920-30 - The annual Minor County match allowed many a famous name to display his skill to the Chester public. For example, the great Sydney Barnes appeared for Staffordshire (1911 and 1933) and AC MacLaren (1922), JT Tyldesley, Eddie Paynter (1926) and Cyril Washbrook (1931) all played for Lancashire 2nds.

The pavilion as it was between the wars.

> **1939** - The next generation of the Jones family - Bill, Leslie, Bryan and Bruce - had become playing members and the occasional appearance together of all six for a team must have been a scorer's nightmare. 'A plague of these Joneses' ran a headline in a local paper as the reporter struggled vainly to avoid his report looking like a page in a Welsh telephone directory. (Also see Tattenhall entry about WE and LN Jones).

1945 - The owner of Boughton Hall died and the club were given an option of buying the ground for £3500. A decision was taken to raise the money by an issue of debentures in the Company, at 4% interest, redeemable after 30 years. The face of the ground had changed. Army Nissen huts were now on the tennis courts and car park and became a source of concern as they were occupied by squatters until 1947 when they were demolished.

1950 - The 1st XI debut of 14-year-old Bob Barber. It was clear he would go on to achieve greater things and his Boughton Hall appearances were restricted, but he did occasionally play between 1950 and 1966. After Cambridge University he joined Lancashire and subsequently Warwickshire. He played 28 matches for England and the pinnacle of his achievements was his innings of 185 against Australia in Sydney in January 1966. This match was a mere four months before he had his final innings for Boughton Hall. On 6 May 1966 he played against Southport & Birkdale and had a significant influence on the outcome, top scoring with 28 and then taking 3-39 (CBH 123, Southport 102). Remarkably, he was playing Test cricket again in August 1966 when England entertained the West Indies at Headingley and he bowled Garfield Sobers for 174. His last Test appearance was in 1968.

1955 - A change of name! It's now Chester Boughton Hall CC and a change of pavilion was also required as the ancient building was classified as virtually beyond repair. £4500 was needed and nearly half that sum was raised by selling off the land where the Nissen huts once stood. By 1960 the dream had become a reality after a loan from the Nomads FC and the issue of 'pavilion bonds'.

> At the club dinner, Mrs Reg Stockton gave members a glimpse of being a 'Cricketer's wife'. 'She must see that the flannels were ready and there must be no major domestic crisis before a big match. She must not tread the hallowed ground of the pavilion, yet might be permitted to help with the tea and cut sandwiches. After the game, she must steal away. Further, she was expected to produce further cricketers. Her husband, she said, had reproached her for having a daughter, when the club so badly needed a left-arm bowler!'

1985-86 - Soon to be West Indian Test cricketers, Winston Benjamin (1985) and Curtley Ambrose (1986) had successful seasons with the club.

2000+ - Under the shrewd and enthusiastic steerage of Chris Fleet, the club strives for excellence at all levels. The Cheshire Cup was won in 2012/13/14/15/17, the coveted Cheshire Premier League title was secured in 2013 and 2017 and, most prestigiously, they became National T20 Club Champions in 2014. For variety they won the Liverpool Echo Cup in 2016.

The new pavilion, pictured in 1960.

Chester County Officers

Mannings Lane, Upton. Chester CH2 4EU

THE CRICKETERS first came together in 1933 when the Chester-based staff of Cheshire County Council started a cricket section. They played at the garrison sports ground in Eaton Road, Handbridge until after the war, when the County Council developed a brand new sports ground at Newton Lane with facilities for tennis, hockey, football cricket and bowls. This was a fine ground, but in 1974 following local government reorganisation Chester City Council made a decision to abandon that facility. Cricket continued at the ground for a couple of years until the move was made to the current site.

The new Cheshire County Sports Club was state of the art and catered for multi-indoor sports, but the cricket ground was spartan, a large field with a basic brick changing room and a subsequent exodus of players weakened the side.

In 2006, a fabulous new two storey clubhouse was built on the ground thanks to a Football Foundation grant totalling £800k. All the sections have benefitted greatly from this superb facility, which is now managed by a private company formed by the members of the Sports Club itself.

At the opening of the new pavilion in 2008 Tony Collard, a club member since 1967, addressed the large gathering and related some clippings from the cricket club archive.

He shared a note from the minutes of a 1950 meeting when five bats were ordered at three guineas each, and five balls were purchased to last the season for both 1st and 2nd XI teams at a cost of £1.40 each. He went on to say after a good season in 1957 the following year was a near disaster, the crowning ignominy being all out for 16 against Lymm Oughtrington Park. A plea for new young cricketers was answered in the late 1960s as a whole crop of schoolboys joined, "many of whom are the old men you see littered around this room." A new steely resolve developed with the then captain Dave Castle, who bowled the last over at Stretford and ran out the non-striker for backing up to win the game, engendering some serious scuffling as the players left the field. Ouch!

This new toughness was demonstrated again in the last match of 1973 when CCO were playing at Barnton, needing not to lose to take the aggregate trophy and with Barnton themselves needing to win to take that same award. This was the era of time cricket when declarations were made. CCO simply did not declare and batted through until there was insufficient time for Barnton to bat, whereupon they walked off the field. CCO were champions. Another ouch! Of that group Peter Glover was at the dinner along with bowling maestros, ex-Lancashire player Peter Greenwood, left arm spinner Alan Wilks (90 wickets in the season) and express Welshman Dave James.

The late 1980s was described as another golden era with league championships being secured in 1986 and 1989. Twenty years later nine of that playing squad attended the dinner and were heartily congratulated as highly successful all-rounders. Most had completed the double of 500 pints and 50 curries in the season. Happy days!

Tony Collard invited the assembled crowd to toast the club and its future. Nearly ten years on, and with fifty years membership to his name, Tony is still central to most things within the cricket section and thoroughly deserves a loyal toast of his very own.

CHESHIRE COUNTY CRICKET CLUB HONORARY OFFICIALS 1908-2017

PRESIDENTS
1909-53	Dukes of Westminster
1954-67	Lord Leverhulme
1968-70	C.J. Sparks
1971-73	H.S. Brown
1974-76	Rev. Canon H.S. Randle
1977-79	A.M. Wolstenholme
1980-82	Rev Canon H.S. Randle
1983-85	A.M. Wolstenholme
1986-88	P.A.C. Kelly
1989-91	B.M. Lowe
1992-94	B.S. Jones
1995-97	J.A. Sutton
1998	R.A. Richardson
1999-2001	B.S. Jones
2002-2004	J.B. Pickup
2005-2007	A.G. Hall
2008-2010	G.C. Hardstaff
2011-2013	A.B. Percival
2014-2016	J.B. Pickup
2017	D.W. Sharp

CHAIRMEN
1908-11	C.J. Hughes
1912-13	F. Fairbank
1914-31	*
1932-39	G.B. Eaton
1946-48	L.N. Jones
1949-64	J.D. Worthington
1965-83	B.M. Lowe
1984-98	R.A. Richardson
1998-2004	G.C. Hardstaff
2005-2013	J.B. Pickup
2013-	D. Bailey

HON SECRETARIES
1908-11	H.P. Rigby
1912-29	J.J. Pendlebury
1930	H.W. Hodgson
1931-46	A.R. Crooke
1947-48	G. Bull
1949-51	J.B. Pimlott
1952-57	L. Wilson
1958-59	Rev Canon H.S. Randle
1960-79	B.S. Jones
1980-2004	J.B. Pickup
2005-2009	A.B. Percival
2010-	D.E. Hastings

HON TREASURERS
1908	W. Bibbey
1909-11	W. Stonehewer
1912-18	D. Reddrop
1919-29	G.A. Starkey
1930	G.B. Eaton
1931	J.H. Beilby
1932-57	C.J. Sparks
1958-63	L. Wilson
1964-82	W.E. Smith
1982-2012	A.G. Hall
2012-	K.S. McGuffie

CAPTAINS
1909	Rev F.C.L. Hamilton
1910	None Appointed
1911	Selected each match
1912-13	F. Fairbank
1914	F.L. Eaton & V. Hope
1919-26	V. Hope
1927-28	W.E. Jones
1929	H.W. Hodgson
1930	E.G. Parker
1931-34	L.N. Jones
1935-47	J.D. Worthington
1948	L. Wilson
1949	A.M. Wolstenholme
1950-53	W.H.R. Jones
1954-58	B.M. Lowe
1959-73	F.W. Millett
1974-76	D. Bailey
1977-86	J.A. Sutton
1987-90	N.T. O'Brien
1991-2001	I. Cockbain
2002-2011	A.J. Hall
2012-2014	J.A. Duffy**
2015	D.A. Woods
2016-2017	L.F. Dixon

No Minor Counties cricket was played 1915-18 and 1940-45
*Between 1914-31 a Chairman was elected from the committee members present at each meeting
** In J.A. Duffy's absence, D.A. Woods acted as Captain in Championship Matches.

Cholmondeley

Castle Grounds, Cholmondeley SY14 8AH

IT'S NO SURPRISE that opponents are content to travel significant distances for the privilege of playing in his Lordship's garden. The ground is situated within the Cholmondeley Castle Estate, which has been owned by successive generations of the Cholmondeley family.

The club was founded in May 1886 after a meeting at the then Cholmondeley School. The 'founding fathers' were local men, farmers and estate workers and during the early years Merrill, the butler, and Hughes, the local blacksmith, were in the team. Run scoring was not easy. The surviving records for 1913 show that in seventeen matches Cholmondeley only scored 936 runs, a mere average of 55 per match. The square, such as it was, had iron hurdles placed around it to keep off the sheep, so the first task before play was to remove them and place them in stacks which served as boundary markers.

For a good number of years there were no changing facilities, but in 1924 Lady Cholmondeley gifted a tent. This was the changing facility until 1928 when the then Marquis of Cholmondeley provided the greater part of the funds needed for the erection of a pavilion with a thatched roof. The building was erected on stilts at the water's edge and had to be reinforced several times to prevent it toppling into the water. The roof remained thatched until it was replaced with a tiled one in 1967. In 1975 the Club erected the present pavilion with money raised from loans, debentures and a grant obtained from the National Playing Fields Association.

> The club was disbanded during WW2 although it is thought some Polish refugees billeted at the castle played some casual matches.

Inevitably, after the war some improvements were made. A permanent fence was erected in 1948 with timber provided by the Estate and the first sight screens appeared in 1949, but the pleasure of playing here has always been the beauty of the surroundings. The backdrop of the castle peering down on the white-clad cricketers is unrivalled.

Arthur Jones waiting to serve you.

Every club needs a loyal stalwart and Cholmondeley can look back with pleasure and remember Jack Blake, who was a member for more than sixty years and club chairman for over twenty. A retired solicitor and former Chester city councillor, he made his debut for the club in 1926 as a 16-year-old schoolboy. He valued friendship and his sportsmanship and sociability did much to preserve the traditions of the game. He was at the club to oversee the centenary celebrations in 1986 when a splendid cricket week was organised. Among the opposition were Neston, the Spasmodics, a Shropshire Xl, a Cheshire Xl and old Wrekinians.

The club's most famous 'old boy' is the celebrated best-selling author Dick Francis, who was a playing member in the 1940s and 50s. He became champion jockey and jockey to Her Majesty the Queen Mother and in that famous Grand National of 1956 was robbed of victory in the last 50 yards when Devon Loch collapsed for no apparent reason. He wrote 42 crime novels and sold more than 60 million copies in 35 languages. He died age 89 in 2010. Talking after his death, his son Felix acknowledged that his mother was the real author. Dick was known by the publishers to be two people. "My Mother was Mary and my Father was Richard. Together they were Dick".

When you visit this stunning ground nip into the pavilion. It's very likely Arthur Jones, a veteran of 500 2nd XI matches, will be waiting to serve you at the bar and Eric Cliff, 28 years in the 1st XI, will be keeping him company.

Christleton

Little Heath, Christleton CH3 7AH

WHO WAS the BBC Sports Personality of the Year in 1975? The answer is David Steele of Northamptonshire, who at the age of 34, bespectacled and prematurely grey-haired, surprisingly debuted for England against Australia in the 1975 home Ashes series. He was selected to blunt the Aussie speedsters, Dennis Lillee and Jeff Thomson, and in the three Tests he played in that series he recorded scores of 50, 45, 73, 92, 39 and 66. Given his new celebrity status, it was a feather in the cap of Christleton CC that they were able to persuade him to open their new pavilion on 17 April 1976. There is still a brass plaque and photograph on the wall in the bar area which records the occasion. Also in the photograph is Gordon Williams, who was club chairman at the time, and that is the clue to Steele's attendance. Gordon's son, Richard, played alongside Steele in the Northamptonshire side and as a youngster played some of his early cricket at Little Heath.

1870 - The Club was founded in this year but then became defunct for a short period until it was resurrected in 1899 by the Parish Rector, Reverend Garnett, who was a fine player himself. The original ground was at the Park, now part of Christleton High School. The outfield was kept short by grazing cattle. Teas were served 'alfresco' under an enormous chestnut tree. Records show that 26 teas cost £1 plus an extra 3 shillings for the hire of a pony and trap to transport the tea lady and food to the ground.

1947 - No cricket was played during the war, but soon afterwards the King George V Playing Field became available. This is the play area immediately before the entrance to the current ground and the club remained here until moving to its present home in 1976. A small shed was built for changing and doubled up as a machinery store. Only friendlies were played until the 1960s. The players travelled to away games by bicycle, car or train. A game played at Elworth had to finish early for the players to catch the last bus back to Chester!

1963 – Joined the Cheshire Association. It was the first time that the club had played in competitive matches. A tea room was added to the old pavilion.

1975 – The cricket and football clubs joined forces to form Christleton Sports Club and an enthusiastic group of members, led by Gordon

Williams, who had moved to Christleton from Bangor where he had undertaken a similar project, set about raising funds to move to a new ground and develop modern facilities. The pitches were laid at no cost by club president Sid Dandy, a local farmer making use of his equipment and workers.

1989 - A Richard Williams Testimonial game was hosted when a Northamptonshire team played a Christleton Select XI. The Northants team included Curtley Ambrose and England players David Capel and Nick Cook, who had both played in the sixth Test v Australia at the Oval only the day before.

2005 - After two successive promotions the club finished third in the Cheshire County League Premier division, the highest position the club has attained.

> Richard Williams (born 10.8.1957) played for Northamptonshire between 1974 and 1992. In 284 matches he scored 11817 runs with a highest score of 175 not out. Additionally, he took 376 wickets with a best of 7-73. He first played for Christleton when he was 12 and scored a club century when he was only 14.

2010 - The Bunbury Under 15 Cricket Festival was held in Cheshire. Christleton hosted the South and West v Midlands game. England selector David Graveney was in attendance.

The ground is approached down the side of that lovely pond in the heart of this picturesque village and the resident swans have been adopted on the club badge. If you can't score runs on this lovely batting track retirement might be imminent!

The Christleton swan

Compstall

Ernocroft Road, Marple Bridge SK6 5DY

IN THE 1800s the textile industry and a coal mine in Ernocroft Wood provided gainful employment for the villagers. They would have been expected to work long hours, but cricket offered the menfolk some relief from the tedium of their repetitive jobs.

Prior to the formation of the present club in 1870, no fewer than three clubs played in Compstall. They were Royal George, Compstall Improvement and Compstall United. Where the latter two teams played remains a mystery, but Royal George played its matches on land behind the present George Hotel before reforming as Compstall CC and moving to the present ground on Ernocroft Road. The Compstall Band regularly played during matches and up to 150 locals would take tea, listen to the music and watch the cricket.

By the end of the nineteenth century Compstall were

The old pavilion

playing in the North Derbyshire & Stockport District League and I have found the league table relating to 1893. Compstall were runners-up with 5 points from 14 matches. This might seem an odd outcome but of the 14 matches played they won 8 and lost 3. A point was awarded for a win, a defeat incurred a one point deduction and the three drawn matches resulted in no points being allocated.

1911 - Playing in the High Peak League, Compstall convincingly defeated Hyde. The headline read 'Derby day at Compstall – Hyde checked by the villagers'. The visitors batted first and were all out for 53. In reply Compstall reached their target by quickly putting 56-4 on the board. Sam Cheetham recorded figures of 6-26 and 17 not out. Compstall went on to win the league. Played 18, won 11, lost 1, drawn 6, points 28. Obviously there was a more conventional points system in this league!

1952 - Joined the Derbyshire & Cheshire League having previously played in the Glossop & District League.

2009 - In the National Village Cup they progressed to the regional final of Group 16 (Dyfed) but lost to Northop CC. In June, former Middlesex and England captain Mike Gatting, opened the splendid new pavilion.

This is a lovely ground with super views and definitely worth a visit. You will be extremely fortunate to call in when Compstall player Stuart Jackson lands his army helicopter on the pitch, but you will be able to look at the plaque on the external pavilion wall dedicated to Dr Hibbert, who died during a match. A longstanding member of the club, in May 1919 he was playing in a game and attempting to retrieve a ball which had been hit over a fence, slipped and broke his neck. Subsequently the ground was purchased by members and friends as a lasting memorial.

1893 North Derbyshire & Stockport District League – final placings

	P	W	D	L	Pts
West Gorton	14	9	1	4	5
Compstall	14	8	3	3	5
Hadfield	14	7	4	3	4
Strines	13	6	1	6	0
New Mills	14	5	3	6	-1
Newton Bank	14	4	3	7	-3
Stockport Great Moor	13	3	2	8	-5
Hazel Grove & District	14	4	1	9	-5

The Sportsman, Mottram Road, Hyde

Congleton

Booth Street, Congleton CW12 4DG

THE BEARS have been at Booth Street since being established in 1870.

The nickname derives from a centuries ago notoriety with bear-baiting. Folklore has it that when the Congleton dancing bear died just before the Wakes were due to start a new one was acquired with money that had been put aside to buy a new bible for the town!

The thriving south-east Cheshire market town has a centrally located compact little ground with a neat and well-equipped clubhouse. The building sits below the dominating roof of the parish church, St James the Great, at the West Street end of the ground. The club joined the North Staffordshire & District League in 1910 and won a good number of championships before eventually joining the Cheshire structure in 1998. Similarly, the Juniors played with regular success in the Kidsgrove & District League.

Congleton have not been without Cheshire representation. Born in the town, wicketkeeper Albert Bratby (b 1873, d 1950), represented both Cheshire and Staffordshire between 1910 and 1926. He made a total of twelve Minor County appearances, mostly for Cheshire. He actually played for his home county against Staffordshire on two occasions and was dismissed by former fiery England international SF (Sydney) Barnes in both matches. Rather earlier, brothers Henry and John Latham are credited with appearances in the 1860s.

After his Lancashire career ended, Ken Shuttleworth, the former Ashes winner who played in Ray Illingworth's victorious 1970-71 England touring side, plied his trade here for a while. Congleton veteran, Mike Kitten, recalls a benefit match being played for Ken in 1975 and Clive Lloyd making history with a six hit that cleared the church. Unsurprisingly the ball was never seen again!

In the late 1990s the Club made an unsuccessful bid for lottery funding, but undaunted they went ahead with a brewery-assisted venture and a new pavilion and function room emerged. A recent refurbishment and redecoration will impress you when you visit the ground.

Crewe Vagrants

Newcastle Road, Willaston CW5 7EP

CREWE VAGRANTS were formed in 1933 and adopted the name given their nomadic existence.

In 1976 they merged with Crewe LMR, a club with quite a history. Their particular origins go back to the 1850s/60s when a group of railway clerks set up a club which they named Crewe Alexandra. Initially they played on a ground in what is now Stewart Street but subsequently they moved to Earle Street. In 1888 the cricketers hosted the England football team when they played Wales (England won 5-1) and in 1887 and 1889 they, respectively, also entertained Aston Villa v Glasgow Rangers and Blackburn Rovers v Wolverhampton Wanderers in the FA Cup semi-finals. Both those finals were held at the Kennington Oval so intriguingly both the semi-finals and finals were played on cricket grounds.

1940-46 - The advent of WW2 presented Alexandra with the obvious difficulties of fulfilling fixtures with the result that an amalgamation was formed with Nantwich, the new club operating as Nantwich Alexandra. After the war the ownership of the ground passed into the hands of the LMS Railway Company and eventually the club came to be badged as Crewe LMR.

1960 - Dennis Cox, the former Surrey player, (in 42 first-class matches he scored 660 runs with a top score of 57 and took 68 wickets, best bowling 7-22), was appointed as the railway team professional and it proved to be an inspired choice as he led them to a number of trophies in the early 1960s.

After the 1976 merger with Crewe Vagrants the club continued to prosper with a well-developed junior section which helped to produce John Morris, who went on to play for Derbyshire, Nottinghamshire and England. In June 1994, in the Warwickshire v Durham fixture at Edgbaston, he bowled the ball that Brian Lara hit to reach his quintuple century. Many will have forgotten Morris scored 204 in his only innings in the same match.

The new Shavington bypass took a good chunk of the club's land, but Highways Agency and Sport England funding resulted in creating the opportunity to replace the old wooden clubhouse with new clubhouse facilities in 1995. As part of the Crewe Vagrants Sports Club squash and hockey facilities are also available. The club is also used as a base by Crewe and Nantwich RUFC and South Cheshire Harriers.

> John Morris was born in Crewe on All Fools' Day, 1964. He might well have played more than three times for his country had he not 'buzzed' an England XI playing in an up-country match during the 1991 Ashes tour in a Tiger Moth piloted by David Gower.

Davenham

Butcher's Stile, Hartford Road, Davenham CW9 8JG

INDISPUTABLY DAVENHAM CC existed in 1877 as an article in the *Chester Chronicle* of 7 April reported as follows: 'Although so early in the season, the club commenced operations on Saturday last, and succeeded in thrashing the Crewe Albion CC in the match, played in a field again placed at the service of the Davenham club for this season by Mr Minshall. Davenham CC 78; Crewe Albion CC 61.'

That ground was known as New Hall Farm but by the end of that season it seems they had moved on. In 1888 there is some evidence to suggest they played at Hartford Hill Park (near Hartford Bridge) but by 1904 they were hosting matches at Eaton Hall Farm. The historical detail is extremely hazy but the parish magazines of the period help to confirm there was a very close link with the church, and it is clear that the local clergy held various senior cricketing posts beyond the turn of the century. Indeed, when the Reverend JT 'Jimmy' Vale left Davenham for Egremont St John's, Wirral he was instrumental in arranging annual games between St John's and Davenham. They took place on Whitsun and August Bank Holiday Mondays from 1911 until 1927. It was not until the autumn of 1951 at an Extraordinary General Meeting that the club voted to allow Sunday cricket. A previous motion was put to the spring AGM under 'Any other business', but the Chairman ruled that such an important and controversial subject could not be taken as a subsidiary item.

At the 1904 AGM two important resolutions were passed:
1. Resolved that the Secretary convene a meeting of the old members and that they be asked to convey the materials belonging to the old cricket club to the present one.
2. Resolved the committee be empowered to draw up bye-laws for the management of the club.

Perhaps the club was reconstituted when it moved to Eaton Hall Farm? We shall never know! Nor shall we understand how 1885 has come to be accepted as the founding date.

1912 - Despite making worthy headway, a crisis struck on the eve of the season when an Extraordinary General Meeting was called to decide whether the club could continue in view of the loss of players and lack of interest. It was resolved to continue and, promisingly, the playing record was rather better than could have been expected.

1915 - 'All fixtures cancelled owing to the Great war of the Nations' as thoughts and efforts were directed to other less pleasurable fields. One of the club's staunchest supporters, Lieutenant-Colonel FC France Hayhurst, was killed in action at Richebourg in France on 9 May 1915 at the age of 41.

> 1912 W Swindells took 50 wickets at an average of 5.4. A footnote says: 'Reported to be quite a character. He was often thought to be a thrower'.

1920 - Although the ground had been given over to agriculture and the equipment dispersed, some matches were played. A new tenancy agreement was negotiated.

1921 - A Christmas Draw made a profit of £12 13 shillings. The first prize was one ton of coal.

1922 - A novel 'in-house Top Hat challenge match' took place with both sides travelling from the village centre in three lorries led by the Davenham Band, who also played musical selections during the fixture. Cigars were provided for the players and a bottle of 'Vintage' for the best bat in each team. The ground landlord agreed to take the old pavilion in lieu of two years rent and a new one was donated by Major Denton. The accounts showed an entry for 'new pavilion – tip for joiners - 2 shillings 6d'.

1947 - The *Northwich Chronicle* reported that despite opposition from the tenant, who regarded it as agricultural land, the Council had acquired two fields under compulsory purchase powers and deemed them to be for cricket and housing. The Council decided to instruct the Clerk to write to Mr Arnold prohibiting him from ploughing the land. This, of course, was the start of cricket at Butcher's Stile.

1949 - The first home match played on the new ground was against Barrow-for-Tarvin. On 28 May the *Northwich Guardian* reported the match was won by 93 to 74. The President was called upon to formally open the ground and did so by raising the club flag to the masthead.

> 1950 - At the AGM tribute was paid to GB Towers, who had given a lifetime of service to the club. A former player and vice-captain, he had served as Secretary from 1908 to 1919 and as Treasurer from 1919, a post he held until 1956. Tribute was paid to the 'meticulous care with which the accounts had been kept and the expert guidance he had given to the club'. Both Mr and Mrs Towers were made Life Members in recognition of their work.

1953 - At the AGM the Treasurer took the opportunity to draw attention to the unsatisfactory arrangement which allowed Mr Foden grazing rights on the ground at £1 per annum; the payment did not cover the nuisance of having cattle on the field. He agreed to pay an additional £2.

1956 - A 28-year lease was secured and, perhaps by way of celebration, Reginald Minshall scored the first century on the new ground against Mobberley. The scorecard reveals Peter Chapman, the current Mobberley President, played in that match for the visitors. On this occasion he did not unduly trouble the scorers!

1968 - The President's XI played the club in an evening fixture to officially open the new pavilion. The President's team was captained by TA Wych and included Reginald Minshall (see 1956) and league stalwart Mike Talbot-Butler, who scored 41 and pinched a wicket without conceding a run. Poor old Reggie got a duck on this occasion.

1983 - The club's first ever tour. South Wales put on high alert! Others have followed. In 2007 the tour to Worcester coincided with the River Severn flooding and all the fixtures were washed away. After one Huddersfield tour match the players ended up in a lap-dancing bar. The detail is as scant as the participants were inevitably dressed.

1995 - A big push on youth cricket based initially on Kwik Cricket paid dividends. A production line to the senior teams was established and by the 2000s Dave Ashley and Louis Bentley were scoring prolifically and quickly. Ashley had a trial at Essex CCC and Bentley was a very stylish left-hand batter who went on to play for Lancashire 2nds.

2010 - I could find no detail about a centenary celebration, but revellers certainly enjoyed the 125th anniversary at a hugely successful dinner dance held at Portal Golf Club. The following morning it was brunch, champagne and a T20 at the club!

No club can be successful without committed volunteers who beaver away behind the scenes. In this respect Davenham are very fortunate to have a team of willing helpers steered in the right direction by Bob Floyd, their enterprising Chairman. The club has come on leaps and bounds in recent years and while cricket remains at the core its extended facilities actively engage the community. The excellent new extension to the club-house, which now features in CAMRA's Good Beer Guide 2017, was opened by former Grappenhall, Lancashire and England cricketer Neil Fairbrother in June 2015.

Didsbury

860 Wilmslow Road, Didsbury M20 2ZY

THE CLUB was founded in 1858. Originally they played on a leased ground now partly covered by Beaver Road School. This land was sold for housing development at the end of the 19th century, forcing a move to the present ground at East Didsbury.

The existing ground was also on a lease and the owners decided to sell it in 1923, again for housing development. Having nowhere else to go, the club developed a plan to buy the land by forming the Didsbury Cricket Club Ground Company Limited in 1924 and local people, mainly members, bought shares.

The required sum of £1700 was raised to make the purchase. The ground company still exists today and has proved its worth several times over, particularly in raising capital to build the new pavilion and also to add subsequent extensions.

In 1933 the Stockton Trophy was won. The Manchester Association Centenary brochure reports: 'One of the curious features of the first team was the uncommonly large number of those committed to temperance'. How things change!

The austerity of the post-war years was in marked contrast to the attractive cricket played by the club in the ten year period from 1948 to 1957. During that span they won the Stockton Trophy on four occasions. The outstanding players of that period were batsman, Ronnie Fairhurst and Fred Allen who was a prolific wicket-taker, claiming 97 wickets in 1954 and 124 at an average of 9.05 in 1956.

The old wooden pavilion which was opened in 1900 was destroyed by an arson attack in April

> In 1939 just after the outbreak of WW2 the minutes of the general meeting record "that due to the grave national emergency the forthcoming darts match would be cancelled". Inevitably formal cricket competitions were cancelled for the duration of the hostilities but some friendly games were played. Matches were staged to raise funds for war charities, involving such teams as the North of England, London Counties, Lancashire and the Royal Air Force. These games attracted large crowds to watch leading players such as Learie Constantine, George Duckworth, George Pope and Winston Place. In 1940 more than £64 was raised for the War Comforts Fund and another £27 for the Red Cross. In 1943, the sum of £207 was handed over to the War Relief Fund and £1535 given to the RAF Benevolent Fund.

1981. A special sub-committee was formed to plan and build a new pavilion on a much more ambitious scale than the old one, and it was opened to members on 23 December 1982. This was a tremendous achievement considering the capital had to be raised, architects appointed, plans approved, some land sold and a contractor employed.

Over the years a good number of benefit matches have been organised. The Cricket Writers' Association, usually led by EW Swanton, played mostly on the vacant Sunday of the Old Trafford Test match to raise funds for the Lancashire beneficiary of that year. As many as 5000 spectators crammed into the ground to watch matches attributed to Cyril Washbrook, Dick Pollard, Brian Statham, Jack Bond, Ken Higgs and, in the last such game, Peter Lever.

Long-standing members of the Manchester and District Cricket Association, (they joined in 1906), they played attractive cricket in the sixties and early seventies but without conspicuous success until the HC Smith Cup was won at Old Trafford in 1975 against league champions St Helens. They left the MDCA in 1999 and in 2001, their annus mirabilis, they won the County League Premiership, the 1st XI Cup and the Cheshire Cup.

Today the club has a buoyant and successful set-up, with six senior men's teams, two women's teams, seven junior sides and a girl's academy playing in the differing league structures of South Manchester and Cheshire. The multi-sport club comprises Didsbury Cricket Club, Manchester Waconians Lacrosse Club, Didsbury Greys Hockey Club and an active social section that benefits from being a regular venue for jazz and comedy events.

Of course, Didsbury is not in Cheshire but they qualify for inclusion as a long-standing member of the Cheshire pyramid.

> ### DIDSBURY CC PEOPLE
>
> George Harold White loomed large over the club in the first half of the 20th century. He was treasurer 1902-04, secretary 1905-35, captain of the 1st team 1911-27, Alderman of the City of Manchester from 1937, Lord Mayor in 1940 and a JP. He was a member for 53 years from 1900.
>
> Until he died earlier in this decade, Richard B. Atty had been the longest-serving member of the club having been elected on the 28th April 1951. His father and grandfather were also members, the latter being a committee member before WW1.
>
> The Andersons have clocked up 50 years of service between them. Current Chairman, Duncan Anderson, has been at the club for 35 years, a 1st XI player for 22 years and at the helm since 1995. Son Nick, an all-rounder who has represented Cheshire, has been club captain since 2011.

Disley

Jacksons Edge Road, Disley SK12 2JR

THE 'MODERN' Disley Club was formed in 1987 as a section of the Disley Amalgamated Sports Club at their home on Jackson's Edge.

The opening game was a star-studded affair between a Clive Lloyd XI and a Peter Lever XI. The club joined the Derbyshire & Cheshire League in 2016, but in the thirty-year period since that auspicious re-birth they have played in a number of local leagues, and then with notable success, for an extended period, within the Cheshire pyramid. Between 2006 and 2014 the club enjoyed a period of real prosperity as the 1st XI won four league titles and three cups with a team largely made up of homegrown players.

The club has nurtured an Overseas friendship and have enjoyed a link-up with Wollongong, New South Wales, Australia. The relationship has included player exchanges and fundraising activity for both UK and Australian charities.

From around 1900 there is very clear evidence of cricket being played in nearby Lyme Park. In fact, a book sub-titled Estate Workers at Lyme Park, 1898-1946 was actually called *Cricketer Preferred*. Such was the popularity of the game that Lyme Park job advertisements explicitly stated that cricketers would be advantaged!

Today the workers of the National Trust still point to an area of the park close to Lyme Cage where matches were played. Disley CC supports the legacy of cricket in Lyme Park by running coaching sessions for visitors in the summer months.

The rise of the game eventually saw the founding of the first cricket club in the village itself in the early 1900s. They played their last season in 1939 before the team disbanded due to WW2 call-ups. Sadly it was nearly 50 years before cricket returned to the village.

Before going up to Jackson's Edge a visit to stunning Lyme Park to pick out the former ground is a prerequisite. Perhaps linger and visit the much-loved home of the Legh family for more than 600 years. The great estate and imposing mansion is a reminder of the Edwardian 'Golden Era' - the heyday of aristocratic life. You are bound to be impressed.

Extracts from: *Cricketer Preferred Estate Workers at Lyme Park, 1898-1946, Edited by Kedrun Laurie (1979)*

We used to run a cricket team at Lyme. Peter used to play and Francis was a bowler. We used to have a good team. Lord Abercrombie played. All the fellows in the garden were in the team. When they advertised for a gardener they used to put Cricketer Preferred. We used to play the local teams round Stockport.

Offerton were frequently opponents. Lord Newton was the captain when he played. I was when he wasn't there ...Bert Maling

That's another thing Frank looked after – the wicket. That used to be his pride and joy ...Oswald Stokes

I know the ground is very rough now, but the actual wicket there was as good as any County ground ... Frank Walton

Dukinfield

Clarendon Street, Dukinfield SK16 4LP

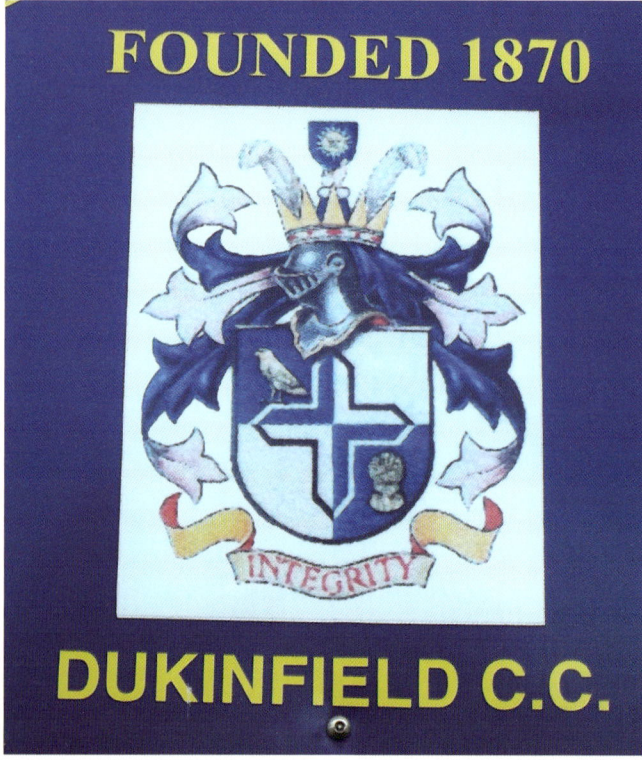

CEDRIC RHOADES, Chairman of Lancashire CCC (1969-86), contributed a one-page article to the Dukinfield centenary brochure in 1970. He wrote that he had spent many happy hours at the club when he was a Levenshulme player. He went on to say, '...it is becoming increasingly difficult for officials to administer clubs in the world of sport mainly due to the fierce competition for leisure time, from, in particular, the motor car. Some clubs look rather askance at the question of sponsorship – far more work could be done in this field'. How things change!

Dukinfield born Norman Oldfield (b 1911, d 1996) was also a contributor and recalled with pride starting his playing career at Higher King Street. He recalled being selected for his 3rd XI debut and staying off school to make sure he was fit for the match. He went on to say he scored 10 and got a good hiding from his headmaster the following day for his truancy! He could not resist mentioning Bob Howard, who was the club scorer for 50 years. 'A very dogmatic man who called a spade a spade but who asked no more than to mark the scorebook and have the honour of singing *Molly Malone* at the Annual Dinner'!

Modestly, 'Buddy' Oldfield makes no reference to his own career in the first-class game, but he achieved considerable success with both Lancashire (pre-war) and Northants (post-war). He played for England, but only on one occasion, against the West Indies at the Oval in 1939, the long war period spoiling other opportunities. In his debut innings he went to the wicket when Keeton was dismissed and England had only two runs on the board. He joined Len Hutton and they added 131. He was eventually out for 80, dismissed by Learie Constantine. At the time I doubt whether it ever occurred to him he was both partnered and dismissed by future knights of the realm! After he retired from playing he was a successful coach and umpire.

1857 - An Ashton team scored 77 against a Dukinfield side who could only manage 15 and 25. Not much is known about the match, but we can infer a great deal a few years later about the fierce rivalry when a newspaper made merry about the defeated 'noble lords and titled gentry' of Ashton losing to the 'plebian Dukinfield masses'.

1893 - The club become champions of the Ashton and District League. A dinner was held in celebration and a local newspaper reported on the event, lavish menu and all. Unfortunately it was placed below a report entitled 'Destitution in Dukinfield' revolving around a coal industry lock-out and an appeal to the charitable people of the town to provide funds for the soup kitchens.

CAREER STATISTICS OF NORMAN 'BUDDY' OLDFIELD

Matches	Runs	H/Score	Average	100/50s	Caught	Wickets	Career span
332	17811	168	37.89	38/101	96	2	1938-54

He also officiated in 277 first-class matches including two Test matches.

> In 1908 the Club finished third in the Central Lancashire League. It was reported that the wicketkeeper, Harry Bennett, went through the season without conceding a bye. In 1918 JO Scholes took 40 wickets at 5.54, including 10 for 27 against New Moss. He suddenly and tragically died during that winter.

1930 - The Mayor of Dukinfield launched an appeal for the purchase of the cricket ground. £700 was required and concerts, socials and various other events were arranged. One cinema gave the proceeds of a matinee performance. Remarkably, the money was very quickly raised despite a period of acute depression in the cotton industry.

1941 - At the end of the season Dukinfield and Denton St Lawrence sat at the top of the table and a play-off was arranged to determine who would be the champions. The 2000 Dukinfield spectators were dismayed to see their team dismissed for 54, and when Denton were 42-6 home supporters were seen to be leaving... but wait. All out 43! It was reported the cheers could be heard in Hyde market!

1953 - A curious incident occurred during a match at Longsight. After the Longsight skipper bowled an over of full tosses he called for a chain to find the pitch was only 21 yards long! After a re-marking exercise he took 6-24, but Dukinfield still won by 133 to 116 runs.

> In 1961 David Myers was the victim of an umpire who apparently could not count for he allowed him to bowl 16 successive, perfectly legal balls before 'over' was called.

Dukinfield are now members of the Greater Manchester Cricket League.

> Norman Oldfield concluded his article by hoping another Dukinfield-born player could make the grade and play for Lancashire ...In 1962 a young teenager by the name of Tony Durose (b 1944 in Dukinfield) won the club bowling award and by the following season he was in the Cheshire side before spending five years on the Northants staff, taking 150 first-class wickets. In 1968 he took 7-23 in the first innings of a championship match against Leicestershire at Peterborough. In the second innings he followed up with 3-78. A coveted ten wickets in a match. Dukinfield will have been delighted that their young starlet progressed to play first-class cricket, even if it was a variation of Oldfield's particular Red Rose wish.

Eaton Hall

Eaton Estate, Eccleston CH4 9JD

GIVEN THE splendour of the Duke of Westminster's estate, the pavilion is rather a modest one despite it being built in 1895 and registered as a listed building. Before the 1960s the pavilion steps afforded a breathtaking view of the now demolished massive, multi-pinnacled palace. The modern day hall is out of sight.

Quite when cricket was first played on the estate is open to doubt, but the *Cheshire Chronicle* of 14 August 1818 reported on a match which took place on 7 August – at Eaton Hall, the seat of the Earl of Grosvenor, several gentlemen of the County beat Lord Belgrave, Earl Wilton etc. A great number of people from Chester were spectators. What is clear is that by the mid-1870s big matches were being hosted. Indeed, in 1875 the United South of England played a three day match here and a good number of column inches were devoted to the game in the *Chronicle*:

The morning opened inauspiciously, the recent rains which had made the ground sodden and uncomfortable being followed by a keen east wind, which was searching and dispiriting in the extreme. His Grace the Duke of Westminster, captain of the Club, interested himself in the arrangements for the comfort of the visitors and the result was that everything was done by the committee which could be suggested. Long rows of seats had been laid all round the enclosed area, and planking, on which the feet could be accommodated instead of being allowed to saturate with wet on the grass, had been placed in front. The England XI who went first to the wickets were represented by WG Grace and Lillywhite, to the bowling of McIntyre and Sharp. Grace took up the parable and got a single. Runs were made slowly for a time, and then McIntyre sent Grace's stumps flying with a splendid ball, to the gratification of the home team and to the intense disgust of the spectators, who, by the by, were anything but numerous.

The full scorecard reveals the rain relented and when stumps were drawn on the third afternoon the scores were: United South of England 168 and 63. The XXII of Eaton Park 48 and 56-13, Match drawn! On the final day a fair sprinkling of visitors put in an appearance. The band of the 30th Regiment, under the able direction of Herr Standhaft, performed some excellent selections of music on all three days.

> **Records held at Eaton Hall include a comprehensive list of matches played in 1899. It is handwritten and shows that Dawpool were entertained on 20 May. The Secretary of Dawpool is shown as James Ismay. He was the son of Thomas Ismay, the owner of the White Star Line. That company, of course, owned the ill-fated Titanic. The Ismays resided at Dawpool (Thurstaston, Wirral).**

An article in *Cheshire Life* published in the late 1980s reports that the 6th Duke was a regular player in his twenties and quotes him as saying: 'There is nothing, frankly, more English than watching cricket being played in a park environment on a summer's evening'. To this day cricket continues to be played at Eaton Hall, but by comparison with bygone days in a rather more low-key way.

Elworth

London Road, Elworth, Sandbach CW11 3BF

ELWORTH CELEBRATED their centenary in 2013. One hundred years before that significant anniversary they were founded as a result of a meeting between Alec Palmer, a Liverpudlian who came to the area to work in the salt industry, and two fellow members of the Elworth United Methodist Church. The first match was played in 1914 at Hollinshead field, which was regularly used for Sunday school treats and the Village Fete. There was no pavilion, but they did have sightscreens - old bed sheets tied to poles!

1914 - In July a victory was achieved over Vale Royal, the highlight being a bowling haul of 5-13 for George Hodgson which included the first-ever Elworth hat-trick. Some suspected George was a 'chucker'!

1920 - The *Crewe Chronicle* reported that an Elworth batsman was given out by the Sandbach umpire but he refused to leave the batting crease protesting he was not out. After much argument he remained, so the entire Sandbach team and their umpire left the field and went home. The following year there was no dispute with the umpires, but Sandbach did put in a written protest about the state of the pitch. A fierce competition with near neighbours Sandbach has continued over the decades!

1923-25 - Progress was being made but in no match in 1923 did the Elworth total score ever reach 100. In 1925 Len Johnson was captain for the third consecutive year, but he also played the violin at Sandbach Town Hall for the silent films and hoped for early finishes. He was seldom disappointed!

1927 - By now the club had moved to Boothville and the first home match was played on 14 May against Weston. A good crowd had been attracted and for the first time an admission charge was made.

1928 - A novel means of raising funds; the Secretary arranged grass-track motorcycle racing in a local field. Over 850 attended on the first night and another 1100 on the second. It is questionable whether Elworth had ever been more roused! A profit of £50 was made.

1935 - To coincide with the Silver Jubilee of the reign of King George V a number of events were arranged by indefatigable Frank Poole. He persuaded Harry Mortimer, the world famous principal solo cornet player with Fodens Motor

1927 pavilion opening

Works Band, to play. The event was a huge success and made a welcome profit. Elworth beat local rivals Sandbach but included three Lancashire players in their line-up – Ernest Tyldesley, Len Hopwood and Len Parkinson! In June the 2nd XI played Doddington Park and after three balls of the match were 0-3! A hat trick for the opening bowler and Elworth all out for 5.

1938 - Ever wanting to push the club forward, Frank Poole wrote and published a booklet called *Village Cricket* with the sub-title 'Suggestions for the Running of the Small Cricket Club'. It was on sale at a price of one shilling. The foreword was by Ernest Tyldesley. The book concluded with the prophecy that by 1941 the eight-ball over would be in universal use. By that time, of course, there was no cricket at all.

WW2 forced a break but in 1946 things got underway again, albeit with just one team. Sunday cricket was out of the question, the club still being regarded very much as a church-based side. In fact the Church Elders were adamant that they should have a say in the scrutinising of potential members. Once the Cricket Committee had approved a member, the Trustees insisted on a vote of veto.

1949 - Against Langley, Harold Scragg was given out lbw. He vehemently protested that he had hit the ball and the opposing skipper withdrew the appeal. Back in the pavilion his batting partner said to him, "You never touched that ball Harold", to which he replied, "No, but I meant to!"

1958 - In a match against Whitmore & Newcastle they were dismissed for a very low score and during the tea interval 'their' umpire expressed the view that even such a modest total would take some getting. Elworth fell short thanks to seven lbw decisions by 'their' umpire!

1965 - A very significant development. The church recognised it no longer had any influence over the club and landlord Frank Poole was persuaded to re-draft the lease in favour of the cricketers but not to allow a bar (that followed in 1973). At last Elworth Mount Pleasant CC was re-badged, quite simply, as Elworth CC. Alec Palmer, the founding father, had serious reservations about the new arrangements but was persuaded to continue his membership of over fifty years (and gratifyingly he became President in 1966).

1971 - The new pavilion was officially opened by Jack Ikin, former Lancashire and England all-rounder but son of North Staffordshire. In opening the pavilion he said, "Cricket for me, and to many of you here, is the greatest game in the world, and it is clubs such as Elworth who are the backbone of cricket". The match was won against old rivals Sandbach.

1976 - As members of the North Staffs & District League, Elworth played league cricket for the first time in their sixty year history. In 1980 they applied for membership of the expanding North Staffs & South Cheshire League, but this was not without some acrimony. The District League took exception to such potential departures and decided to expel all those clubs that sought to move. In the event they were elected to the NS&SC League and participated from 1981.

1984 - A year to be remembered. Two pinnacles within a month in two different counties! Division 1, Section A of the NS&SC League was won as

---

NOTABLE ELWORTH PLAYERS

Bert Sproston (1914-2000) was a very fine batsman immediately before WW2. He was born in Elworth and earned his living as a professional footballer. He played for Leeds United, Manchester City, Millwall and Tottenham Hotspur. He also played for England in the same side as Stanley Matthews.

New Zealander **Martin Crowe** played just one match as a deputy professional in 1989. He scored 79 against Knypersley.

Matt Winter joined Elworth when he was six years old. In 2011, at the age of 17, he scored 200 not out against Hem Heath for the 2nd XI. He now has four Blues having played for Oxford University in the 2013/14/15/16 Varsity matches. He was captain in 2015.

Yasir Ali (b 1985) has given sterling service to Elworth in recent years. He has played 69 first-class matches with a top score of 129. He has taken 200 wickets at this level with a best bowling analysis of 5-22. He played in one Test match in 2003 against Bangladesh.

Other Elworth players that have played the game at first-class level – Keith Semple, Paul Persaud, Kevin Darlington, Andre Percival (all Guyana), Vanburn Holder (WI), Derek Walker (Central Districts, NZ, Sultan Rana (Punjab), Keith Smith (Warwickshire), Andrew Lawson, Ian Mitchell and Murray Ranger (all Border).

well as the prestigious Cheshire Cup. The latter match was against Birkenhead Park and played before a home crowd estimated to be around one thousand made up mainly of enthusiastic home supporters. Brian Statham was the 'Man of the Match' adjudicator.

1992 - For over thirty years Gerald Bennion had been associated with Elworth as a player, Secretary and later Vice-President. After his playing days finished he took to umpiring and it was both a club and personal honour when he was appointed as an umpire at Lord's for the Village Cup final match between Hursley Park and Methley.

1997 - Being located close to the boundaries of Staffordshire and Cheshire has always presented an issue over county affinity. At this point in time there was overwhelming support for Cheshire County League membership and an application was duly made but rejected on a technicality over the date of receipt of the application.

1999 - Sir Richard Hadlee was the guest speaker at the Elworth CC Sportsman's Dinner held at Sandbach Town Hall. Over £2000 was raised.

2000+ - Never a club to sit back on their laurels, a lottery grant was lodged for the purpose of a substantial pavilion refurbishment and this eventually resulted in a successful bid. The former Olympic javelin star Tessa Sanderson handed over a cheque. The eventual award totalled £103,243. What a start to the new Millenium! The downside was that the club had to find £67,156. By dint of hard work that target was achieved and says much about Elworth CC.

The attractive ground is now in the ownership of this thriving club.

If you want to read an in-depth history of Elworth CC, Allan Littlemore's 120 page book, published in 2001, is a gem. Allan has been associated with his local club for more than 66 years and has contributed so much as both a player and administrator. A year or two back he had the thrill of hosting England cricketers Katherine Brunt, Paul Collingwood, Liam Plunkett and Moeen Ali when Elworth won a Waitrose award. Now here is something no other club official has achieved, surely? He persuaded Cheshire East Council and the Developers to use the names of twenty stalwarts of Elworth Cricket Club as the street names of a housing development close to the ground.

Europa Exiles

Mere CC, Warrington Road, Mere WA16 0PU

POP A SANDWICH into a tupperware box, fill your thermos with coffee and head off to Mere. You'll be watching Cheshire's newest recruits.

In 1980 the North West HQ of the Central Electricity Generating Board formed a cricket team and they badged themselves as Europa Sports (so named as they were based at Europa House, Cheadle Heath). Initially they were a Works midweek T20 team, but by 1983 they were playing league cricket having been accepted into the Denton & District competition. Subsequently they played in the Ashton League, later the Ashton & Oldham Cricket Alliance, and much more recently in Greater Manchester Amateur Cricket League. Without an established home ground over the years, they have camped out at Scholes Playing Fields, Gatley with shorter spells at Silver Wings BA Club at Timperley and Woodford recreation ground. The break-up of the CEGB in 1990 meant that a vital funding stream was severed, but they have survived despite all the odds. The subtle name change from Europa Sports to Europa Exiles coincided with the company severance.

The highlight in terms of performance was winning the Ashton Cricket League First Division in 1991, but the main attraction has always been the friendly spirit in which Europa have played the game. Any display of over-competitiveness by an individual has always been dissolved with good humour!

Vital to its continuity has been the presence of Secretary, Barry Harwood. With the exception of 1996 he has captained the team every season from 1984 through until 2017. That really is some record. Even Lord Hawke only captained Yorkshire for 28 consecutive years! (1883-1910).

Mere was their Saturday home in 2017. On Sundays they have formed a partnership with Flowery Field in the Greater Manchester set-up.

Flowery Field

Throstle Bank Street, Hyde SK14 4NT

CRICKET HAS been played here since 1838. Flowery Field is a district to the north of Hyde town centre. It is mainly a residential area once dominated by the Ashton Brothers Textile Mill. In fact an Ashton Trust was formed in 1913 and land was given in perpetuity by the family specifically for cricket. Beyond the well-appointed ground is the local church, which also benefitted from the generosity of the Ashton family. In the 1870s Ashton insisted that villagers raised the seemingly impossible sum of £1000 and when, some years later, they duly advised him they had collected that amount he was so impressed that he promised to build them a church at his expense and return the £1000 on the condition that it was invested to augment the Minister's stipend.

1888 - Some of the best cricketers in England were seen at Flowery Field. In the August Wakes the local club were assisted by Tom Emmett, aged 47, and described by a local reporter as 'the veteran of the Yorkshire County team'. Some years later Arthur Mold of Lancashire, reputed to be one of the fastest bowlers at the time, also played. Both played for England. Another to play for his country was Hyde-born Len Hopwood (b 1903, d 1985), but two brothers who actually started their careers at Flowery Field and went on to play for Derbyshire were William (b 1861, d 1913) and Joseph (b 1867, d 1886) Chatterton. The latter died before he was 20 but by that time had already played 11 matches for his county. His older brother played for England on one occasion and scored over 10000 runs and took over 200 wickets in the first-class game. *Cricket Archive* reveals William died in Flowery Field and that Joe was buried at the Hyde Unitarian Chapel.

> 1908 Having won the North Cheshire League in 1907 the club joined the Glossop & District League and both the 1st and 2nd XI won their respective divisions. There is an account in the *North Cheshire Herald* which tells how the players paraded in two wagonettes through Mottram, Hollingworth and Hadfield with the Cup which was filled with 'not teetotal stuff'.

1915 - Joined the Saddleworth League and had continuous membership until they opted for the Lancashire County League in 2004. They left as champions, repeating a feat they had previously achieved in 1947, 1948, 1952, 1954 and 1992.

1930-32 Flowery Field won the Parliamentary Cup. As its name might suggest the tournament was played on a knock-out basis between teams located in the old Stalybridge and Hyde parliamentary division.

1976 - Remembered by most as a heatwave summer, but not in rainy Offerton! A Tanner Cup quarter-final match took eight evenings to complete! John Rice opened the batting, went on a week's holiday, and returned in time to claim three wickets in five balls to take Flowery to victory.

1988 - The club's sesquicentennial year. Events were scheduled throughout the season. In conjunction with Arnie Sidebottom's testimonial, an April Sportsman's Dinner was arranged. The speakers were footballers Steve Kindon and Malcolm McDonald and England cricketer Frank Tyson. Other events included a pub and company six-a-side competition, a challenge match between Flowery Field Past and Present and a Saddleworth League XI and a coach trip to Fylde, which included four free hours in Blackpool before a forty-over match at Thornton Cleveleys.

1990s - Flowery reached (and lost) the final of the Tanner Cup in consecutive seasons, both times to Delph & Dobcross. but a remarkable semi-final saw substitute professional, West Indian Phil

> The sesquicentennial brochure includes a letter from Aussie Robert Zadow (b 1954), who spent two summers with the club. When he returned Down Under he played for South Australia (1979-87). He recalled that in his first game for Flowery Field a tray of drinks were brought onto the field which balanced thirteen glasses of squash and two of shandy. He fancied a beer but a quick tap on the shoulder advised him in no uncertain terms they were for the umpires!

Simmons score 115 as the Field defeated Moorside whose pro was Joel Garner. There was a fitness doubt about Garner before that match and they had Roger Harper at the ground in case a substitute was needed. A real Caribbean bonanza!

1998 - The club sold land and built a new pavilion. Inevitably these improvements were masterminded by chairman John Ellis. He passed away in 2015 and the pavilion was re-dedicated specifically to him in 2016. In nearly half a century at the club he truly became 'Mr Flowery Field'. He was a player for two decades and chairman for as long again.

2016 - The Club moved to the newly formed Greater Manchester Cricket League.

Then there are eight Vice-Presidents but they are little seen
Are rarely come to test their powers upon the field so green
But their subs are always ready, which cheers the Treasurer's heart
And thus I think that in the game they fairly bear their part

extracted from a poem in 'A History of Ashley CC, 1888-1988'

Frodsham

Monument Park, Moor Lane, Frodsham WA6 7AE

TUCKED AWAY just off the High Street not far from the Bear's Paw is Cricket Field Lane, where the noble game has been played for many a year. The club has some 1873 match details, but it is speculated in those very early days the games were played 'up the hill' in Overton. Again the detail is hazy but it seems likely by very late Victorian times they had occupied Cricket Field Lane. Alas, play has not been continuous as the club disbanded sometime before WW2 through a lack of players.

It reformed in 1983 when the late Don Mellor, patron of all things Frodsham, called a meeting at the community centre to gauge the interest of local people. After a positive vote a committee was appointed and during the first year some friendly games were arranged. Home matches were played at the Halton Sports Club in Runcorn. The club joined the West Lancashire League the following year, playing there with some success for three years before moving to the now defunct Cheshire Club Conference. At about this time the club moved to Frodsham High School's pitch on the marshes at the bottom of Moor Lane (Cricket Field Lane) and in effect returned to the site they had occupied from around 1900. From the Conference the club joined the Cheshire Cricket Association in 1991. A close relationship with the school was fostered until it closed in 2009. The club is now the sole tenant. Don Mellor often trumpeted, 'the youth of today are the players of tomorrow' and since the club reformed it has endorsed that sentiment by promoting a keen youth policy.

The club endeavours to be an integral part of Frodsham life and for 30 years, right up to 2015, they organised a highly successful donkey derby at the community centre. Carnivals and bonfire evenings have been other local fund-raisers. The proceeds from many years of fund-raising finally paid dividends in April 2004 when the club opened its new pavilion. The expenditure was in excess of £60000 and was made possible by a grant of £25000. Significantly, the pavilion was constructed almost entirely by club members - under the ever-watchful supervision of the late Keith Stubbs and after whom the pavilion is appropriately named - which dramatically reduced the costs and has provided a valuable facility for both the cricketers and the community.

Travelling westwards on the M56, when the trees are not in full leaf, it is sometimes possible to spot a match in session. Keep your eyes on the road to avoid an unwanted shunt!

Glazebury

Hurst Lane, Glazebury WA3 5LS

IF YOU HAVE never been to Bents Garden Centre on the outskirts of Glazebury, call in on the way to the cricket. You are bound to be amazed at its size. It is huge (and I do mean huge). Is there a bigger one in Cheshire or even further afield? I doubt it. It all started in 1937 when Alfred and Margaret Bent started growing and selling roses in the front garden of their terraced house at 404 Warrington Road, Glazebury. Not far from their old residential address is the cricket ground, tucked just behind the village school in Hurst Lane.

In its current format the club was formed in 1962, but its origins date back to 1896 when it was founded under the name of All Saints Glazebury Cricket Club with a link back to Bury Lane Cricket Club, which existed as far back as the 1860s. Mention of Glazebury & Bury Hill might ring a bell with railway enthusiasts as it was a station on the first inter-city passenger railway in the world - the Manchester to Liverpool line - constructed in 1830. There is a link with the local cricket inasmuch that the players use the Chat Moss hotel, situated on the site of the old railway station, as their drinking hole.

World Cup-winning footballer Roger Hunt (b 1938) strutted his stuff on the Hurst Lane ground as a youngster when the field was used for football. He lived in the village where his parents had a haulage business. When on 22 August 1964 he scored a first half goal against Arsenal in a home win it became the very first goal to be shown on *Match of the Day*. On my visit to the ground I met Frank Nelson, a former Glazebury player, who lived next door to the old Liverpool favourite.

When former player and hardworking groundsman Tom Milmine died in 2013, aged 64, the pavilion was named after him. Tom's sister Rita Tongue presented the club with a memorial plaque. It was not possible to name the Hurst Lane ground after him because it is already a memorial to Glazebury soldiers who fell in the First World War.

First team bowler Sam Stanier has been a model of consistency in recent seasons. In 2016 his efforts were rewarded with a trio of awards at the club presentation evening. He collected the Bowling award (averages), the Wicket-taker trophy and he was also nominated as Players' Player.

Year	Wkts	BB	Ave
2014	54	7-20	10.76
2015	66	7-23	10.06
2016	48	8-27	9.98
2017	25	5-11	17.48

Grappenhall

Broad Lane, Grappenhall WA4 3ER

HOW COULD you not eagerly anticipate a trip to Grappenhall CC? There are a couple of nice pubs in the heart of the village and a warm welcome at the ground is a given. Nick Sharp will be out on the square waiting to pounce on an unsuspecting emerging weed, and if you pick the right day his lovely wife, Pat, might be hidden away in the kitchen producing yet another splendid tea. Steve Wright resists the temptation to embrace online scoring technology and steadfastly hangs on to his trusted pencil and green-covered scoring book. Dear old Les Fairbrother, the octogenarian father of Neil, Grappenhall's most famous cricketer, will be lurking around somewhere in his very familiar white cap waiting to shake hands. Neil played 366 first-class games for Lancashire and ten for England. With remarkable symmetry he once scored 366 for Lancashire. Surrey were the victims and this innings remains the highest score in England by an English-born player since AC MacLaren scored 424 against Somerset in 1895. Despite his significant achievements at the highest level he has remained fearlessly loyal to his home club and has continued to play Over 40s cricket for them. Occasionally he has enticed his good friend Wasim Akram into his whites as well. What a thrill for the ageing opposition – whacked around by Neil Fairbrother and pummelled by Wasim Akram!

Other Grappenhall players to make their mark in county cricket have been Steve Titchard, Richard Green, Duncan Martindale and Steve Bramhall. Steve Titchard played 107 first-class matches for Lancashire and Derbyshire between 1990 and 2001. On one notable occasion he and Steve Stubbings batted the whole of the final day for Derbyshire against Kent in a Championship match at Canterbury. Both remained undefeated. After his first-class career came to an end he played for Grappenhall for over a decade. Richard Green played 31 matches for the Red Rose county and then captained Grappenhall for a good few years up to 2015. Duncan Martindale played 55 matches for Nottinghamshire and Steve Bramhall, perhaps the best wicketkeeper ever to play in the Cheshire County Premier League, played a total of 12 first-class matches for Lancashire and Nottinghamshire.

The club have been resident at Broad Lane since 1892. The existing pavilion sits beyond the car park and offers a prime view of the cricket. Tucked on the far side of the pavilion is the Candice Roberts Memorial garden. She worked behind the bar at the club and died prematurely, aged only 26, in 2010.

Grappenhall CC the first 125 Years (1881-2006) is essential reading for those wanting to learn more about the club's intriguing history. Gerald Hudd is the author and his thoroughly comprehensive lovely little book is the source document for most of the following information.

The first recorded match involving a team called Grappenhall took place in 1878 when Wycliffe

Pavilions in Splendour

Sunday School beat Grappenhall. In fact, the club itself affiliated to the church towards the end of the 1880s and, until the time of the WW1, it was referred to as Grappenhall St Wilfrids CC.

Grappenhall has had three grounds. The first was in Glebe Avenue, the second was in Goss Lane but closed to make way for the Manchester Ship Canal and the third became the eventual long-term home.

1890 - A match aroused the ire of the *Warrington Guardian* when Grappenhall dismissed Padgate Wesleyans for six. In the event Grappenhall refused them a fixture the following season. As fate would have it Grappenhall were then bowled out for just four against Warrington Post Office. The *Guardian* was scathing: 'Perhaps Saturday's result will take a little conceit out of Grappenhall'.

1911 - A local map shows the pavilion was at the north end of the ground, opposite to where it is now. At the end of each season a working party would be organised to bury the contents of the lavatory.

1914 - Grappenhall (135) play Warrington (131) for the very first time. A young George Duckworth, later to be the Lancashire and England wicketkeeper, batted at number four for Warrington and was out for 0.

1920-30s - The three Tipping brothers, Frank, William and Percy, feature strongly in the record books. In 1931 Percy headed the batting averages, scoring 365 runs at 40.5 and taking 17 wickets at 11.7, William scored 352 at 32 and Frank 226 runs at 17.38. In June 1932 William scored the first ever century made by a Grappenhall player when he recorded 102 not out against Middlewich. Later in the season Percy scored 140 not out against Davyhulme. In 1935 he went one better by scoring 154 not out against Newton Heath. In 1936 Percy topped the batting with 549 runs at 36.6 as well as 41 wickets at 7.5 and William was second with 229 runs at 28.6. Frank was fourth with 211 at 16.2. Percy was tragically killed in a motor cycle accident on Christmas Day 1937.

1939 - Grappenhall were founder members of the North Cheshire League, together with Altrincham, Burnage, Manchester YMCA, Moorside, Newton Heath, Roe Green, Stockton Heath and Winton. The outbreak of WW2 meant that all the September fixtures were cancelled and the League was never reformed after the conflict.

1940 - Instructions were received from the War Agricultural Committee to plough up the cricket field. Mr HJS Dewes entered into negotiations and what probably helped the club avoid that action was a good relationship with the Royal Navy Air station and other local Service Corps who used the ground for matches and practice. The junior section was reformed in 1943 and one notable player was JG (John) Dewes, son of HJS, and a future star for Cambridge University, Middlesex and England. When Oughtrington Park were the host club in 1942 father and son opened the batting for Grappenhall. HJS scored 6 and JG 24.

1950 - The AGM voted for Sunday play. Major Parr stated he had no objection provided matches finished by 6pm so that players could go to church. Hereabouts the club purchased the ground from the Major for £585.

1956 - A building which now forms the main part of the clubhouse was purchased for £190.

1962 - First season in the Manchester Association. It was not practical to play all 36 teams and Grappenhall finished 14th on a percentage basis with 51.42%.

1975 - Founder members of Cheshire County Cricket League.

1976 - Neil Fairbrother's first appearance for Grappenhall, age 14.

1982 - For the second year running the First Division of the Manchester Association was won, along with the HC Smith Cup against Didsbury at Old Trafford.

1992 - Andrew Sharpe hits 100 against Sale in the same weekend as his brother, Will, hit 114 versus Birkenhead Park - a unique event in the history of the club. The Cheshire Cup was also lifted.

2000s - Two superb 'legend day' events were organised in 2011 and 2013. Big crowds enjoyed the great entertainment. In 2011 David 'Bumble' Lloyd hit Murali for two consecutive sixes, one of them breaking a car window. In 2013 the Warrington Wolves played a Grappenhall XI before Wasim Akram turned out alongside Jeff Thomson, Simon Katich and Damien Martyn in the green and gold of an Australia XI. It could only happen at Grappers!

The Candice Roberts Memorial Garden

Great Budworth

Arley Cricket Ground, Arley Green CW9 6LZ

IF YOU ARE planning a visit take a good map, a compass and a survival bag! The eventual outcome was, of course, very rewarding as a splendid ground emerged through the trees after my lengthy woodland search. I (wrongly) approached the ground from a private lane with a signpost which read

> *This road forbidden is to all*
> *Unless they wend their way to call*
> *At Mill, or Green or Arley Hall.*

As I sat on a pavilion bench cursing my satnav, which went into meltdown mode, I concluded most visiting teams must be obliged to start a match without eleven players!

Great Budworth CC was established in 2006 and has an attractive programme of friendly matches, but cricket has been played here for well over a century. 'AD 1902' is cut into a beam immediately below the clock-face, which appears to confirm the age of the pavilion. The original club played under the banner of Arley CC and there is a photograph of the 1971 team in the pavilion. The captain is shown as the late Ron Jones, who many Cheshire umpires will recall was a leading light in that organisation after his playing days ended. There is also a lovely old bench on the verandah endorsed 'The Doctor's Seat' and an associated framed picture of a distinguished group, including Lord and Viscountess Ashbrook, unveiling the seat in 1972 in memory of Dr Gilbert Love, who was the Arley captain between 1946 and 1955 and President from 1964 to 1970.

Arley Hall peeps at the cricketers through the trees just a field away. The scene is a timely reminder of country house cricket as it was in the 'golden age'. I loved it.

(The) Groves

Groves Sports & Social Club, Whitby Road, Ellesmere Port CH66 2NX

THE CRICKET club emerged in the early 1970s as a section of the former Castrol Sports & Social Club. The club went into private ownership about a decade ago but the cricketers have continued to use the site facilities.

They were Cheshire Alliance Division 1 winners in both 2004 and 2010, but on each occasion failed to make a significant mark in the higher company and were relegated back to the Alliance, the last time being after the conclusion of the 2013 campaign. Martin Flanagan, the current chairman and a former captain, has been around for a long while and has consistently scored runs and taken wickets. The same goes for Mike Garvey. Another consistent run-scorer for a good few years has been Mike Caulfield and new the captain, Neil Percival, clearly has a keen eye – he recorded two 2nd XI centuries in 2015, taking 116 off the Kerridge attack and biffing the Appleton bowlers for 136 not out.

Former England and Somerset pace bowler Andy Caddick went to the club in July 2013 to take part in an 'Ashes Breakfast'. The assembled gathering watched the second day's play of the Lord's Test on TV and participated in a Question & Answer session. Inevitably the breakfast session turned out to be a mere aperitif for an all-day marathon! The following day the 1st XI had to travel to Pott Shrigley and a check of the match results reveal that the Groves were skittled for 50 when chasing a Pott Shrigley total of 149. The biggest partnership (14) was for the tenth wicket. A probable case of sore heads!

Hale Barns

Brooks Drive, Hale Barns WA15 8TN

PROPOSED BY Councillor Davies, seconded by Mr Roberts and unanimously resolved by the meeting 'That Hale Barns CC be, and is hereby, inaugurated'. So there can be no doubt about the formation of the club as this extract taken from a public meeting held on 12 June 1947 demonstrates. Early on all the matches were played on an away basis. The very first match was against Bowdon Vale. A home ground was eventually found when a Brooks Drive resident, Mr Noel Nichols of 'Prestwood', offered the use of his meadow assuming his neighbour Wing Commander Rhodes had no objection. It transpired the resident of 'White Acre' was a supporter of the noble game and raised no concern. A brew hut from Helsby was acquired as a pavilion for £200.

When transport was not readily available in the post-war period the players used to resort to the bus or bicycles. On one occasion half the side were unable to board the bus for Pott Shrigley and returned home for their bicycles. The match started without them, but fortunately the five early arrivals were able to hold out until their colleagues turned up after an arduous bike ride. Occasionally the team would travel in Geoff Barnes' ancient 15cwt Morris van, and with the full side and all the kit on board it was a very tight fit. The 'to' journeys were much less hazardous than the victorious 'from' trips!

> For some of the Sunday friendly matches selection was often influenced by the owning of a car and not necessarily an ability to sing but a willingness to sing, rather than any out and out cricketing skill.

> One had to have certain qualifications to play in a Cheadle match and a non-drinker stood no chance of selection. We always played our 'thirst' eleven!

1950 - Legal proceedings were considered against the owner of a racehorse which had damaged the ground.

1957-58 - In an attempt to raise funds the dance committee booked Eric Delaney for September at a fee of £200 and Ken Mackintosh for October at £180. The result was a complete disaster. Better news for January, the Johnny Dankworth dance showed a profit of £120 2s 10d. Mr Nichols was prepared to sell the ground for £1400. In the event the lease was renewed for five years with an option to buy in that period (Eventually purchased in 1960 for £1450).

Frank Hayes, David Lloyd and Clive Lloyd open the new pavilion in 1974

> **1958 - Geoff Barnes bowled a ball so wide it clipped gully's left ear, raced to the pavilion and subsequently ended up in the visitors dressing room. Wicketkeeper Tony Holland uttered one word that was often used by the Reverend John Stacey, but in an entirely different context on a Sunday!**

1972 - The twenty-fifth anniversary was celebrated with a Dinner & Ball at the Bowdon Assembly Rooms. Planning permission was received for a new pavilion.

1974 - The new pavilion was opened by David Lloyd, accompanied by Lancashire colleagues Clive Lloyd and Frank Hayes. It was subsequently extended in 2015.

1996 - Dave Molloy took 102 wickets in a season.

2017 - The club's 70th anniversary was celebrated with a 1st XI promotion and a Mad-Batters (!) tea party, the highlight of which was a T20 match between the long-serving Dave Saddington's All Stars and Steve Hough's Vets XI. A single trestle table accommodated the 94 revellers – 47 aside!

> Tim Cooper, 2nd XI captain in the 1970s ...A captain sometimes has a bit of luck. Mike Eardley, a new member, was picked as a batsman in his first game for the club. Being short of bowlers the ball was thrown to him with a request that he bowled a few overs. The net result was a hat-trick with his first three deliveries and Prestbury were back in the hutch for 36! (Subsequently Mike demonstrated he was a good bat and in 1971 scored an unbeaten 157 against Mossley for the 1st XI.)

The Mad-Batters tea party

Hartford

Grange Park, off Bradburns Lane, Hartford CW8 1LU

VICTORIAN CLUB cricket was regularly played on unreliable surfaces and team totals were generally best described as modest. This point is well demonstrated by a Hartford CC AGM report which appeared in the *Northwich Chronicle* in March 1900. In all matches Hartford totalled 1065 runs for 147 wickets, at an average of 7.24 runs per wicket, and the opposition aggregated 789 runs for 149 wickets at an average of 5.29. Another point about this period is that it is never easy to establish the exact founding date of a club. Hartford is no exception, but the *Northwich Chronicle* of 16 May 1885 does reveal that Norley Hall beat Hartford by an innings and 18 runs. As no previous newspaper had mentioned the club it is reasonable to assume that particular year as their founding one.

1886 - During Hartford's second campaign the local press drew attention to a fundraising event in aid of the cricket club which was held at Grange Park. This took the form of an athletics festival and a football match between Blackburn Rovers, holders of the FA Cup, and Davenham FC, holders of the Cheshire Challenge Cup.

1887 - Hartford drew with Northwich 2nd XI. Northwich and Middlewich were the longest established of the mid-Cheshire clubs and they tended to play their second eleven against the newer clubs. Hartford must have performed creditably in their first encounter because in 1888 Northwich fielded their first team in two matches against them.

1904 - The 'old shed' was replaced in 1901 by a new pavilion costing £40 and this season's newspaper preview described the club as only having a small deficit to pay off. The ground was reported to be in beautiful condition and the pavilion 'spick and span'.

1908 - The preview to the new season in the *Northwich Chronicle* (2 May 1908) mentioned that Hartford would again play at Grange Farm, the club's ground for 'so many years'. JFL Brunner, son of Sir John Brunner, co-founder of Brunner Mond, was the new President.

Sometime between the wars the club was forced to move away from Grange Farm as Brunner Mond had purchased the land to build houses for its senior management (on a road now known as 'The Grange'). As an alternative Sir John Brunner offered a ground at Sandiway House on Littledales Lane for a peppercorn rent and that remained home until 1957 when the site was acquired by MANWEB.

In the early 1950s the parish council had been keen that the cricketers moved back to the heart of the village, but they enjoyed the idyllic surroundings in Littledales Lane and declined that invitation. However, around 1956-57 MANWEB informed the Club that it now wanted to use the ground on both days of the weekend for their own teams. In the circumstances the cricketers had to re-approach the parish council with a view to playing at 'Grange

Park' and fortuitously they were welcomed back with open arms. This particular site was, of course, not the original Grange Park but their current home off Bradburns Lane.

The club started playing here in 1957. The parish council acquired a concrete building for £200 from the Prees Air Force base which was used as the pavilion.

1975 - The Club decided that a new pavilion was required. Although permission was given by the Parish Council the club raised funds and managed the project themselves. The parish clerk, William Morris, opened the new facility on 11 September 1977 when a match was played between the club and the President W R Wollen's XI.

Over the years the lease has been renewed a number of times and a proviso remains that the site be used solely for cricket, but for more than 20 years now the pavilion has been sub-let to Hartford Bridge Club and more recently to other local organisations.

> ## HARTFORD'S ENGLAND CAPTAIN
> ### – written by John Prew in 2010
>
> During the mid-1950s I used to collect the vice-president donations. Joe Sorton, a gentleman in his 80s, was a contributor and he told me the following story:
>
> One week Aubrey Brocklebank, a Cambridge University student, brought his friend Stanley Jackson to play. After this game in which Stanley Jackson did well, they asked him to play the following week but he declined, saying that he could not play as he was playing for Yorkshire.
>
> I researched this story and established that:
>
> The Hon. Sir Francis Stanley Jackson (b 1870, d 1947) played for Cambridge University, Yorkshire and England. He captained England in 1905 against the Australians.
>
> He was at Trinity College, Cambridge with Aubrey Brocklebank (b 1873, d 1929) who became the third Baronet of Greenlands and Springwood in 1911. The Baronetcy was created for his grandfather on the 22 July 1885. He was the eldest child of five children of Sir Thomas Brocklebank and Agnes Lydia Allport. Sir Aubrey was a director of the Cunard Steamship Company, the Suez Canal Company and the Great Western Railway.
>
> He was believed to have lived in Abbey House, Abbey Lane in Hartford and Nunsmere Hall in Sandiway, which was built for the Brocklebanks in 1900.
>
> I was also able to verify that Sir Stanley Jackson's sister, the Hon. Grace Mary Jackson, married the above Sir Aubrey. Thus the story is believable as marriage, the area, and the friendship at the same university college neatly linked them together.

The old pavilion with the new pavilion taking shape.

Haslington

Clay Lane, Haslington CW1 5SE

PLAYING AS 'the mighty squirrels' (the club badge), Haslington CC took on the TV *Eggheads* in January 2013. £18000 was at stake and the cricketers came very close to victory, taking the contest into a sudden death situation. The killer question was: "Which Samuel Beckett play features the quotation 'Give birth astride of a grave, the light gleams an instant and then it's night once more'?" Regrettably, (but very understandably!) they couldn't come up with *Waiting for Godot*. No doubt the Haslington slip cordon have cursed Samuel Beckett ever since!? The worthy Haslington team was Jon Gledhill, Tom his son, James Blake, Andy Harrington and Richard Brown. Oh yes, and James disclosed to Jeremy Vine he had once sat in every one of the ten thousand seats at Crewe Alexandra FC. It took him 5 hours and 28 minutes!

As well as being a prominent member of that team, Jon Gledhill is a key figure in the day-to-day running of the club. He is the current chairman and is extremely committed to continue overseeing the development of the south Cheshire outfit. They have four senior teams and junior sides from Under 9 through to Under 18. They have a large ground on the edge of the village and a sizeable, modern and attractive pavilion which has been home to the club since before the millennium. Ever ambitious they have plans to introduce a women's team 'the does'!

In 2014 the club inflicted a defeat on Wirral CC which was reported worldwide. At tea Haslington, having posted a modest 108 all out off of 41.4 overs, could not have envisaged the eventual outcome. Wirral dismissed for 3 made from 9.2 overs. They lost 8 wickets before a run was scored. The star Haslington bowlers were Ben Istead 6-1 and Tom Gledhill 4-0. Ben (1) and Tom (26) had scored a combined 27 runs with the bat so contributed nine times more than the final Wirral total. (See Wirral CC entry).

Haslington on Eggheads

Hawk Green

Rhode Fields, Upper Hibbert Lane, Hawk Green SK6 7HQ

THE CLUB was founded in 1909. They joined the High Peak League the same year. They moved from their original ground, adjacent to Marple Golf Club, in the mid-1920s when the golf club purchased the land. Their new home was on the village green itself, opposite The Crown public house.

However, with the restrictions of a publicly-owned ground, not to mention locals walking across the outfield in the middle of a game, the club purchased their present ground in April 1956.

Moving right up to date the club has a splendid new pavilion which serves not just the cricketers but also a number of local organisations. A fire all but destroyed the old one in September 2008. The late Roy Cartledge, a former chairman, groundsman, coach and all-round good guy, who had been at the centre of operations since joining the club from Birch Vale in 1990, was devastated. He explained that he was in a nearby house when he got a call, just after midnight, telling him that the pavilion was alight. "When I arrived at the ground, the fire had really taken hold. It was just awful to see. All our history gone up in flames. The cause was never established. The fire service and police forensics suspected foul play but no evidence was ever found."

For the following two seasons the club survived in a large marquee at the far end of the ground and really had to make do. Roy added: "The members were brilliant and all rallied round to help."

A substantial ECB grant along with the eventual insurance pay-out and a small bank loan funded the new building, which was eventually finished in 2010.

In August 2013 the club had the good fortune to play a Twenty20 match against an England Legends XI, which included Michael Vaughan, Adam Hollioake, Neil Fairbrother and Devon Malcolm. Over a thousand spectators turned up. The match resulted from the club entering a Nat West competition. It was a great prize but they only had four weeks' notice of the event!

For the record, England, batting first, made 194-6, which included a century from Mal Loye. In reply, Hawk Green made a very respectable 165-8. Justin Blackhurst scored 88 not out for the home team.

2015-16 - The club have had recent successful runs in the National Village Cup. In 2015 they were the Group 8 (Cheshire & Clwyd) winners, defeating Northop Hall in the regional final. At the national last eight stage they lost to the eventual winners, Woodhouse Grange. In 2016 they defeated Tattenhall in the Group final but lost to Cleator at the last 16 stage.

Hawk Green have played in the Derbyshire & Cheshire League since 1967 but enter the Cheshire Shield on a Sunday. In 2016 they lost in the final to Northwich. Hawk Green 186 all out, Northwich 190-4. In 2017 they became the Derbyshire & Cheshire League champions.

Hazel Grove

Wesley Park, Newby Road, Hazel Grove SK7 5DR

A CELEBRATORY 50th Anniversary Dinner was held at the Cheshire Conference Centre, Edgeley Park, Stockport on 29 March 2008. We learn from the dinner brochure that developing the ground in the 1960s was not all plain sailing. Money was needed and an ambitious event was planned in conjunction with Norbury CC ...*Someone once said 'if you are going to have a disaster have a big one'. We certainly had a big one, the biggest marquee we could hire, nearly half of it wooden floored, an integral tented area for the bar, lights, staging, amplification and three jazz bands. Organisationally it was good, some of the too few fans (700 attended but 1000 was the breakpoint) said 'superb', but one bad mistake cost both clubs dear, we forgot the weather. On Friday evening it was akin to being on the 'Cutty Sark' under full sail.*

A few years later the Social Committee were back in business, but this time with a more modest event; the 'Seven Arrow Challenge' for enthusiastic dart players.

1984-85 - In consecutive seasons the Derbyshire & Cheshire First Division was won, which made a nice change for one member who had a memory of the League Wooden Spoon Trophy being displayed in the Hazel Grove Post Office window!

1991 - Of all the challenges faced, none tested the resolve of the club more than when an arsonist struck on 21 April. The wooden pavilion, which had stood for 54 years, was reduced to a pile of rubble. At an emotional meeting at the Grapes Hotel the members pledged that cricket must continue. Delivery vans arrived as temporary dressing rooms and a caravan served as a kitchen. Unwittingly the arsonist, a tragic figure who subsequently committed suicide, did the club a favour in the long run, but it did not feel like that at the time.

1995 - Chairman Phil Glennon demonstrated his commitment to fund-raising by walking from all the Derbyshire & Cheshire League grounds back to Wesley Park.

2006 - Ken Daniels died after a lifelong involvement with the club and in September 2007 his wife performed the ceremony which re-named the pavilion in his honour, marking both his name and the memory of his service to the club forever.

> Chris Ashling, now of Bowdon, started his career as a Hazel Grove junior. He went on to play six first-class matches for Glamorgan (2009-11) with a top score of 20 and a best bowling analysis of 4-47. The family connection remains to this day as Ralph, Chris's grandfather, is a club patron. Paul, Chris's dad, was also a very useful Hazel Grove player in his day.

The club has a thriving junior section. Is there another Chris Ashling in the pipeline?

The ground is accessed through a sizeable industrial estate, which contrasts vividly with this lovely little cricketing oasis.

Heaton Mersey

The Heatons Sports Club, Green Lane, Heaton Moor, Stockport SK4 2NF

IN 1879, HEATON Mersey and Heaton Moor were semi-rural suburbs of Stockport on the one hand, and Manchester on the other. Fields separated the fine new villas and the old cottage property from Manchester's growing sprawl, and industry crept along the Mersey valley out of Stockport. Gentlemen rode to business in their carriages, or used the train from Heaton Moor and Heaton Mersey stations. They were pleasant districts, appreciated by early commuting businessmen and growing in popularity for their social desirability. Farmland surrounded the area and it was on one of these farms that Heaton Mersey Cricket and Lacrosse Club had its first home on Didsbury Road.

Funding the cost of a pavilion and equipment was always an issue, but lots of social events were organised and a troupe of entertainers known as 'The Minnehaha Minstrels' were firm favourites. In 1886 two sketches were presented at the Conservative Hall with over a thousand attending the three performances. It was, therefore, a huge blow when the club was given notice to quit in 1890 and this led to the move to the existing ground. The new home hosted its first match in May 1893. The *Stockport Advertiser* reported that the club President 'received the first ball before a large and fashionable assembly'. In 1895 a huge bazaar which ran for four days raised £1835 towards the purchase price of £1987 of the site. The newly-acquired ground was placed in a trust.

1900 - The AGM was told that several cricketers had played on a Sunday and hoped it would never happen again. Mr Purdy was one of the most vociferous voices when the subject was raised again many years later. (In 1933 'He felt sure that it would be a very bad move for a club of our standing which had always received the support and respect of all the best people in the neighbourhood, a support which would undoubtedly be withdrawn if the resolution was carried'. It was put to the vote and the motion was carried. Three resignations followed).

1901 - AN Hornby, captain of Lancashire, opened the newly-refurbished pavilion and commented that it was his preference to open 100 pavilions to one bazaar as it was cheaper! There was a rousing chorus of 'For he's a jolly good fellow'.

1902 - Croquet was added to the other sports which already included tennis, hockey and lacrosse. The President hoped its provision would prove to be an attraction for those declining athletes who might otherwise be tempted to stray away in pursuit of the mixed pleasures of golf!

1911-13 - Taylor, the groundsman, was shirking his duties and in no uncertain terms was threatened with dismissal without notice if he did not mend his ways. He was later sacked. In 1913 a magnificent Chippendale design eight-day grandfather clock was presented to the Chairman in appreciation of 21 years of service to the club. The dark clouds of war gathered.

1948 - The pavilion had been refurbished with basket chairs, new curtains, heaters and a wireless set. The kitchen now boasted a new sink, an Ascot heater and some long-awaited new lino. In the same year the club was taken to court by a resident whose property bounded the ground, complaining of damage to trees and bushes. The judge, however, found in favour of the club and 'the Mersey contingent in the court could scarcely refrain from throwing their hats in the air'.

1973 - David Humpage, now a long-serving officer of the Cheshire County Cricket League (Treasurer 1985-95 and Chairman 1995 and ongoing), scored 104 not out in an innings against Moncton when the next highest score was nine. The 'other' batsman was Sandy Scrimgeour, who much later served the County Club with distinction as Team Manager. David actually joined Heaton Mersey as a junior in 1955, but prior to that date can recall his father taking him down to the ground to watch the matches and meet some of the club characters of the day. The first team opening batsman was called Alan Jordan, who had a wooden leg. He always fielded at first slip and the opposition always allowed him a runner. His fellow opening batsman was Harold Briggs, who batted in a trilby and fielded at third man in front of the pavilion where he kept a half pint of beer by the gate to sample between overs!

1986 - Having been a founder member of the Cheshire County League (1975) the 1st Xl were crowned County League champions for the first (and only) time.

2006 - The club merged with the Heaton Moor Rugby Club and the Heatons Sports Club was born. Through a deal with a national house builder, both clubs exchanged some land for the construction of a new joint clubhouse, tennis courts and extensive parking. The club continues to field four senior sides each weekend and has an extensive junior structure, now fielding sides at all age levels.

> The Committee minutes of September 1883 state "It was resolved that E Oldham having used the cricket field for an unauthorised match, and also wilfully broken a tennis pole, the property of the Club, he be charged 10/6d for the use of the field, and 9d, the net cost of the tennis pole, and that he be reprimanded by the Secretary".
>
> At the 1884 annual meeting the club colours were changed from navy blue to canary and claret. Later that year "a person named Pearson had been going about soliciting subscriptions for the Club, the said person having no connection whatever with the club". Advertisements were placed in the local newspaper warning people against subscribing to bogus collectors.

The following are Cheshire-based clubs who played in the South Lancs League when Heaton Mersey Village were members:

- Cheadle Heath (Stockport-based, since folded)
- Hans Renold (factory-based team)
- Heaviley Sunday School (later changed name to Davenport but subsequently folded - Stockport-based)
- Post Office Telephones (played on the well-appointed civil service sports ground at Timperley)
- Woodlands (played at Woodbank Park, Stockport, later merged with Cheadle Heath)

Heaton Mersey Village

Harwood Road, Heaton Mersey SK4 3AW

DO YOU KNOW of another club that has had four variations of its name? At the outset it was known as Heaton Mersey Parish CC, later Heaton Mersey Beech Road, subsequently Harwood CC and, finally and currently, Heaton Mersey Village.

The origins of the club go back to 1924 when local church members played in a farmer's field near to the old Renold chain factory on Burnage Lane. By 1934 a substantial piece of land was secured near the clay pits of Jackson's Brick Yard at the side of Beech Road. The new location justified the first name change. In 1960 a decision was reached with the local corporation to use the site as a refuse tip. Two of the clay pits were filled in and the ground was raised by about 20 feet. The club received about £4000 in compensation but had an expectation of returning to the ground rather sooner than actually occurred. In the event it was 1972 before cricket was played on the new surface and the facility was now to be shared with the local footballers and lacrosse players. The trustees negotiated with Vaux Brewery and a new lounge was built adjacent to the changing rooms. Given the ground entrance was on Harwood Road, the title of Harwood was a natural choice, but it seems that name was never very popular and in 1982 the present name was adopted. In 1983, after settlement and enduring drainage problems, the ground was re-laid at a cost of £30000.

Before finally settling in the Cheshire pyramid, the club had played in the High Peak League, the Cheshire Association and also the South Lancashire League.

I'm obliged to Keith Seddon for turning up a 1987 newspaper article which included an overview of the club. He served the club for 27 years up to the millennium and for two score years was captain of either the 1st or 2nd XI. Les Chapman wrestled with the demands of being the groundsman for just about 20 years but has now passed the baton to Rob Samuel.

In 2016 the club won the 2nd XI Central Division of the Cheshire Alliance.

Approaching the ground along the A5145, Didsbury Road, look out for The Griffin public house on the corner of Harwood Road. It was built in the 1830s by members of the Thorniley family and assumed to have been constructed with bricks from their family brickworks. This building is within the Heaton Mersey Conservation Area, although the cricket ground, slightly to the north, is just outside the designation. Appropriately enough Harwood Road was originally Pottery Lane. A stroll around the heritage trail and a trip to the cricket sounds like a neat combination.

High Lane

Middlewood Road, High Lane SK6 8AU

WHEN HIGH Lane celebrated their centenary in June 1985 they marked the occasion with a cricket week. A Cheshire Cricket League Representative XI were the Sunday visitors. On Monday the programme shows that the Chairman's XI included the recently retired Bob Willis, for whom the club had hosted a highly successful benefit match in 1981. The Cheshire Cats were the Tuesday visitors. Cheshire provided the opposition on Wednesday and the XL Club on Thursday. On the Friday evening a six-a-side competition was hosted. Warwickshire CCC were one of the participating teams, with the evening's proceeds being shared between the High Lane CC Centenary Appeal and the Dennis Amiss Testimonial Fund. In his programme notes the Chairman, Peter Johnson, said that the cricket club had been an enduring part of High Lane life over the century when the village consisted of just a few houses and farms.

I'm grateful to Vernon Addison, former sports editor of the *Manchester Evening News*, who told a tale against his own club in a book he published in 1971. He claims a one time High Lane player, Jack Cliffe, holds the doubtful distinction of being the king of the dobbers (the act of running up to bowl but instead running out the non-striking batsman without the courtesy of a warning). He recalled a match in which Jack acknowledged the opposing captain with a nod and then dobbed him before he had faced a ball. Even this, however, was not his *piece de resistance*. Previously, in an away game against Mirrless when High Lane were going for a title, feelings were beginning to run high as they felt the hosts were making very little effort to get the match started following morning rain. Eventually the umpires positioned the bails, but no sooner had they done so Jack had them off again. He had pulled his master stroke ...a dobbing with the first ball of the match! (I confess to not being aware of the term 'dobber' being used in this context. The modern day terminology is a 'Mankad').

By the way, if you are planning a visit to High Lane, don't panic, be persistent. It's a fair way up bumpy Middlewood Road. Look out for the direction post. You'll get there eventually!

> **Mention High Lane CC and there is a good chance you will immediately think of the late Arthur Cash - High Lane legend in every sense. A resident in the village from the age of five, he was a one-club cricketer. He played here with distinction until he was 60, but his contribution was not just confined to the field of play, he was a genuine and dedicated clubman. He died in the summer of 2016, aged 90. At his peak he was a quick bowler and a top order batsman who regularly featured at the top of both sets of averages. In his early years his brother, Ernie, was in the same side and then later he played with his son, Garry. Of course, his sporting prowess was not just restricted to cricket. He was already a skilful footballer when he undertook his period of National Service and he was quickly appointed as a physical training instructor. He played football on a semi-professional basis, primarily for Hazel Grove Celtic in the 1950s. He qualified as a FA Coach and continued playing and coaching until his mid-forties, latterly with Cheadle Rovers until their demise in 1965. When he retired from cricket he took up Crown Green Bowls, eventually qualifying as a referee, although he continued to play rather than officiate!**

Hollingworth

Thorncliffe Hall Road, Hollingworth SK14 8LW

I WAS DELIGHTED to be able to chat with Alan Sidebottom, who has been involved with the club for seventy plus years. His first association with his local team was as a 7-year-old. He played until he was 60 and is the current President. He told me the club was formed in 1890 and that they originally played in Woolley Lane. The current ground was purchased by Mr Redfern for £245 (x 5 acres) in 1947. He recalled the 1990 Centenary match when some of the Manchester United players turned out. Danny Wallace, Paul Ince and Lee Martin all played. Lee Martin (b 1968) was a local boy. He, of course, scored the deciding goal in the 1990 Cup Final replay after United had been held by Crystal Palace to a 3-3 draw in the first Wembley match.

> **On the side of the pavilion is a signboard displaying the club badge and confirming 'Established 1890', but Lillywhite's Annual of 1880 discloses they played 23 matches (9 wins, 9 draws, 5 defeats) in that particular year, a decade earlier. H Harrop was top of the batting averages, scoring 288 from 20 innings. The captain, W Howe, followed him with 230 runs from 18 matches. G Platt took 35 wickets for 188 runs. It is recorded they had 110 members at the time. With such a level of detail available and with a substantial number of matches played, it might suggest the club is even older? Lillywhite's also provides statistics for subsequent years. All are before the accepted foundation date.**

> **A sign of the times ...the 1955 annual handbook of the Club and League Cricket in Lancashire & District sets out the dates for Cotton Town holidays. Hollingworth was allocated 23 July-6 August and 17-19 September.**

An earlier foundation date is apparently validated by *Cheshire Cricketers 1822-1996*, which informs that Thomas Pointon (born in Hollingworth in 1863) played 60 matches for Cheshire 1883-1895. His clubs are declared as Hollingworth, Staley and Castleton Moor. *Cricket Archive* shows he also played for Rishton and that he appeared at Lord's on at least eight occasions. The same source also shows Sylvester Sinfield (born in Hollingworth in 1861) also played a single match for Cheshire in 1889. Hollingworth is shown as his only club.

At one time Hollingworth played in the Glossop League, but the current senior sides now play in the Derbyshire & Cheshire League. Links with local schools help to maintain a healthy junior membership. The club holds fundraising events which have included a Sportsman's Evening, Comedy & Curry Night as well as a Duck Racing at the Roaches Lock, Mossley.

The ground is situated at the top of the village with stunning views over the Derbyshire hills.

Holmes Chapel

Victoria Sports & Social Club, Victoria Avenue, Holmes Chapel CW4 7BE

THE PEMBERTON family lived in Congleton and moved to Holmes Chapel between the two world wars. Their relocation occurred so that George could occupy a house belonging to his employers. He worked at the Victoria Mills factory, which had opened in 1911 and originally traded as the Holmes Chapel Wallpaper Company. Eventually it became part of the huge Crown Paints & Wallpaper group. Although now in a different ownership the factory exists to this day on the Macclesfield Road by the bridge over the railway track. Just about the same time as the family moved so the sports club in Victoria Avenue was built for the employees' use and it was here that George played his cricket. When he was old enough, his son Cyril was recruited and, in time, he became a wicketkeeping 2nd XI captain. Grandson Craig joined up to represent the third generation of the family. My informant was Helen Birchall, granddaughter of George and mother of Craig. Her brother Brian and his son Ian were also members. In her time she has kept the scores, prepared the teas and sorted out the administration for the colts team tours to Devon. Husband Alan was the junior coach and the mini-bus driver between 1989 and 1994. Daughter Kirsten was an occasional tea-lady. Work at the factory and an involvement in the cricket club was a key part of family life. That's how it was in those halcyon days of yonder.

Of course, the ownership of the club has now changed and the facilities have expanded, offering the local community a wide variety of activities across the age range, but the cricketers still occupy the back field. They were promoted to Division 1 of the Cheshire Alliance in 2013 and in recent years have secured mid-table finishes.

Preceding the 'wallpaper' ground by a good number of decades was another cricket field on the north east corner of the London Road and Station Road crossroads. Undoubtedly William George Armitstead (b 1833, d 1907) would have played on this old ground. He was born in Holmes Chapel and educated at Westminster School and Christ Church, Oxford. He played 14 first-class matches, mainly for Oxford University, where he acquired four cricketing Blues in the 1850s, but perhaps his greatest claim to cricketing fame revolved around the introduction of the umpire's white coat. He was a founding member of the Free Foresters club and during one of their matches against a United England XI in 1861 he protested that he could not see the ball against the dark clothing of the umpire. His complaint was upheld, and, in the words of the day, 'the umpire was vested in a nightshirt'. The rest is history! Armitstead was the vicar of Goostrey from 1862 until he died.

Hyde

Werneth Low, Gee Cross, Hyde SK14 3AA

HYDE CC EMERGED from the ashes of Hyde Chapel CC. Mr James Hampson, who had been Secretary of the chapel team, was instrumental in taking the initiative forward and his work was generously acknowledged at the first annual dinner held at The Grapes Hotel, Gee Cross in November 1901. The *Herald* reported there was a loyal toast for King Edward VII after which a humorous song was contributed by Mr Handforth and a good number of speeches interspaced with pieces on the gramophone and more songs. The Secretary was presented with a very handsome Davenport writing desk in recognition of his good work. (In 1906 he also received an ebony writing table!) He responded by saying that there were certain times in a man's life when his feelings were too deep for words, and this was one of them to him. He thought he had better content himself with thanking them all for this kindness.

The original ground was at 'The Gerrards', Pole Bank, Stockport Road. That remained HQ until 1948.

1906 - Hyde (40) v Tintwistle (40). The Tintwistle innings included seven ducks.

1908 - F Ward won the 2nd XI batting prize and additionally a gold mounted umbrella(!) for the highest individual score in the club (68).

1916 - With a view to raising funds for the Hyde division of the Red Cross, a match was organised between the Ladies and the Gents. The ladies were victorious but the writer in *The Reporter* had a suspicion, let it be said gently, that in the closing stages they were helped by their chivalrous opponents. When the gents fielded they could only catch the ball using their left hand and when batting they had to use pick-axe handles! The ladies wore full VAD uniforms and the saucy scribe suggested that in any future fixture the ladies might venture to turn out in knickers similar to those worn by our smart young lady tram-guards. He suggested the ground would be full and the Red Cross coffers would overflow!

1919 - Talented Ernest Bardsley scored a 100 not out against Strines. Having joined the Manchester Pals in 1914 he was later commissioned and attached to the West Yorkshire Regiment. He was wounded three times during the hostilities and awarded the Military Cross.

1930 - Having joined the High Peak League in 1907 Hyde won the title for the very first time. The championship was secured in front of a record number of spectators at Pole Bank against New Mills, who finished as runners-up. After a good number of disappointments in previous

The new pavilion in 1928

The current pavilion under construction in 1967

years when they looked well equipped to win the competition, this success came as a pleasant surprise given that Ernest Bardsley had stopped playing and the genial but formidable old stalwart, Joe Higginbottom, had retired before the season started. He had played with Hyde for 20 years. Apparently offended that Hyde had won the trophy without him, Joe decided to play again in 1931, but the selection committee decided that he must start off in the 2nd XI; he took 6-30 in his first match back and followed that up with 8-29, but when he was not selected for the 1st XI the following week he went off to play at Bredbury! (At the end of the season he was made the first Hyde honorary Life Member).

1936 - Nineteen-year-old 2nd XI player Frank Schofield took 10 wickets for 5 runs (all bowled) against Buxworth.

1939 - For some years the renewal of the lease at Pole Bank had been a concern and a new home was a priority. At one stage Smithy Fold on Stockport Road had been earmarked, but eventually Werneth Low was identified as the best option despite its distance from the town centre and the fact that very significant levelling of the ground would be needed. Just as the mechanical diggers were about to commence work WW2 started and that was that for six years.

1948 - The new facilities were officially opened on 12 June after a herculean effort. Many thought the conversion task was impractical in terms of both the workload and costs (£2000). Mr JC Fallows (see Romiley entry) cut the ribbon.

1949 - A drought year. NO matches lost to the weather at the Low! Has this ever happened since?

1952 - The Committee authorised the purchase of one ton of railway sleepers to provide additional seating.

1962 - After a number of modest years on the field of play the Committee enlivened things off the park by seeking permission to build a bungalow and open a caravan park at the ground. (The caravan park was to be located near the existing net area). After the application was refused an appeal was lodged but subsequently lost.

1963-66 - On 11 September 1963 the pop group The Hollies, supported by The Meteors, were playing at Hyde Town Hall (admission 5s 6d), but the Hyde CC 'top of the bill' the previous evening had been the Building Sub-Committee Chairman when he announced outline planning permission had been granted for a new pavilion. Exactly a year later two thousand people, mostly teenagers, attended a fund-raising barbecue and dance at the ground. Arranged jointly by Hyde CC and Hyde Round Table it raised £400. There were concerns about potential trouble from Mods and Rockers, but the only incident was from a high-spirited youngster who attempted to dislodge the main pole holding up the marquee! The Meteors were on

> **In 2000 Lee Brown wrote a 270 page Hyde CC centenary book. It's a masterpiece of research and entitled *Station yer fielders down by the shed*. The origin of the title relates to a visiting Aussie who suggested that very phrase was appropriate whenever he batted. In the event it transpired he could barely hit the ball off the square!**

duty again. The barbecue became a regular event and in 1966 another two thousand came along. George Best was in attendance with David Sadler and his Manchester City friend Mike Summerbee. He left early saying he needed an early night!

> Jim Allen first played for Hyde in 1977. What a signing! He joined the Kerry Packer West Indian team in 1978. An Australian newspaper reported ...we were treated to another remarkable display of fierce driving by young Jim Allen from Montserrat, the least known of all the West Indian players. Following his 83 in Sydney against Australia, he hit the first ball he received from Gilmour for six, put both Viv Richards and Clive Lloyd in the shade, and reached 58 off 45 balls before he was bowled by Ray Bright.

1969 - The new pavilion, built at a cost of £10k, was officially opened. A match was played between Hyde Past (103) v Present (78-6). Rain denied the 'yesteryear boys' a victory?

1970s - After 58 years in the High Peak League Hyde joined the Lancashire & Cheshire League. In 1979 the club were First Division champions and winners of both the Thompson Trophy and the Parliamentary Cup. A great triple! Alan Berry won the League bowling award with 60 wickets at 11.35 and Jim Allen finished top of the professional's batting averages with 989 runs at 65.93.

1980s - Membership of the Central Lancashire League commenced in 1981 and the title was won at the first time of asking with significant help from New Zealander Bruce Edgar, who scored 1658 runs, took 35 wickets and held onto 20 catches. After that great first season it was increasingly difficult to compete financially with a good number of sides making very big payments to a battery of West Indian fast bowlers – Andy Roberts, Franklyn Stephenson, Ezra Moseley and Joel Garner were all employed by Central Lancashire sides.

1990s - After a period of under-achievement in the cash-crazy CLL there was a determination to begin a new era and that was in the Cheshire County League from 1993. In that first year they collected the wooden-spoon. When the 1996 season dawned they had spent £20000 on new practice nets, which were officially opened by former England star Derek Randall. Chairman Peter Hardman said the club was committed to bringing on the youngsters. John Ashley was an early product of that initiative. By the end of the century other now familiar names were emerging – Mark Leathley, James Duffy, Rob Brierley, Mark Makin and Danny Berry.

2000s - A period of sustained success at all levels, but for the 1st XI, T20 Cup wins in 2007, 2011 (culminating in a national finals day at Essex CCC), 2012, 2013, Cheshire Cup wins in 2008, 2011 and 2016 and the coveted ECB Premier League title in 2015.

Irby

Mill Hill Road, Irby CH61 4XQ

IRBY CC, UNDREAMT of six weeks ago, is already a flourishing concern, with eighty members, a ground replete with kit, and in a very sound financial position. So said the local newspaper in 1948.

When the club was founded in that year the home venue was the municipal park in Sea View Lane (just about half a mile from the current HQ). For the first few years tents were erected and utilised for both changing and as a tea area. When the club applied to the District Council in 1950 for planning permission to build a pavilion, they replied: 'the Council are reluctantly obliged to decline the proposal but propose as an alternative to themselves erect dressing room accommodation'. What a stroke of good fortune!

1950 - Playing membership had increased rapidly and a 2nd XI was formed with a 3rd XI added in 1953.

1955 - ANP Gifford had the distinction of scoring the first hundred for Irby, albeit for the 2nd XI, a feat that stood until 1957 when, playing for the 1st XI, MR Brearey took 105 off a Wallasey XI. Earlier that season he had taken all ten wickets in a match against Odyssey.

1957 - 'Move to ban Irby Sunday cricket fails by one vote' is the local newspaper headline. By an 11-10 vote the club are allowed to play four home matches. *The News* has another report some years later when the Council debated the subject again and, evidently, with some passion. Councillor Fletcher, speaking for the motion, accused the opponents of 'a façade of seeming broad-mindedness as a screen for narrow-minded Victorianism'. He concluded: 'I don't know for what unutterable guilt the Lord has condemned England to the weekly punishment of Sunday.' The vote was conclusively in favour of Sunday play by 11 -1.

1964 - The long search for a private ground was successful and negotiations commenced for the purchase of five acres of land off Mill Hill Lane.

1965 - The most successful season so far for the 1st XI. Captained by JDO Hughes, of the 33 games played, 27 were won, 4 drawn and only 2 lost.

1970 - The new ground at Mill Hill Lane was formally opened by the Right Honourable Selwyn Lloyd, MP for Wirral. The back pitch to accommodate 3rd/4th XI cricket came 25 years later.

1972 - The *Heswall & Neston News and Advertiser* carried a photograph and report of the Silver anniversary dinner held at the Kings Gap Hotel in Hoylake. The Chairman congratulated Arthur Marsden, who had umpired the 1st XI throughout the first 25 years, and to Roy Thomas, who had served on the committee for 20 years. During my research I was fortunate enough to be able to meet Roy, who is now the only surviving member from the founding year. Now 90 years old, he joined the club immediately upon returning from completing his National Service in India and Singapore.

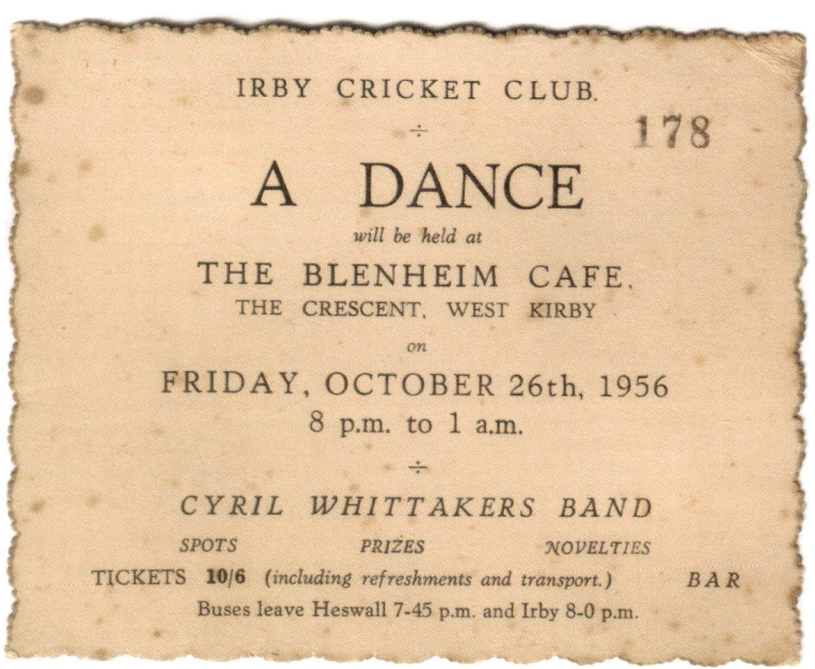

1976 - A fundraising Summer Fete was held on 26 June. The gates were opened at 1.45pm with the music of a piped band followed by a gymnastic display by members of the YMCA. At 3.45pm a mock battle was performed by the company of the Cheshire Regiment. The sideshows included a fortune teller, 'beat the goalie', a coconut shy, a ping pong nerve test and darts roulette! Presumably the cricketers had a day off?

1981-1993 - Inspirational captain Jeff Spence led the club during its most successful period, with six Merseyside Competition league titles and five Lever Cup wins as well as scoring over 10000 runs.

In 1998, to celebrate the 50th anniversary they played a Cheshire XI. Inevitably on that day in the Irby team were the Newman brothers, Mike and Dave, who have contributed so much to the club, both on and off the pitch, since they joined up in the 1970s. Between them they have contributed more than 25000 runs. Now that Mike has retired he has passed the Irby baton to his son, Mark, who is now 1st XI captain.

The club has had a long history of organising successful dances, dinners and Hot Pot suppers. Frank Woodhead (Nottinghamshire) spoke in 1965, Harold Rhodes (Derbyshire) in 1967, Freddie Millett (Minor Counties & Cheshire) in 1971, Tony Nicholson (Yorkshire) in 1974, Nasser Hussain in 2001, Graham Lloyd (Lancashire) in 2003, Kim Barnett (Derbyshire) in 2004 and Richard Hadlee in 2008. The latter was a 60th anniversary celebration lunch attended by a good number of old members and friends.

By the way, the Irby Mill pub is a mere five minute walk from the ground, so a pre-match lunch is an inviting option.

The Irby CC 'welcome stone' at the entrance to the ground

Kerridge

Clarke Lane, Kerridge SK10 5AH

THE CLUB was founded in 1923 and originally played in the field at the side of the War Memorial on Oak Lane. In 1962 the club moved to its present location on Clarke Lane.

The club played in the Adlington and District League until 1964 when they joined the High Peak League. In 1977 they became founder members of the Cheshire Cricket Competition. They continued in that league with some success, the 1st XI winning the knockout trophy in 1993 and the 2nd XI a trophy two years later. Ironically both teams played against Wilmslow Wayfarers in the finals.

The 75th Anniversary of the club coincided with the amalgamation of the Cheshire Cricket Competition and the South Cheshire Cricket Alliance, which merged to form the Cheshire Alliance, an integral part of the emerging Cheshire pyramid.

2004 - When a journalist from the *Macclesfield Express* arranged to meet a club representative to discuss recent vandalism at the ground they got a shock on their arrival as the arsonists had set the pavilion alight. So extensive was the damaged it had to be demolished.

2017 - Kerridge CC got a very unexpected mention on *Sky Sports News*. During their Division 5 1st XI match against Mossley on 24 June a cow escaped from a neighbouring field and scuttled across the ground. A mobile phone video-clip showed the beast building up a good head of steam and making a bee-line for the umpire, Ken Hockenhull, before declaring his brief innings closed. As the Sky newscaster aptly pointed out, the animal left the field via cow corner! This is the second time Mossley have been involved in such a scene (see Saughall entry). The Kerridge captain, Adam Banks, said: "It was scary at the time, but I can see the funny side now. At first I just thought 'hello, what's this?' as it was just plodding around the pitch. But then it took one look at me and started charging. I thought 'stand your ground', but that's not so easy when you have a half tonne bull (or was it a cow!) running towards you." Adam, 38, added: "I went one way and he tried to turn, but because the ground was wet its legs went from under it. Then it got up and headed for the umpire." He continued: "We have kids coming to the games, so you always have to be wary of where the balls are flying, but we've never had to worry about bulls!" Supporter Geoff Allen, 74, said: "I've been at the club for more than 40 years. We've had the odd dog running onto the pitch and causing havoc, but never a bull. It will definitely stick in the memory of the players."

 (The) King's School, Macclesfield

Cumberland Street, Macclesfield SK10 1DA

THE KING'S School has been selected as one of the 2017 Top 100 schools in the UK for cricket by *The Cricketer* magazine for the second consecutive year.

The judging panel of the world's number one cricket magazine based their selection on the quality of coaching, the range of fixtures, the extent of facilities and the quality of cricketers making their way into the professional ranks and league cricket.

Steve Moores, King's Head of Cricket and a long-standing Macclesfield CC member, said: "We are delighted to again be chosen by the magazine as a Top 100 cricketing school. Generations of former cricketers remember their days playing King's cricket with great affection and we want to maintain that long tradition." Simon Hughes, Editor of *The Cricketer*, said: "I heartily commend the commitment that the school dedicates to coaching pupils in our wonderful sport and hope it continues long into the future."

The school was established in 1502 and cricket dates back to at least 1865. A photograph of that particular year's team is displayed inside the pavilion, along with other team photos from the last 50 years.

In any one season the first team will play around 22 fixtures, with teams coming from as far away as Edinburgh, but the annual 'local' matches against sides like Manchester Grammar School, Sedbergh and RGS Lancaster are always eagerly anticipated. The school has a main pitch on Cumberland Street, which is a prominent feature in the town centre, an all-weather pitch and nets on the Westminster Road site, three more grass squares at the Derby Fields, pitches for junior and girls' cricket at Fence

The King's School, Macclesfield from the air

Avenue and use of the Leisure Centre for winter indoor training.

The school has produced a handful of first class cricketers, most notably Steve's brother Peter, who is the former England coach and as a player was a stalwart of Sussex. The school also has a good record of producing Minor Counties cricketers and supplying plenty of players into the local leagues. Freddie Millett (see Macclesfield entry) was an early example, but more recently former King's captains James Lomas, Tom Foreman and Alan Day have all made their debuts for Cheshire. James Duffy and Khalid Sawas are other well established Minor County players. In 2016 Jonny Marsden captained Oxford University to a unique treble in winning the varsity four-day game as well as the One Day and T20 matches.

> **Johnny Marsden has won four cricketing Blues at Oxford University, 2013-6. In the defeat of Cambridge University in 2016 he had bowling match bowling figures of 40.4-8-92-8. In all he has played seven first-class matches, taking 21 wickets and has recorded a best score of 27 not out.**

In addition to the top quality cricketing staff, the school uses skilled young Australian cricketers to help coach King's young talent, plus it also recruits specialist coaches such as former Lancashire opener Andy Kennedy as 1st XI batting coach as well as top local coaches.

In 2016 the school was visited by cricketing legend Sir Garfield Sobers, who met with players and staff and gave a talk about his time playing for the West Indies.

Steve Moores said: "Our advice to any father or mother wanting their son or daughter to play cricket is to get a bat and ball in their hands at an early age. Many local clubs run superb U7, U8 and U9 sides and we often see cricketers come to us already with high skill levels. Above all allow them to enjoy the game, enjoy the competition and don't over coach them. Some youngsters will come to us with a good shape at the crease and good technique but don't want to hit the ball; encourage your son or daughter to hit the ball hard."

The school has toured extensively with trips to Sri Lanka, Grenada and Barbados in recent years and there are more in the planning.

Kingsley

The Croft, Mill Lane, Kingsley WA6 8HH

THE CLUB has made great strides since the ignominy of a first match defeat against a bunch of 'mixed village no-hopers'! The detail of this friendly match played in 1971 has (conveniently?) been lost but the founding seed was sown. Within a couple of years things were formalised under the chairmanship of Martin Mann and the captaincy of Nick Crosskell and the picturesque ground at the Crossley Hospital was adopted as home. By the early 1980s more players had been recruited and two sides were being fielded. Despite the attractive site, in the lee of the Victorian hospital building, the ground was too small and, no doubt a factor, the annual re-licensing arrangement was restrictive.

A new ground was required and where better than in the heart of the village. By June 1993 the new premises, temporary portakabin and all, was sufficiently ready to accommodate the cricketers. To the credit of the members all the work had been carried out by them and with little 'outside' funding. By 1994 the new pavilion was in place. At this point the club were members of the South Cheshire Alliance, having previously played in the Flintshire League, the Cheshire Conference and the Cheshire Association.

By 2007 a significantly extended pavilion was in place and the ribbon cut by local MP Mike Hall. It was a great day with lots of stalls, face-painting and a bouncy castle. There was some hilarity when a boot in the welly-throwing competition went considerably off course. Miraculously it missed the large crowd gathered in front of the pavilion before ending up on the roof. The culprit, a certain Roger Ollier, father of the cricketing trio, was quickly frog-marched back to the safety of the beer tent!

> In the early days fundingraising was high on the agenda and some very successful and remunerative discotheques had been arranged in Kingsley, but on one occasion the Frodsham Community Centre was chosen as the venue. In the event the staff closed the bar at 9.30pm and 175 angry attendees demanded their money back (which was not forthcoming!) The revellers laid siege to the building and windows were broken ...end of detail!

Why not visit this vibrant little club with an emerging junior set-up. If you can't make their next beer festival, how about a weekend fixture and a swift half at the club bar?

Current Kingsley chairman, Keiron Ollier pictured with Tessa Sanderson at a British Olympic 1988 Appeal event.

I'm indebted to Carol Rees for the following tale

My husband, Ceri joined the cricket club in 1974, soon after we moved to the village. He needed no persuading to play, and I found myself spending many a long Saturday afternoon up at Crossley Hospital.

I can remember the ground was on a slope and there was a small tree just inside the boundary.

The cricket teas were a haphazard affair. Occasionally one of the wives/mothers/girlfriends would turn up with a pre-prepared tea, but mostly the lads took turns buying a couple of loaves and a box of cakes from the village shop on their way to the ground which resulted in a 'make your own sandwich'. Goodness knows what the visiting teams thought! It was suggested that I might like to organise a tea rota amongst the ladies. Looking back, I think I must have had 'mug' written on my forehead.

Before doing the first rota, I felt duty bound to familiarise myself with the facilities available. I was hoping for some sort of kitchen, but the only building, jokingly called the pavilion, was little more than a shed. There was a central area between the changing rooms, mostly taken up with a huge rusty old roller which doubled up as the other leg of a trestle table for serving the teas. There was no water and no electricity. The only nod to modernity was a jumbo-size tea urn with no lid and so heavy it took two cricketers to lift it. What amazed me was that the lads saw nothing strange about this at all.

Undaunted, I did produce a rota. For health reasons the teas were exclusively prepared at home and we used paper cups and plates as there was nowhere to wash-up. Two cricketers had to fill the urn and they were obliged to remove their boots at the hospital entrance before going into the kitchen.

The tea rota worked quite well. One or two of the helpers harboured a degree of competition, resulting in some very fine home-baking. Margaret Oultram, who had two boys playing at that time, out-shone us all. She must have been baking for days. Rob Coward could be relied upon for some delicious pies and meats; Sue Coward was very glamorous and could distract the visiting team!

For some reason Tom Leather found it extraordinarily amusing to criticise the quality of the tea. He did it time and again, with no regard for the difficulty the tea ladies had with the basic facilities. One afternoon, unable to curb my irritation any longer, I had the temerity to interrupt play by insisting Tom tasted the tea on-field to assure himself it was in accordance with his apparent high standards. The tense intermission was broken when Tom professed himself to be well satisfied!

We managed this system of teas for a few years. Looking back, there was a fantastic 'village cricket' atmosphere up at Crossley. Set amongst woodland, surrounded by rhododendron and azalea, who could ask for a better setting for village cricket. They were good times. We were all young. Our children played while the match was on – even though one of them once locked his brother in the boot of their dad's car!!

Knutsford

Knutsford Sports Club, Mereheath Lane, Knutsford WA16 6SZ

THE CRICKET ground is within the parliamentary constituency of Tatton. Until his 2017 resignation the serving MP was George Osborne, who actively promoted the 'Northern Powerhouse' and that term could, perhaps, have applied to the Knutsford cricketers of the 1800s. *Cheshire Cricketers 1822-1996*, so painstakingly compiled by Tony Percival, reveals that more than twenty of them represented Cheshire before 1882. Like Osborne, one of that number was also a Member of Parliament for Knutsford; Alan de Tatton Egerton (b 1845, d 1920), who played one game for Cheshire in 1873. The match was against Incogniti and played at Chelford. He batted at number 11 and contributed 1 not out. He did not bowl. He was educated at Eton and eventually became the 3rd Baron Egerton. He died at Tatton Park. Also in that Cheshire team was a subsequent MP for West Cheshire and Eddisbury (1881-1906), Henry James Tollemache (b 1846, d 1939), who played for Nantwich and the Free Foresters. A wicketkeeper, he represented his county on 44 occasions during the period 1865-76. Educated at Eton and Oxford University, he was born at Dorfold Hall, Acton, Nantwich and died at the same place.

The club claims a foundation year of 1881, but it is very evident from the above, and other persuasive supporting documentation, that the date was as early as 1861. John Brandreth Long (b 1844, d 1866) was born in Knutsford and died in his home town aged only 22. He played for Knutsford and Cheshire (1861-66).

These days Knutsford CC is an integral part of the Knutsford Sports Club, which as a community club additionally offers facilities for tennis, squash and archery.

Given that Alan de Tatton Egerton played local cricket and lived at Tatton Park, a pre-match visit to the 1000 acre deer-park is a prerequisite. For nearly 400 years the estate was the property of the Egerton family until it was bequeathed to the National Trust in 1958.

Langley

Cockhall Lane, Langley, Macclesfield SK11 0DE

I MAKE NO apology for starting off with David Frame's statistical record. He joined the club straight from school, invited by one of his schoolteachers who was the 1st XI captain at the time. That was in 1984. By the end of the 2017 season he had played 983 matches, had 778 innings and scored 13042 runs for an average of 23.258 with a top score of 107 not out. In addition to three centuries he has contributed 42 fifties, hit 1211 ground boundaries and whacked 300 sixes. Oh yes, and 62 ducks. Howzat! A one-club man and he is rightly very proud of it. (He does play midweek for Macclesfield Over 40s along with some other Langley players).

The cricket club was established in 1864 and has a fascinating history. By 1918, the firm of William Whiston had become the largest silk printing, dyeing and finishing company in the country; screen-printing was used for the first time in Britain at his Langley Print Works. Whiston encouraged his workforce to play the summer game by providing facilities within the grounds of the factory. This situation prevailed for many decades, but eventually the factory was sold on and subsequently closed. In the event the cricketers became homeless in the 1960s, but they survived for a decade as a nomadic team. During this period local people interested in cricket and

The Langley Log

natural justice attempted to demonstrate that the factory ground had been set aside for cricket in perpetuity. A long innings was finally settled in the London law courts, and found in favour of the club, who subsequently were given the parcel of land that is now the present ground and a small cash settlement. They started playing at Cockhall Lane in 1973 when the players changed in a caravan and tea was taken at the St Dunstan Inn in the village.

> An article about the club in a 1980s edition of the *Cheshire Life* magazine refers to the one-time honorary captain, George Williamson, who at the age of 78 was said to be the oldest player to ever appear in the National Village Cup competition. A reference is also made to one of his notable bowling performances when he was in his 70s; Nine overs, five maidens, six wickets for seven runs.

I am very grateful to Dave Belfield, who once worked in the old silk factory, for this information. He's been playing here since he was 14, is still making the occasional appearance on the greensward, and is approaching 60 years of membership.

The Langley Flag

Langley is a pretty suburb of Macclesfield with several small reservoirs and woodland above the village to the east. There is a forest park in the woods above Langley and this is a good point from which to make an ascent of Shuttlingsloe - the 'Matterhorn' of Cheshire - and to access Tegg's Nose Country Park.

You'll find it difficult to resist a weekend visit here.

David Belfield

Lindow

Upcast Lane, Wilmslow SK9 6EH

WHEN 'LINDOW Man', as he came to be known, was unearthed in August 1984 at Lindow Moss, not far away from the cricket ground, it caused a media sensation. It was regarded as a most significant archaeological discovery and, maybe, the best-preserved bog body to be discovered in Britain. The body had been conserved in peat for nearly two thousand years. Disappointingly, when, in September 2015, Lindow CC were promoted to the top echelon of the Cheshire pyramid the press were less enthusiastic, even though their elevation represented the highest placing that the club had achieved in its one hundred and thirty seven year history.

Intriguingly, in 2016 they finished off the season with a rather unusual occurrence, one of those cricketing oddities we all enjoy discussing while supping the post-match jug. On the last day of the season at home to Stockport, Lindow set their opponents a target of 247. Stockport reached 244-9. Would the match have a dramatic conclusion? Well, yes, it did but not in the way you might have imagined. A delivery from the bowler evaded the wicket-keeper and struck the helmet which was lying on the ground some distance behind him. The five penalty runs provided Stockport with a one wicket victory! When was the last time your team, on the last day of the season, lost to a five run penalty?!

When I visited the Upcast Lane ground the club President, John Williams, proudly showed me round the splendid pavilion. He remembered his introduction to the club in 1971 when the original 1920s building was a 'rotting heap' and he had a strong recall of his wife being recruited to the tea rota and told to make sure she went to the loo before arriving at the club, such were the facilities!

Lindow are a club on the up and were shortlisted for the title of Cheshire East 'Club of the Year' in 2016. Lindow were the only cricket club to be listed and were up against four other clubs for the top honour – Macclesfield Harriers & Athletics Club, Satellites of Macclesfield Swimming Club, Egerton Youth Gymnastics Club and South Cheshire ABC Boxing Club from Crewe.

The judging panel recognised Lindow's all-round achievements over the 12-month period, including all three senior teams playing in the Cheshire County League for the first time, having a club record number of junior members, the introduction of girls-only sessions, the creation of the 'Lindow Cup' for local primary schools and the fundraising and investment of almost £90000 into new facilities. David Kendrick, Club Chairman, commented: "We're thrilled that our hard work as a club run by volunteers has been recognised by being shortlisted for this award. It's been another wonderful year for the club in so many ways."

The origins of the club date back to 1880 when a local resident decided to place the land in trust for the use of recreational sport. Of course, it is very, very different now. Why not take a look at the modern version of this lovely little ground located in this leafy corner of south Wilmslow, inspect the new nets which were officially opened by former England captain Michael Vaughan in May 2016, and then nip into the pavilion, funded by a Sport England grant in 2001, and try out their highly regarded teas while enjoying the late afternoon sunshine on the newly-added sun terrace?

Lymm Oughtrington Park

Oughtrington Lane, Lymm WA13 0RB

1884 IS REGARDED as the formation date and for the first thirty years of its existence the club was largely under the influence of the Dewhurst family. The Hall and surrounding estate was bought by George Dewhurst, a Manchester cotton merchant, in 1862, and on his instigation a separate parish of Oughtrington was formed in 1869.

The new parish needed a church and St Peter's was built. The recreational activities of the parish fell, in part, to the Reverend WG Knocker and club records suggest the first cricketers were his choir and parishioners. The club's centenary document suggests the very first name of the club was St Peter's Oughtrington (but the prefix was soon dropped). The clergyman was the first President, but from 1891 until the start of the Great War the post was held by a member of the Dewhurst family.

Country house cricket was becoming very fashionable and many large property owners were anxious to establish a ground within their estate. By 1889 things had advanced sufficiently well for a fixture card to be produced. By 1894 a 2nd XI was in place. Typically, the tea was prepared in the Hall and brought across to the ground in a large wicker basket which was full of buttered buns and slab cake and served on a trestle table in the open air.

1906 - A surviving scorebook revealed the opening match of the season was against Flixton and their opening batter was JT Tyldesley. The Lancashire and England cricketer, who had scored 3000 first-class runs in 1901 and made a century against Australia in 1905, was not quite so successful in this match. He was bowled for 11 by J Thomason, who modestly suggested Tyldesley had been deceived when the ball pitched on a daisy! Intriguingly, in the back of that scorebook was the sheet for a match played in 1935 against Whalley Range and it revealed Frank Hindley had played in both those matches more than 30 years apart.

1911 - The Dewhurst family sold up and although the Hall was lived in as a private residence the club was left much more to its own resources.

1914-19 - No cricket was played during WW1, but fortunately the ground was spared from agricultural ploughing, a fate suffered by Lymm CC which never resumed. (Lymm CC was on Rush Green Road).

1920 - An energetic committee got things underway quite quickly after the hostilities, but it became clear that to maintain the fixture list improvements would need to be made and permission was granted for the ground to be enclosed with a post and wire fence. A tea pavilion was added to the main one. A pony was hired from the local greengrocer to pull the mower, but within a decade a motor mower had been purchased. The £50 cost was covered by a garden party held at 'The Old Tannery', the home of the President, HM Johnson (1920-39). At that time a bat cost £1 10s and a ball 10s 6d.

1940 - By this time Oughtrington Hall and the estate was owned by Mrs S Frankenburg. She was the 1940 President and it was expected that she would then pass the lease of the ground to the cricket club when the estate came into the ownership of Cheshire County Council after the war. It seemed to be widely acknowledged that was the intention, but perhaps the legal costs of separation dictated otherwise? Eventually the Council intimated the lease renewal might be in question until a local campaign by members and friends eventually secured the freehold in 2000.

1950s - Other than in 1951 Paddy Saville captained the team throughout the 1950s. He was a popular and extremely talented all-rounder and good enough to play for Cheshire. He skippered a very strong team and for three consecutive years (1957-59), Pakistan Eaglets visited Oughtrington. The 1958 team was strengthened by the inclusion of Hanif Mohammad before a crowd of several hundred.

> Julian Knowles made a welcome return to the club where he had been a member of the 1st XI in the early 1960s. The fire of his earlier years had subsided, but replaced by control and movement and in 1976 he took 62 wickets at under 10. In 1978, now aged 44, he captured 91 wickets at 11. The records show he achieved 10 -24 v Prescot in 1989.

1960s - The club maintained a strong fixture list, but disaster struck in 1963. A pile of rubbish which had been set alight by the groundsman was safely smouldering when he left the ground, but it is thought that when a high wind sprang up, the fire spread and the pavilion was completely destroyed. Despite providing modern amenities the replacement contrasted sharply with the traditional appearance of the old one.

1970 - An application to join the Manchester Association was answered favourably. In the same year Mr Harry Holt stood down from the Presidency after 24 years of distinguished service. He was replaced by HB Whitelegg in recognition of his tremendous contribution to the club. Since joining in 1922 as a player he had been Secretary (1930-39) and was regarded as an unrivalled expert on the preparation of pitches, which he supervised for more than 20 years. When in his late seventies 'Bert retained the erect carriage of his earlier years, when the arc of his straight bat was reminiscent of the Corinthian Age'. At about this time a car park was put down behind the pavilion. Access was from Oughtrington Lane by means of a paved track and this entailed the sacrifice of a six foot strip along the length of the northern boundary.

1984 - The centenary year. The celebratory booklet concludes by hoping that the traditions of the club continue and that the members enjoy the best of games under summer skies in the presence of the 'soundless clapping host' of those who had gone before.

1987 - After several meetings and much emotional debate the club resolved that it should be called Lymm Oughtrington Park CC.

The old Hall is a listed building and is now part of Lymm High School's administration block.

The ground is unusual having a 100-year-old beech tree within the field of play. Local rules are that if the ball strikes the tree only a four is scored.

Macclesfield

Victoria Road, Macclesfield SK10 3JA

ALTHOUGH DETAILED documentation is not available, it seems entirely reasonable to accept 1847 as the founding date of Macclesfield Olympic CC. The justification is twofold. The existence of a club letterhead showing an 1853 date and, more particularly, the existence of a match played against Leek CC in 1848 for which the scores are recorded in the annals of the Staffordshire club. The clubs played each other twice in that year. In August Macclesfield travelled to Leek and scored 48 and 82. Leek replied with 31 and 44. In the return match a month later Macclesfield won again. Home matches were played at West Bank Field, Prestbury Road, a large ground on the site now occupied by West Bank Road and the cemetery. 'An attractive tree–lined ground'. In 1862 the club moved to Beech Lane, where they remained until the land in Victoria Road was acquired. The descriptor 'Olympic' was dropped after the 1874 season.

1854-1860 - During this period the All England team were entertained on three occasions. The All England side in 1854 included all the big names of the day – HH Stephenson, (captain of the first team to tour Australia), George Parr, Tom Box, William Clarke and the opposition was provided by '22 of Cheshire'. Every effort was made to make the match a memorable occasion with the attendance of the Macclesfield Brass band and refreshment tents provided by the Spread Eagle and the Angel. The morning trains brought large contingents of spectators from Leek, Stoke, Crewe and Sandbach.

> There is a 1831 reference to a cricket match played at Poynton, a half-way venue, between a Macclesfield team and one from Stockport. The Courier remarked there was no disgrace in 'losing the first match they ever attempted to such a well-disciplined team'. Later in that decade other matches were played in the grounds of the Ryle family residence. John Ryle was an important Macclesfield businessman with banking and textile interests. He became the MP for Macclesfield in 1832. His son JC Ryle, an Etonian, played cricket for Oxford University and was probably the instigator of these friendly matches. Intriguingly, JC Ryle not only played seven first-class matches for the University (1835-1838) but in 1880 he became the first Anglican Bishop of Liverpool. (Please don't assume David Sheppard was the first cricketing Bishop of Liverpool!) In 1839, 'in the presence of prominent ladies and gentlemen', Macclesfield met Knutsford at Ryle's Park and after the match both teams were entertained for dinner.

1879 - The arrival at the club of 'Blaster' Jimmy Bates. Born in the town in 1862 he became a popular sportsman in Macclesfield. Bates was a prolific batsman and the first town player to play for Cheshire. He was also a star footballer for the town football club.

WW1 - Mr Frost said at the 1915 AGM the club did not share the view that sport should stop. 'Sport is the national safety valve, and if it were true that Waterloo had been won on the playing fields of Eton, it was equally true that endurance, pluck and daring of our troops in France and Belgium were developed on our playing pitches of football and cricket'. Not everyone agreed and Hewetson, the Secretary, resigned in protest. Macclesfield CC mounted a full programme throughout the war and raised generous sums for war charities. By this time thirty-seven members were in khaki and by 1917 this number had grown to sixty-seven. There were 200 members in 1914. Mr Hope had been raising guest XIs made up of popular and famous sportsmen like Joe Makepeace and Jack Sharp, both double internationals, James Tyldesley from Old Trafford, Albert Lawton, the former Derbyshire captain, and David Denton and Schofield Haigh from Yorkshire.

1919 - Vernon Hope became skipper 23 years after he first appeared at Victoria Road. He was the Cheshire captain and his position might have influenced the allocation of a county match, against Northants, to the ground for the first time.

> Freddie Millett dominated Macclesfield cricket for many years. He was educated at King's and played for his home town from the late 1940s through until 1974. He regularly sat at the head of the batting list but in 1959, 1963, 1964 and 1971 he topped both the batting and bowling averages. He played for Cheshire between 1949 and 1973 and was captain between 1959 and 1973. He led Cheshire to their first Minor Counties championship title in 1967. He also played for the Minor Counties and was their captain between 1969 and 1973. He served on the MCC Executive and Cricket Committees, and represented the Minor Counties on the Test & County Cricket Board. He received an MBE for services to the game. When the Cheshire County League was founded in 1975 he was Chairman for the first four seasons and then became the Patron from 1979 until 1991(he died in office). Fittingly he died in the town of his nativity.

> The local newspaper of 25 May 1929 reported the official opening of the new pavilion and extensions. The ceremony was performed by Sir William Bromley-Davenport, KCB, CMG, CBE, DSO and Lord Lieutenant of the County. Sir William told his large audience he hoped his words would sink into their hearts and his hand into their pockets! It was a real happiness to do anything in his power to encourage manly and healthy sports and he thought cricket was the finest game in the world.

1921 - Macclesfield played in the Manchester Association from 1921 to 1933. Thirteen years of continuous success. During this period the ground was purchased (for £900 in 1926) and a new pavilion constructed (replacing the 1876 model). A tea pavilion was also built.

1923 - Cheshire played the West Indies in July. This was the most prestigious match ever played at Victoria Road. Learie Constantine was in the West Indian team. The visitors were provided with a motor cavalcade, cinema tickets and a six course banquet at the Town Hall. When Constantine played for Macclesfield in 1929, in a fundraising match against Derbyshire, he received only five balls but hit three sixes.

1926 - Vernon Hope retired. Now in his late 40s it seemed like a fitting time to stop playing as he had been named the new Mayor of the town. He had captained both his club and county with distinction. Undoubtedly one of Macclesfield's greatest cricketers, he had made his debut in 1896.

1931 - To accommodate the widening of the ground and to build a boundary wall it was deemed necessary to remove a number of trees. Suffice to say this led to protracted debate, significant acrimony and unwanted publicity in the local newspaper.

1934 - The club joined the Lancashire & Cheshire League (members until 1958). They looked forward to the new challenge of competitive league cricket (Champions in 1937, 38, 49, 52, 54 & 57). Despite the undoubted impression of affluence - the ground had been purchased and improved, the arrival of bowls, the consistent success of the teams (photographed in their smart blue and white blazers) - the administrators were struggling to make ends meet.

1949 - No sooner had the season finished, the contractors moved in to begin levelling work and developing the embankments on the town corner of the ground.

1959-74 - Member of the Manchester Association.

1980 to date - The 1980s saw the introduction of overseas players into the Cheshire County League and Macclesfield have had a number of outstanding Australians playing for them. Amongst these were Phil Emery, Darren Berry, Ian Wrigglesworth and Evan Gulbis, all of whom later played at State or international level. Founder members of the Cheshire County League and 1st XI league winners in 1992, 1993 and 1999. In 1992 they secured the 1st XI Cup. Darren Berry scored over 1000 runs in both 1992 and 1993 and set a league record for the highest average at 78.6 and the highest individual score of 196 not out.

1983 - Macclesfield staged the first Minor Counties KO final. Cheshire convincingly defeated Bedfordshire.

The club celebrated its 150th anniversary in 1997 with a programme of events including the annual cup match against the Mayor of Macclesfield's XI and matches against a touring team from Hambledon and an Australian XI. In the early 2000s the club changed its legal status to become a Company Limited by Guarantee and was an early mover to Community Amateur Sports Club status.

Macclesfield CC 2014 in front of the new changing rooms

The club has been very successful in developing and supporting activities for junior cricketers with the formation of the Macclesfield Academy in conjunction, initially, with neighbouring Parkside CC.

Post millennium the two clubs came even closer and now play exclusively under the banner of Macclesfield Cricket Club. The Academy has had up to 140 junior members in age groups from 7 to 18 and has been fortunate to have retained the services of a number of retired senior players as coaches.

In 2014 the new changing facilities were opened with the most well-known of the Moores' clan, Peter (in the England hot seat at the time), in attendance.

Three Cestrians opening up for England

When England played the West Indies at the Oval in August 1984 the first three England bowlers in their opponents first innings were all Cheshire born. Jonathan Agnew, born in Macclesfield, opened up (12-3-46-0) and shared the new ball with Paul Allott, born in Warrington (17-7-25-3). First change was Ian Botham, born in Heswall (23-8-72-5).

The match was won by the West Indies by 172 runs. In their respective innings Agnew scored 16 and 4, Allott 5 and 2 not out and Botham 14 and 54.

Malpas

Wrexham Road, Malpas, Cheshire SY14 7EJ

THE NEIGHBOURING parish church of St Oswald's is a fine 14th century construction with a superb bossed ceiling, Flemish window panels, and a magnificent 13th century oak chest. The church also contains a 15th century octagonal stone font and choir stalls with carved misericords. The cricket pavilion is rather less ornate but has its own charm, sitting on a slightly raised platform and affording a good view of the cricket. The ground is surrounded on three sides by open fields. It's a pleasant scene in a picturesque village adjacent to the Shropshire and Welsh borders.

1868 - Malpas Cricket Club was originally founded and it remained the sole sport to be played on the Wrexham Road ground for the next 90 years.

1958 - A radical change took place when football and tennis facilities were introduced to the site. This was made possible by gaining a lease for an additional seven acres of adjacent land. A key intention was to ensure the survival of each section by laying down a permanent residence with funding being achieved through one central club, with one large membership, rather than three small clubs all fighting for their existence. It was re-named the Malpas and District Sports Club Ltd.

1964 - The cricket playing area was re-developed and increased to its present size. This involved removing tons of earth which now lies alongside the bowling green and the hard-surface training area.

1968 - Malpas CC celebrated their Centenary year with a match against the Cheshire Gentlemen.

1975 - The club's first venture into league cricket was in the Cheshire Conference. Prior to this time Malpas CC had forged a reputation as a formidable mid-week knock-out side, but weekend cricket had been restricted to playing friendly matches.

1976 - The aforementioned seven acres of leased land was eventually purchased from the local Church Diocese.

1977-1997 - From within the Cheshire Conference a new league was formed. The South Cheshire Alliance emerged, predominantly made-up of South Cheshire clubs, plus a small number of bordering Staffordshire sides. Malpas were one of the founder members. The South Cheshire Alliance continued up until 1997, at which time the nucleus of the Cheshire clubs joined the Cheshire pyramid.

1981 - Further adjoining land was purchased to accommodate the increase in parking requirements.

1997-2015 - The Cheshire Cricket League, which Malpas had joined in 1997, provided an exciting rollercoaster ride. The pinnacle was two promotions to the County League in 2006 and 2011.

2000 - A junior section was formed. Membership has increased year-on-year and they now compete at various age-group levels in the North-East Wales Junior Cricket League. In 2016 the number of children registered was approaching one hundred.

> Tony Percival's compilation of *Cheshire Cricketers 1822-1996* discloses that Charles George Cholmondeley (b 1829, d 1869) was educated at Cambridge University and played one match for Cheshire in 1865. His club side is shown as Malpas but also records he played for Devon and Hampshire Gentlemen. Clearly loyal to his home area, his place of death is shown as Malpas Lodge, albeit in Torquay, Devon. His single match for Cheshire was against Bullingdon, Oxford. He opened the batting in both innings and recorded a pair. He was a regular MCC player and played a good number of matches at Lord's.

2016 - Due to a series of difficulties and setbacks, Malpas resigned from the Cheshire Cricket League, being unable to sustain both a 1st and 2nd XI team, but they successfully re-joined for the 2017 season at a lower level and fielding just one team.

The view from the pavilion

David Bailey, Cheshire CCC - Chairman (from 2013 and continuing)

When 'Bails' captained Minor Counties North against Middlesex in the Benson & Hedges Cup at Lord's in May 1979, he scored 52 and captured three wickets (11-4-31-3). His victims were Mike Brearley, Graham Barlow and Mike Gatting. This performance won him the Man of the Match award. Four years later he won another one, again in the Benson & Hedges Cup, when he scored 51 not out for Minor Counties against Sussex at Hove. In 32 first-class appearances, primarily for Lancashire, his highest score was 136 and his best bowling figures 3-67.

Maritime

The Green, York Street, Bromborough CH62 4TY

HERE IS A club with a real difference. It's modern, multi-cultural and had the most unusual of beginnings. The journey originated in 2002 on the shoreline at New Brighton when a group of Sri Lankans living on Merseyside played social cricket together on the beach. From these very humble beginnings they progressed to playing in nearby Central Park, Liscard and subsequently to their current home at historic Bromborough Pool in 2005. Before competing in the Cheshire pyramid they played in the old Merseyside Competition. The club name emerged, quite simply, from Merseyside's long-established sea-faring links.

In conjunction with their landlord, Riverside Housing, they have recently refurbished the old pavilion, which had started to show signs of structural decay. The Housing Association was persuaded to work in partnership with the club given the time and effort the membership had dedicated to the maintenance of the ground and the pavilion. In doing so it has re-established the rich heritage of cricket within the environs of the village.

Bromborough Pool is located on the eastern side of Wirral and stands in history as one of the splendid villages constructed by wealthy industrialists who revolutionised the working and living standards of their workers. It was developed in 1854 to provide homes for workers in the nearby Price's Candle Factory. The development of the village continued throughout the rest of the century to incorporate a school, hospital, village hall and church - all of which remained in the ownership of the factory. Although now much changed, it can still be regarded as a fine and early example of English private company philanthropy.

A pictorial information board on the edge of the green informs that the ground was first used by Bromborough Pool CC in 1856. Even from that early date a brick built pavilion was in place, although it was subsequently demolished and replaced by another in 1884. The board goes on to say 'the very games added to the skill and manual dexterity of the people; cricket exercised its influence on candles; the good cricketers acquired a fineness of hand which gave them increased facility in their work …the sympathy and confidence bestowed upon them inspired many a heart with an interest in the factory distinct and above what mere wages can create'.

Watch some cricket, browse the pictorial information boards and take tea in the attractive café attached to the garden centre run by the Wirral Autistic Society.

Marple

Bowden Lane, Marple, SK6 6ND

THE DETAIL is hazy but it appears that the club originally came into existence in 1864. The first reported match was against fourteen players from the Marple Academy, who were made up of two masters, three old pupils and nine students. The match was played at a site below the Railway Hotel on Stockport Road (now occupied by Oak Drive, Kayswood Road, Beech Avenue and Hawthorne Avenue).

1874 - Marple staged a match against Brabyns Hall before a large crowd. Marple 80, Brabyns Hall 49. The latter was an old estate home subsequently used as a Military Hospital during WW1 and demolished in 1952.

1879 - The *Stockport Advertiser* carried the scores of a match against Poynton, who made 108. Marple replied with 57. Three years later the clubs are referred to as Rose Hill, Marple and Poynton Vernon.

1904+ - An old scrapbook shows a photograph of the Marple team tagged as League Champions in 1904. There is also a menu card of a dinner held in the Jolly Sailor pub in 1908 to celebrate another League Championship. At the onset of WW1 eight players enlisted. The ground was eventually ploughed by the tenant farmer and all the equipment was sold. A heavy roller was leased to Strines CC and subsequently to Buxworth, but it eventually found its way back to Marple in 1951!

1950 - Although Marple CC existed in name there appears to have been no cricketing activity between the wars despite the efforts of Fred Hoole and his old committee. Some new ground options were explored, but cost and unsuitability of the sites were regular factors. An application to play in the Memorial Park or the Recreation Ground were rejected by Marple Urban District Council and even a proposal to merge with Hawk Green CC was rejected by members of that club! However, in 1950, Mr Newton, the Manager of the local branch of the District Bank, and Mr Roberts, an Estate Agent, probably through professional opportunity, were in a position to explore an option to acquire land in Bowden Lane. On 18 July 1950 'a spontaneous meeting without notice' of twenty-two like-minded people, including some from the old club, met in the Jolly Sailor. The group resolved to take the initiative forward under the chairmanship of Mr Newton with Mr Roberts providing the secretariat. They soon formalised arrangements with members of the old club, who for thirty six years had closely guarded the assets. Hereon things moved apace and a public meeting attended by 200 people at the Willows School (now Marple Sixth Form College) elected a Committee of twenty-four made up of movers, the old committee, other worthies and four local councillors.

1951 - The astonishing energy created by these events resulted in the resumption of High Peak League second division cricket. Two hospital chalets from the local Nab Top Sanatorium were donated to create the first pavilion in the Seven Stiles/Bowden Lane corner of the ground and the cricket square was created by progressive re-turfing. Largely this was achieved by voluntary labour, spurred on by the ambition to 'put Marple on the cricketing map'. An amateur cine-film, later transferred onto videotape, recorded scenes on the opening day of the 1951 season, together with other clips from Marple life at the time. At the end of the first season the adult membership was 324, and there were a further 93 junior members.

1955 - The ground was levelled and a new square was laid, more central to the ground. In 1956 a long wooden hut, which had previously been a works canteen, was erected on the site of the present brick building. Working parties were regularly arranged and the former captain and chairman of the ground committee, Harry Smith, was always in the thick of it. He subsequently became groundsman, a position he held until his death in the late 1980s.

1957 - The club was accepted by the Lancashire and Cheshire League. An early disaster occurred when the first team was bowled out for 13 by Glossop, and at the end of the season the wooden spoon was acquired. However, under the hardworking captaincy of George Booth (captain 1954-1961), the club became runners-up in the competition in 1959. Junior members began to infiltrate the teams. A strong club was emerging.

1963 - Under the influential captaincy of Jack Tighe the club became a real force, winning the League championship in 1963, runners-up 1964, and champions again in 1965. His winning habit was passed onto a succession of captains and lasted until 1971. Eight championships were secured in that nine year period. More to the point the team was based on Marple juniors and the foremost was Frank Hayes, the eldest of four sporting brothers, whose talent took him to Lancashire, where he made his first-class debut in 1970. He scored a century in his first Test against the West Indies at the Oval in 1973. From 1962 the club fielded a third team in the Glossop & District League and in 1963 secured a ground at Pikes Lane in Glossop for the purpose.

> In 1977 in a County Championship match at the St Helen's ground, Swansea, Frank Hayes hit the luckless Malcolm Nash for 646666 in a single over. This was nine years after Nash conceded six 6s in an over to Garry Sobers at the same ground.

> Garry Cash has notched up an incredible 17952 1st XI runs over 36 seasons (19 for Cheadle and 17 for Marple) in the Cheshire County League. Since 2013 he has scored an additional 1776 runs in 2nd XI cricket. Some record! [The totals exclude four seasons that he played in the Cheshire Cricket League].

1970s - At one time lacrosse had been played on the outfield but that fell by the wayside, unlike the rapidly expanding hockey section which now demanded more pitches and the encroachment onto both sides of the square. The resulting acrimonious relations between the sections led to the mass resignation of the men's hockey members, who found a site in Disley and formed the now thriving Disley Sports club (including cricket!). Ladies hockey soldiered on at Bowden Lane until the end of the second millennium.

1972 - The domination of the Lancashire and Cheshire Cricket League came to an end following the loss of key players and the club was relegated to the second division. The third team was allowed to lapse. Off the field, financial pressures led to the sale of the Glossop ground to help to pay for the building of three squash courts as a commercial venture. These opened in 1975 and blossomed into a thriving squash section with a keen social membership.

1975 - The cricket section became founder members of the Cheshire County League in 1975. Mike Hibbert was the captain in that inaugural year. Forty-one years later he is still loyally serving the club but is now running down the pitch with a mower rather than a bat! Against the odds, the first team were runners-up in 1976, but had to wait until 1987, under the captaincy of Chris Lees (captain 1984-1991), before winning the coveted 1st XI championship pennant.

Thereafter fortunes ebbed and flowed for a good period of time, but under the leadership of Matthew Shelton the club returned to the Premier Division in 2012. During his tenure he was most ably assisted by the former Cheshire captain, Andrew Hall, James Ormond, the former Leicestershire, Surrey and England paceman, and the evergreen, wily old bowler, Andy Greasley. They suffered an unexpected relegation at the end of 2015 but they have now regained their premier status for 2018 when they will be delighted to be back amongst the big boys and to show off their splendid pavilion refurbishment and costly ground improvements.

Mellor

215-217 Longhurst Lane, Mellor SK6 5PN

THE MELLOR Sports Club consists of four distinct sections. In addition to the cricket, they provide facilities for tennis, badminton and lacrosse. In fact, Mellor can claim to be a lacrosse hotbed and has enjoyed much success over its long history. The men's North of England championship was won six times on the trot in the 1960s and over the years a good number of members have played at international level. The tennis club will point out that Angela Buxton, who won the women's doubles title with Althea Gibson at both the French championships and Wimbledon in 1956, opened their upgraded courts in 1959, so it is probably fair to say the cricketers have operated from a more modest base. Cricket started at the present site in 1951 when a group of enthusiasts met in the Devonshire Arms. Following that meeting a local cricketing eccentric named Warwick Frost mortgaged his house on the corner of Longhurst Lane and Knowle Road for £2000 and bought the field at the rear of his property. A drill hall was bought for £80 and the grand opening of the clubhouse took place on February 25, 1953. Friendly matches were played for the first few years until the club was elected to the High Peak Cricket League. Steady progress was made until the team won the League title in 1961.

Although spirits remained high, the ground suffered from poor drainage, worms and rabbits. The changing rooms consisted of just two former railway fruit wagons and, in an episode that was later to be repeated by the Derbyshire and Cheshire League, the club was expelled from the High Peak League. Common sense prevailed and the club gained entry to the Glossop and District League, winning the second division titles in 1968 and 1979. The club's resurrection was subsequently helped by the erection of a second-hand prefabricated laboratory building bought from ICI in the early 80s.

Over the years there has been a healthy exchange between the sporting sections and this is nicely demonstrated by current cricketer, Ben McAllister, a lacrosse goalkeeper, who is one of a select group to have represented his country in four World Championships.

The late Laurie Marsland is the father of current captain Nick. Laurie played his best cricket at Marple and Stockport but then dedicated his time to coaching the Mellor youngsters and umpiring. A memorial plaque on a pitch-side bench is a fitting tribute to one who contributed much to the game.

Mellor now play in the Cheshire Cricket League.

Merseyside Sports & Cultural

The Oval Leisure Centre, Old Chester Road, Bebington CH63 7LF

WHAT LINKS Merseyside Sports & Cultural CC with 'Chariots of Fire' (Warner Bros, 1981)? Easy, they both have Bebington Oval connections! The cricketers, largely Indian migrant workers, started to play together just about a decade ago. Initially they played in Mersey Park and also on that delightful green at Thornton Hough, but when they were properly constituted in 2012 they joined the famous old Liverpool Competition (which has its origins date-stamped as 1892) and acquired access to the cricketing facilities at the Bebington Oval.

> Barry Dudleston, who had a successful first-class career with Leicestershire and Gloucestershire, was born in Bebington in 1945. In addition to playing 295 first-class matches (1966-1983), he also umpired 426 first-class matches (1983-2010), including two Tests.

They started playing in the Liverpool Competition, Saturday 3rd XI Division 1 from 2013. At the first time of asking they won their division and were subsequently promoted to the Premier Division. Undaunted they won that top division in 2014 and finished as runners-up in 2015. In 2016 they were fourth. A very new club but clearly heading in the right direction, MS&C CC are keen on developing their own young cricketers and have now set up a junior section.

And now to the other part of the equation. In 1980, during the making of the highly-acclaimed film, the cinder running track and the stadium structure itself were deemed to be very suitable for the filming of the 1924 Paris Stade Colombes Olympic scenes in which Harold Abrahams (Ben Cross) and Eric Liddell (Ian Charleson) so famously competed. The Oval was originally provided for the workers of Lever Brothers, Port Sunlight in the 1920s but was acquired by Wirral Borough Council in 1973. Other Cheshire cinematic 'stand-in' sites used in the film were the Woodside ferry terminal, where its landing stage doubled as Dover for the departure of Britain's Olympic hopefuls, while the film crew also took over the 1920s-style facilities at Cowley Grammar School in St Helens – the changing rooms at the boys' school and the gym at the girls'.

The pavilion in 1924

Middlewich

Haddon Field, Croxton Lane, Middlewich CW10 9EY

THE STORY goes that in the 1950s when a dedicated member of the club died, his wife, resenting the amount of time he had spent at the ground, gleefully burnt all his cricketing papers, which included the history of the club. This spiteful act meant that the documentation which was presumed to have disclosed the founding date, thought to be in the 1870s, went up in smoke. In 1982 the members, recognising the club must be at least a hundred years old, decided to commemorate it in that year. In 2010 another centenary was celebrated, which coincided with the move to Haddon Field.

1870-1910 - The original ground was close by on Finney's Lane on the site of the present cemetery extension.

1910 - The first game played at Haddon Field was on 10 August and was officially opened by Captain FC France-Hayward. Sandbach were the first visitors and spoiled the occasion by defeating the home team by one run. The field was leased from Mrs Haddon, who lived in a house where the three bungalows opposite the pavilion now stand.

WW2/1950s - During WW2 some friendly games were played against servicemen from Byley Airfield, (RAF Cranage). At the end of the conflict a large open-air thanksgiving service was organised on the cricket ground attended by hundreds of people. After the hostilities a good number of top cricketers played on the ground while they were still attached to the Western Command based in Chester. Midweek evening cricket was very popular during this period and teams from the town and nearby localities competed for a handsome trophy. Each team had to contain a certain number of players who did not play regular cricket.

1946-57 - Seven Minor County fixtures were staged at Haddon Field during this period. The

Malcolm Hilton played four matches for England. By the time he retired in 1961 he had taken 1006 first-class wickets and scored 3416 runs, including one century. He was a Wisden Cricketer of the Year in 1957.

Golden Lion in the town played host to some of the players. Malcolm Hilton played here for Lancashire II against Cheshire in a two-day match on 30 June and 1 July 1948. He had match figures of 6 for 50. His appearance on the ground might have been a surprise to the spectators as only a month before he had claimed Don Bradman's wicket twice during the touring Australians match at Old Trafford. He bowled 'The Don' for 11 in the first innings and had him stumped for 43 in the second. Hilton was only 19 at the time and the match against 'the Invincibles' was only his third first-class appearance. Players took their tea in a marquee situated near the main entrance on these big occasions. Temporary seating was erected to supplement the existing facilities and extra work was carried out courtesy of Reg Seddon, who provided people from his salt company to work on the ground for a number of days.

Two Middlewich cricketers represented Cheshire in the early 1950s. John Richard Robinson (b 1924, d 1987) played two matches in 1950 and 1951 and James Allen Hall (b 1932) turned out on nine occasions in 1951 and 1952. He scored 65 runs, took 21 wickets (best 4-67) and held six catches.

A large depression in the outfield was filled in with residue from the salt works pan fires and subsequently grassed over. This area was immediately in front of the main entrance and an integral part of the outfield. The present pavilion was erected in the 1950s to replace the wooden one which was taken down and sold to Crewe Vagrants CC.

Late 1960s - Middlewich played for a year at the Hayes Chemical Works while the ground was levelled. The work was paid for by the Brine Compensation Board. Evidence of the original ground height can be seen in the slope between the backs of the houses on Chester Road and the present pitch level.

1970s - Middlewich Young Farmers played hockey on the ground and before that Dane Rugby Union Football Club, who played nearby, used the ground for changing and socialising.

1978 - Middlewich left the Manchester Association to join the Cheshire set.

2013-14-15 - The club hosted Lancashire in Second XI trophy matches against Worcestershire, Leicestershire and Durham. In the last of those three matches future England starlets Haseeb Hameed and Keaton Jennings managed to score a total 11 runs between them as Durham won convincingly.

On his way to becoming an International cricketer, Joe Root played one match at Haddon Field. In an interrupted two-day match in June 2008 he opening the batting for the Yorkshire Academy against Cheshire A. He was run out for 46 as the visitors made 222 all out. Cheshire A replied with 399-6 off 70 overs with Grappenhall's James McCoy impressively thrashing his way to 187.

Richard Goulding, who prepared a really informative little history sheet in 2010, speculated what Middlewich CC might look like in 2110 and also reflected on the last century: "In the last 100 years cricket has changed dramatically in a superficial sense yet remains fundamentally the same. It is more than a game reflecting as it does the changes in English society. However, what is certain is that if players from 1910 strolled on the ground now to watch a match they would instantly recognise the scene."

Mobberley

Church Lane, Mobberley WA16 7RD

PETER CHAPMAN was Mobberley-born in 1935. He has never moved away. The cricket club has been a big part of his life and in 2008 he published *131 Not Out - A history of Mobberley Cricket Club 1876-2007*. I have taken the liberty of lifting much of the following from it.

The origins of the club date back to 1876 and we learn that the first president and captain was the Reverend George Leigh Mallory. His grandson of the same name died on his third expedition to the world's highest mountain in 1924: '...at last in the flower of his perfect manhood he was lost to human sight between earth and heaven on the top-most peak of Mount Everest'. It does not appear that the explorer ever played for Mobberley, but his sister was married to HM Longridge, the club president between 1942 and 1951, which neatly continued the club/family link.

During Longridge's presidency the Reverend Howard Randle joined the club having been given the 'living' of St Wilfrid's, the parish church which sits close to the boundary edge. Unusually for a clergyman he was a fast bowler and at one time had played a number of matches for Nottinghamshire 2nd XI. His apparent desire to play for his adopted village occasionally caused him some pastoral embarrassment. Peter Chapman related a couple of stories (against his father-in-law); he recalls when a match at Hale Barns was scheduled to start there was no sign of the car-driving clergyman and his two passengers. It transpired that on passing his church he noticed a good number of cars parked outside and stopped to discover he was due to officiate at a wedding! So with his 'whites' under his cassock he took the service before dashing off to the match. On another occasion he was watching Cheshire play when the local Mothers' Union were expecting to be addressed. He was renowned for his wit and good humour and was in much demand as an after-dinner speaker. He died in 2002.

The first surviving minutes of the club date back to 1898 and they report that members 'will be expected to play in whites' and that 'swearing or smoking in a match will be liable to a fine'. By 1900 the club had moved to its existing ground, but the pavilion was nothing more than a sixteen foot long hut with a small verandah. By 1914 a somewhat larger structure had emerged, made of wood, painted white and with a pitched corrugated roof. It was demolished in 1950 and a new one built. Since then plenty of improvements have followed to both the pavilion and beyond. The book describes how in 1995 they benefitted from a National Lottery grant - the very first one ever made to a cricket club - towards the cost of new net facilities. The Prime Minister, John Major, presented a publicity cheque to Peter Chapman at Lord's and all was recorded on national TV.

If you are interested in the full history of the club, Peter's book is a thoroughly recommended read. There are two interesting chapters about exotic overseas tours and so much more. One notable paragraph refers to the payment of players which, perhaps, demonstrates it is not just a modern day fad. The 1893 balance sheet shows a payment of £3 12s to cover two men's wages playing in eight games – 4s 6d each per game. This is the current-day equivalent of a three figure sum.

Mossley

Moss Road, Congleton CW12 3BN

A LETTER FROM the club secretary, dated October 1965, is displayed on the wall in the Mossley pavilion. It informs Mr Yates of Leek Road that the club has been revived and invites him to become the club auditor. Its previous incarnation goes way back to the early 1900s when home matches were played at Henshall Hall. From sometime in the early 1960s, home games were played at Murgatroyds, the old British Salt ground between Sandbach and Middlewich.

Local architect Gordon Ball was Chairman and instrumental in setting up the 'new' club. By 1967 the club had moved to its present picturesque home in Moss Road. At the time of its acquisition it was a farmer's field, but gradually it was transformed into a cricket ground with stalwart Frank Speak acting as Mr 'Get it done'.

They joined the Cheshire Conference League in 1973 fielding two teams. The present club president, John Beardmore, was the 1st XI team captain at the time. By 1977 both teams were well established and around this time there was something of a coup for the club when they persuaded the enigmatic Dave Miller from Macclesfield to join up. He was capable of bowling long spells and regularly contributed wickets, as well as being a prolific and flamboyant middle order batter and an excellent fielder.

Hereabouts a pavilion was acquired from Congleton Golf Club. It arrived on the back of a trailer and its transportation caused some local traffic havoc and a number of trees and lamp-posts were threatened!

New faces were beginning to appear on the team sheet: new captain Howard Cartlidge, best remembered for having some teeth knocked out at Wilmslow (no helmets in those days!), present treasurer John Davies, Dave Moss, Steve Povey, Jack Corrie, Pete Howell and present Chairman Steve Austin.

The former golf club building was destroyed by fire in 1994. The club was practically on its knees when player and local businessman Stuart Seddon came to the rescue with the loan of three container cabins which were used as changing rooms; some opposing teams were not impressed! However, by 1997, mainly down to the fundraising efforts of the treasurer John Davies, the club were able to celebrate the opening of a new pavilion with a 'Past & Present' fixture.

A significant initiative in 2006, led by Adrian Austin, was the formation of a junior section. What began as one team soon blossomed into a thriving section. Adrian, with his infectious enthusiasm, was able to enlist the help of like-minded people who acted as a pool of junior coaches. Such was the progress that coach Phil Stirk even took the U15s to Sedbergh School for a cricket festival. A decade on, some of these young players are still with the club. Gareth Cresswell (present 1st team captain), Charles Wright, Callum Mckinlay, Tom Trevers, and Peter and Nathan Stirk. The 2006 captain was Andy Sadler. Unknown to anyone, he arrived at the club one dreary morning and before long was overseeing a successful team, improving the pavilion and organising training. Suddenly the cricket became rather more serious! In 2008 Mossley won the CCA Division 3. An all-weather surface was installed in the same year. At this time England Deaf cricketer Chris Harrison represented the club with his friend Dave Gregson.

'Golden oldie' Steve Austin is at the helm these days, supported by a committed group of workers. Among that number is groundsman Tony Brown, a past captain and who for many years has looked after the green acres. 2017 is their fiftieth anniversary at this lovely rustic little ground. Do pay them a visit, you won't be disappointed. It's a rural delight.

Mottram

Broadbottom Road, Mottram in Longdendale SK14 6JA

MOTTRAM CRICKET Club was formed in 1878* and apart from St Michael's Church is the oldest institution in the village. A committee, chaired by Joshua A. Hirst, assembled in the old village court room on Market Street and mulled over the various ways of spending some generous donations. The sum of £19 was more than enough to purchase all the necessary playing equipment and there was sufficient funding remaining to secure the services of a professional.

The ground at Broadbottom Road only hosted friendly matches in those early days, although by all accounts they were anything but friendly!

*Records found in the Archives at Ashton and Glossop Libraries clearly show that a Mottram club was actually formed in 1860. Match reports, scorecards and articles appear regularly in both the *Glossop Chronicle* and *North Cheshire Herald* from 1861 onwards. For example, on 7 September Hollingworth provided the opposition and scored 36. Mottram replied with 38 for 4.

1894 - Mottram become founder members of the Glossop & District League.

1900 - The club moved to a new ground just off Hyde Road. The members were obviously not entirely comfortable with these new surroundings as fifteen years later they returned to Broadbottom Road where they have been resident ever since.

1910-16 - The league championship was won on four occasions as the legendary Arthur Marsland wove his magic with the ball. Also playing around this period was John Chapman of Derbyshire. His family enjoyed a long association with the club.

139

> John Chapman b 1877, d 1956 played for Derbyshire between 1909 and 1920 and was county captain for three seasons from 1910 to 1912. An attractive batsman and excellent cover-point, Chapman (165) shared with Arnold Warren (123) in a ninth-wicket partnership of 283 - a world record which still stands - against Warwickshire at Blackwell in 1910.

Only a Rhodes Bowl in 1928 and a league championship in 1936 were captured during the next three decades before the advent of a golden era which began just after the Second World War. Between 1946 and 1967 Mottram were a dominant force at all levels, winning 23 cups in that 21-year period.

After all this success it was very much a case of 'after the Lord Mayor's show' and a bleak period followed both on and off the field. The break-up of the successful sides of the 1960s left the playing resources depleted and the club was also blighted by a spate of vandalism. The tea hut and sightscreens were repeatedly damaged, and in October 1970 the pavilion was burnt to the ground.

A beleaguered general committee set about what seemed the hopeless task of rebuilding the club and what you see today is a testimony to the dedication and sheer determination of those members who put the club back on track. In spite of this adversity the junior side won their league in 1971 and 1972 and a number of these players were in the under 21 team which won the HS Brown Cheshire Colts Cup at Alderley Edge in 1978, appropriately the centenary year of the club.

The finances raised by the many commemorative events held in the centenary year enabled the club to refurbish the new pavilion, which had been erected in 1973. In 1985 the ground was levelled. More trophies followed. During the period 1981-99 another 20 trophies were secured at 1st/2nd/junior levels.

Following the demise of the Glossop & District League at the end of the 1999 season, they joined the Derbyshire & Cheshire League. Currently they run a total of four junior teams at under 11, 13, 15 and 17 levels along with two senior teams and an Over 40s XI.

It's a lovely ground with stunning views. Why not pay them a visit. Spot the weather-vane atop the scorebox.

Nantwich

Whitehouse Lane, Nantwich CW5 6HH

EARLY REFERENCES suggest the club might initially have been known as Nantwich Albion. In the 1840s matches were played on Kingsley Fields. Saturday was a busy day in the Town's shoe and clothing factories and Monday was recognised as a rest day and that was the time those early sporting heroes came out to play. Given the preference for Monday play, a full fixture list was an issue.

By 1890 Nantwich were ready for league cricket and the club's long association with North Staffordshire cricket began.

1927-33 - A hat-trick of Senior 'A' section championships was secured in 1927/28/29. Sensationally, the services of Dick Tyldesley, no doubt looking to top up his splendid 1930 Lancashire benefit of £2027, signed up in 1932 and helped the club to win two more titles. He took over a hundred wickets in each season.

1934 - Tyldesley went off to play at Accrington and was replaced by Vic Fox. An experienced County batsman, he stayed for five seasons and helped Nantwich notch up another championship in 1937.

The 1930s were halcyon days, but it was not only the team that was on fire. In 1935 the pavilion and a considerable amount of equipment went up in smoke, but such was the spirit which abounded at the time that a new pavilion was ready for the start of the 1936 season.

1954-55 - GS Ramchand, the former captain of India, was engaged. What a catch! In his first season he steered the club to its ninth Senior 'A' Championship, scoring 816 runs and taking 60 wickets.

1956 - The battle to retain Kingsley Fields was lost and in 1956 they moved to the Council-owned Barony Park until they settled at their current, well-appointed ground in 1971.

1963 - Nantwich became founder members of the new North Staffs & South Cheshire League,

> **Dick Tyldesley (1897-1943)** was the Wisden Cricketer of the Year in 1925. He played seven matches for England (1924-30) and 397 for Lancashire (1919-31). For his home county he scored 6419 runs, highest score 105, but more significantly he claimed 1509 wickets, best bowling 8-15.
>
> **William Victor Fox (1898-1949)** played 163 matches for Worcestershire (1923-32). He scored 6654 runs, including eleven centuries with a top score of 198. His Wisden obituary records he was a fine footballer who played for Middlesbrough, Wolverhampton Wanderers and Newport County.

Pavilions in Splendour

> Tony Loffill's splendid 2014 publication *Fifty Years On*, which celebrates the fiftieth anniversary of the North Staffs & South Cheshire League, suggests that no summary of Nantwich CC could be considered as complete without a reference to Geoff Bull. He first marched to the wicket for Nantwich in 1934 and played his last match in 1980. In that period there is no doubt that he scored more runs than any other batsman in the area. On one occasion he scored a half century while Frank 'Typhoon' Tyson', who just a year later was ripping the heart out of the Australian batting line-up, was in the opposition's attack. He reports that every time Tyson dropped one short the ball was thumped to the offside boundary. He quotes Bull as saying his finest knock was an innings of 103 made against Freddie Taylor, the Staffordshire bowler who just a few days before had bowled out five Australian batsman (Benaud, Hassett, Craig, de Courcy and Archer) for the Minor Counties against the tourists at Stoke in May 1953. The article claims that Bull went 27 years without missing a match. Some record!

but it was not until 1980 that they won that competition. The following year the Championship was successfully defended, and in 1983, it was won again. The West Indian fast bowler, Vanburn Holder, was the spearhead of the attack.

Staffordshire links were finally broken in 1995 when Nantwich opted to join the Cheshire County competition, but it was not until 2010 that skipper Andy Newton lifted the coveted Premiership trophy, a feat they notably repeated in 2011 and 2012. During this highly successful period the highly influential overseas players were New Zealander Lou Vincent and Aussie Glen Batticciotto.

The pavilion opening in 1936

Ever an enterprising club, Nantwich have had a long-established annual fundraising Boxing Night in the Civil Hall and in recent years highly successful celebrity evenings when David 'Bumble' Lloyd, Michael Vaughan, Geoffrey Boycott and Phil Tufnell have been the speakers.

2016 - Haseeb Hameed made a very successful debut for England, aged 19 years 297 days. He opened the batting with Alistair Cook and scored 31 and 82 in the First Test against India played at Rajkot. In 2014 he had played for Nantwich in the Cheshire County Premier Division. He played six matches, scoring a modest aggregate of 95 runs.

Once a Dabber, then a Lion

2016 was quite a year for Liam Livingstone. He plied his trade with Nantwich between 2013 and 23 April 2016. By the time of his final appearance he had already made his first-class debut for Lancashire, in the previous week, at Old Trafford. He made an impressive start with an innings of 70 against Nottinghamshire. By high summer of that year he had already played for England Lions at Cheltenham against Pakistan A and by July 2017 he had worn full England colours, making his debut against South Africa in a T20 match at Taunton. In 2018 he will be the Lancashire CCC captain.

In 2015 Manchester brewer, Joseph Holt, commissioned a golden beer – Livvy's 350- following his explosive innings against Caldy (see Caldy entry).

Neston

Station Road, Parkgate, South Wirral CH64 6QJ

MAKE NO MISTAKE, the Neston facilities are among some of the finest in the country. The significant acreage provides not only for cricket, but also hockey, tennis (12 courts) and squash.

The pavilion first-floor balcony offers a spectacular view of the cricket field and just beyond the playing area is the magnificent River Dee, nearly five miles wide at this point, and the more distant Welsh hills. Despite it being a superb viewing gallery for those sampling the beer pump products in the adjacent bar, very few visiting spectators can resist the five minute walk to the famous Nicholls ice cream parlour on the Parkgate river frontage.

The pavilion, built in 1971 and enterprisingly extended in 2009, is large and impressive in every respect. Equally, the second pitch facilities beyond the tennis courts are of the highest standard; an ultra-modern dual-sided pavilion is the main feature. One side provides for the cricketers and the other serves the hockey players.

At one time Neston played in the Liverpool Competition but since 1998 have played in the Cheshire County League.

England cricketer and Liverpool dentist Ken Cranston played his club cricket here from before the Second World War through until 1961 and the pavilion's state-of-the-art banqueting suite carries his name. Incredibly, Cranston made his debut for Lancashire on 14 May 1947 and within eight weeks was representing England. He played only eight Tests, but in his second he took four wickets in one over against South Africa at Headingley. Cranston captained Lancashire in 1947/8 and led his country on one occasion in the West Indies in 1948 when the opposition included the mighty Everton Weekes, Clyde Walcott and George Headley. Inevitably, he found some difficulty balancing his sporting activity against his dental profession and he had a relatively short first-class cricketing career, just 78 matches, before concentrating on his dental practice.

Cranston is not the only first-class cricketer to play here. Eddie Bates became the Neston professional in 1932. Previously he had played 406 matches for Yorkshire and Glamorgan between 1907 and 1931. He scored 15964 first-class runs with a top score of 200 not out. For good measure

> In 1924 Henry Beausire took all 10 wickets against Ormskirk for 22 runs off 13 overs, a club record to this day. The other opening bowler actually had the surname of Bowler (JW)! He sent down 13 overs with 6 maidens and only 12 runs, but no wickets!

> Alan Pennington played for Neston for a number of years in the early 1930s, but in 1936, the son of a Mayor of Wallasey, went head to head with one of the greatest Olympians of all-time. Pennington was an outstanding sprinter who boasted national records and medals galore, but in Berlin at the XI Olympiad, he shared a track with the great Jesse Owens.
>
> Despite facing a 20th Century icon, the brilliant young flying machine from the Wirral was far from disgraced. Pennington was entered for the 100m, 200m and sprint relay in Berlin – and in the 100m he registered 10.6 seconds, which was enough to reach the quarter-finals. It was in the semi-finals that Pennington lined up against Owens, but this time he found a searing pace too hot and finished sixth.
>
> Pennington was one of the outstanding British sprinters of his era. A brilliant junior, he went to Oxford University where he won the Varsity 100 yards in 1936 and 1938 and the 440 yards in 1939. In the 1938 European Championships he won a silver medal in the 4×400 metres relay and a bronze in the 200 metres.
>
> The outbreak of war ended his hopes of bidding for Olympic honours in 1940. He reached the rank of Captain during the war before working in insurance on his demob.
>
> He married Margaret Edwards in 1941, sister of the famous comedian Jimmy Edwards.
>
> In June 1961, at the age of 45, it was reported he had been found with gunshot wounds to his head in a hotel room in Lisbon. A pistol and a note were found nearby and a verdict of suicide was recorded.

he took 230 wickets (best 8-93). His father was Billy Bates, the first England player ever to take a hat-trick (Melbourne 1883) and his son was the Southampton footballer and manager, Ted Bates. Arthur Ashwell, who has a clubhouse room named after him, was another Neston professional who played for Kent in 1933-34 (four matches, top score 21 not out).

More recently, first-class cricketers Brad Donelan (Sussex and Somerset), Simon Marshall (Cambridge University and Lancashire) and Jack Smith (South Australia) have played for the Shrimpers.

Lancashire 2nds are regular visitors.

The back pavilion at Neston

New Brighton

Rake Lane, Wallasey CH45 5DE

I AM INDEBTED to Derek Watson, the former Cheshire player (1968-75), for the loan of his copy (No.82 of 100) of a limited edition of *'Battleground', Rake Lane 1856-2006*. Malcolm Barber compiled the 132-page blockbuster in 2006 to mark the 150th anniversary of the club.

We learn that Rake Lane was acquired in 1881 and was the fourth home of the club. Intriguingly, none of the four sites sit within New Brighton proper. As Mr TE Edwardes, a one-time Victorian secretary, captain and life member commented: "If a genius could be tacked up who thought of a name of an adjoining parish for a club in the next one, he would, I think, be entitled to a place in the roll of honour."

It transpires that two Rake Lane fields had been rented and made into one. A local butcher owned one of them and a Shropshire family had the possession of the other. The separating hedge was removed, and so that ownership could continue to be established, a line of stones were buried beneath the original hedge-line. "The early pioneers established the curious anomaly of a 50 yard square in the midst of the hummocky declivity."

> **1865...local press cutting... FATAL ACCIDENT TO A CRICKETER** - On Tuesday afternoon an inquiry was held at the Clarendon Hotel, New Brighton, before Mr Churton, Coroner, upon the body of a young man named Francis Barker. The deceased originally came from Dumfries, he was employed in a Mercantile Office in his town and had been staying at Mr Owens lodgings New Brighton. On Monday eve he met his death under the following circumstances:- Whilst playing cricket upon the ground of the New Brighton Cricket Club he was accidently struck upon the head with a ball. For the moment he staggered and complained of pain, but nothing more took place and in a short time he left the field. Feeling unwell, he returned home and as he became worse the assistance of Dr Par was obtained. He continued to sink and at half past eleven the same evening he died in a state of insensibility. The immediate cause of death being concussion. Meanwhile the cricketer who had thrown the ball was unaware of the serious illness of Mr Barker until Wednesday morning when he was made acquainted with the melancholy circumstances of Mr Barker's death. The Jury recorded a verdict of "Death from being accidentally struck by a cricket ball".

1885 - Gradually the facilities improved and the press were now reporting the club had made their eight acre ground into one of the best in Cheshire. In 1891 it was decided by a group of members to purchase the land and the New Brighton District Cricket Company Limited was formed. A section of the ground was let to New Brighton Rugby Club (and hockey was also played some years later) in the winter months.

1899 - To pull the heavy roller a horse was purchased for £3 10 shillings. Additionally, a double-winged net was acquired for £6 and scoreboard numbers for 10 shillings.

1900 - A strip of land was sold to Wallasey Corporation for the widening of Rake Lane. This was the length of the ground, parallel with Rake Lane and 22 feet wide east to west, reducing the playing area by ten feet.

1913 - In August a fire broke out in the pavilion. The dressing rooms were badly damaged. The local newspaper said there was no suggestion that the fire was the work of suffragettes.

1914-18 - In early September 1914 it was agreed to write to Wallasey CC stating that given the outbreak of WW1 the club thought it sensible to cancel the fixture on 19 September and consider the season closed. At the December AGM the cricketers were congratulated on the way in which the call-to-arms had been responded to, and it was unanimously agreed to hang in the pavilion a roll of honour bearing the names of members who had joined HM Colours and the Regiments to which they were attached. In 1917 the ground was given over to the Wallasey Volunteer Battalion for drill purposes. Sheep grazing rights were also granted to a local dairyman.

1919 - By July cricket was reportedly back in full swing.

1939 - By the start of the season the cricket playing membership totalled 170. There were five participating teams plus schoolboy XIs and top match attendances were up to 1000 spectators. At a meeting on 4 September it was announced: "Consequent on the outbreak of war it was agreed that all remaining fixtures must be cancelled and that the annual meeting be postponed indefinitely."

1941 - During the early hours of 3 May a German landmine was dropped right in the middle of the cricket field causing a five-foot deep crater to be formed. Very significant pavilion damage was sustained. Subsequently the ground was used as a wartime allotment until 1948 and, given the restoration work required, cricket did not return until June 1952. Harrison Park was used as a temporary home.

A devastating scene following a bomb raid, May 1941

1974 - Both the 1st & 2nd XIs win their respective divisions in the Liverpool Competition. Subsequently the 1st XI lifted the coveted top prize again in 1982, 1983, 1991, 1993 and 1998. They had to wait 17 long years for their next success before eventually winning the Liverpool & District Premier League in 2015.

1976 - Tens of millions of ladybirds appeared on the Wirral coastline. Some local matches were abandoned or delayed.

1978 - A crowd of 1500 packed into Rake Lane to watch the full Lancashire side led by Frank Hayes defeat the home side. In 1979 and 1980 further benefit matches were played for Barry Wood and Jack Simmons.

> **1990 - A father and son playing in the same team is not uncommon, but playing against each other is rather more special. On Bank Holiday Monday the scorebook recorded, DJ Watson (New Brighton) lbw PJ Watson 5 (Wallasey), but Dad Derek (Cheshire 1968-75) got his revenge when Paul was caught off his bowling for a duck. For the record, New Brighton 151 all out, Wallasey 130-9.**

The 'white' pavilion... the old pavilion demolished in 2010

1999 - New Brighton were thwarted by their neighbouring rivals, Wallasey, in the final of the Cheshire Cup. They had previously been runners-up in 1981, 1994 and 1997 but had never actually won the knock-out competition. The trend was eventually reversed in 2002 when they defeated Hyde CC. Subsequently they lost the concluding match again in both 2007 and 2015.

2000 - A Millennium match was played against Wallasey. The Liverpool Competition league fixture was chosen and was preceded by a morning Under 13 match. In that special year New Brighton were led by long-serving captain and club stalwart, Tim Watkins. The new scorebox was formally opened.

2006 - The club celebrated its 150th Anniversary. By chance a programme for the 1906 50th anniversary was found. The card revealed that a boot hunt and a needle-threading race for the gents was part of the entertainment. For the former, the competitors were required to remove their black-laced shoes and place them in two baskets at the starting post. One basket was then placed 30 yards distant and the other at 60 yards. The starters were required to run to the baskets, find their shoes, put them on, lace them up and appear at the winning line. When the prizes were awarded special attention was paid to neat lacing!

The second game required a gent's pairing to act as a horse with a jockey on his shoulders, and to run a course threading needles at specific intervals. I doubt whether these games were repeated in 2006!!

2010 - The pavilion was demolished and replaced by a splendid two-tier structure. The new facilities were officially opened at a club dinner on 16 September 2011.

The pavilion terrace is a lively place to watch cricket and affords a great opportunity to sample the local beer. If there is a club in the county that produces a better match programme, I have yet to see it.

The New Brighton wathervane

Newton

Mount Pleasant, Barmhouse Lane, Godley SK14 3BZ

NEWTON CC WAS established in 1912 following a meeting held at the home of Alfred Rushton in Oak Street, Newton. His name became synonymous with the club and its official history records: 'Alfred was the driving force behind our beloved club and without his enthusiasm, steadfastness, vision and commitment it would simply not exist'. He was the President for all his 49 years of involvement. Sadly, he died in 1961 just one year before the Golden Jubilee celebrations.

Originally home matches were played at Clarendon Road. A deal was done to rent a sloping field for £2 per annum. A pavilion was purchased with money that the Rushton family had set aside for a new piano for their daughter!

Initially the club only played friendlies and then WW1 enforced a suspension. A post-war application to join the Glossop & District League was unsuccessful, but by 1920 they were playing their first matches in the Stockport & District competition.

1925 - Newton recorded a score of over 100 for the very first time. They actually notched up 141 all out before dismissing Denton UMC for 28, Alan Kay taking 8-20. Three weeks later the same bowler captured another 8 wickets, this time for only 7 runs when Newton Mill could only score 29 when chasing a modest Newton total of 34.

1926 - Four Wilson brothers played for Newton 2nd XI against Hyde PSA and all recorded ducks.

1927 - The Clarendon Road ground was sold for housing, but it was not until 1934 that the present Barmhouse Lane ground was acquired when Hyde Wesleyans, occupants at the time, disbanded. During that seven year period of homelessness occasional friendly fixtures kept the club together.

1936 - Tragedy struck when the pavilion was burnt to the ground. All the club equipment and records were destroyed. The fire occurred on a Sunday evening, but by the Monday night a new pavilion had been sourced, purchased and delivered. A hen-house from a local farm was in place!

1937 - The Silver Jubilee is celebrated. The local newspaper refers to Mr President as 'Lord Hawke of Newton CC'.

1939-45 - Some league cricket was possible. The members were determined not to let 'Jerry' deprive the

> The impressive *100 years of Newton CC, 1912-2012* book discloses that around this time a Hyde League was set up as a breakaway from the Denton & District League. It had a membership of eight teams, all of them within one mile of Crown Point!

club of cricket and a motto 'like the Whitehall theatre we never close' was adopted.

1949 - An old timber-framed building was acquired from the Co-op. It was transported to Barmhouse Lane and remained as the club pavilion until 1972. At about this time, Joe Pickett, a club member, became a local councillor and successfully led an application for the playing area to be designated as greenbelt.

1950-70 - For two decades Hiram Tagg was the club chairman and his wife was the scorer. She had a theory that was regularly tested - she alleged that if she walked round the boundary in a clockwise direction it would help Newton score runs, but if she walked anti-clockwise it would help the team take wickets. The jury is still out! Ever keen to assist the club, she led the Christmas sing-song while Hiram acted as Father Christmas. Stalwart Joe Chapman, a previous captain and wicketkeeper, was a member of the magic circle and provided the festive entertainment.

1971-1975 - Off the field the club negotiated a 30-year lease for the ground. Previously it had been subject to an annual tenancy arrangement. Two disused pre-fabricated bungalows were acquired, dismantled, brought to the site and re-built. The Water Authority constructed a large underground reservoir nearby and negotiated a deal whereby they would dump their surplus soil from the excavation into the big dip at the bottom end of the outfield. In return they agreed to grade, level and re-seed the entire outfield.

1983-1991 - A fire destroyed the pavilion in September 1983. It burnt with such ferocity that overhead power cables were damaged. Two rented portakabins were a temporary solution until an insurance settlement was negotiated. On receipt of that money, grants and a good number of member loans, a new structure was ready for the start of the 1985 season, but it was really no more than a shell. With no money in the bank the fitting out of the new facility was a huge task and for a good number of years the club functioned within a very rudimentary building until it was officially opened in 1991. Sid Lofthouse, father of former Cheshire minor county umpire John, was singled out as a tireless worker over the extended period. John played for Newton in the 1970s and was captain in 1978. Not only was the development of the pavilion an ongoing concern during this period, the buying of the ground was also on the agenda. Securing its purchase with the freehold was eventually completed in 1989 for approximately £7000, with part funding from the Sports Council. The availability of money was a constant problem and just when the club's bank account was at breaking point there was an unexpected windfall. A new housing development was proceeding apace and it transpired the building work would impinge on the right of way held by the cricket club. In the event a 15k fee was negotiated in 1990 and another parcel of land was sold to a different developer for £20k in 1991.

1935 team picture in front of an earlier pavilion

Newton Ladies in 1954

1990s - A golden passage in terms of honours. The club's most successful period and as members of the Glossop & District League they won five first division championships, two first division cups, five second division championships, four second division cups and the Aggregate trophy for seven years in succession.

In 2000 Newton joined the Derbyshire & Cheshire League. The 2012 centenary was celebrated with a match against their long-standing Peak District opponents from Ashford in the Water CC.

Northwich

Moss Farm, Moss Lane, Northwich CH8 4BG

THE DETAIL is sketchy but the club was reportedly formed in 1826. The earliest recorded scorecard in existence is said to be from 1856 when Northwich played a match at Bowdon. Previous researchers have suggested an early home ground was on a field called 'Fat Lay', which was in the proximity of the current Winnington Park CC ground and, likewise, the second site was in the same locality. By 1881 it is probable the club moved to Hartford Hill Park and then Brewery Meadow.

> **Minutes of a meeting on 18 June 1881**
> **Committee meeting held in the pavilion on the ground (ground not specified)**
> This meeting was called (after the Knutsford match this day) for the purpose of remonstrating with the professional on his unsatisfactory behaviour. He was called into the pavilion and cautioned by Mr Wells and promised better behaviour for the future.

1898 - A much clearer picture starts to emerge. A report in the *Northwich Chronicle* gave details of the AGM held at the Angel Hotel on 5 November when the chairman reported that the landlord of Brewery Meadow had refused the further use of his field, but that he had obtained a ten year lease from Mr Royle of Southport for seven acres of land which subsequently became the established Vicarage Road ground.

1914-39 - During WW1 the entire cricket field was set aside as allotments to aid the war effort, but after the conflict the club managed to secure sufficient finances to purchase the land. In 1931 part of the ground was sold off for housing (Danefields) and the square was relocated on a rather smaller site. The deal represented bad business for the cricketers as the pavilion construction and relocation costs incurred were greater than the sum received. In the years immediately prior to WW2 the club almost folded.

1950-60s - After the War, the club regrouped and thanks to the stalwart efforts of the more experienced members it enjoyed its most prosperous years. A go-ahead committee hosted a good number of representative matches. Among the most notable was a visit of the full West Indies side in 1951, following their epic Test series victory against England the previous summer. The 'Three Ws' - Everton Weekes, Clyde Walcott and Frank Worrell - attracted a crowd of more than 2000. The trio hit 30 sixes between them. It is said they were still finding some of the lost balls 20 years later! In 1955 a Commonwealth XI, captained by Cec Pepper and including Garry Sobers and Sonny Ramadhin, attracted another huge crowd. Mike Talbot-Butler, the current Cheshire County League President, who played for the club from 1951-81, recalls: "People were queuing into the road to get in and the boundaries had to be brought in five yards to accommodate them all. We were instructed to fumble any catches offered ('they've come to watch them, not you'). One hard chance came to me off Sobers and I duly obliged, enabling him to go on to score 90. I was reminded of this 'blunder' in the town for years afterwards!"

Northwich also entertained county teams in testimonial games. Maurice Tremlett brought Somerset to the town before Derbyshire made two appearances for the benefits of Derek Morgan and Les Jackson. Lancashire played there once for Harry Pilling. Harry got a duck, but won twice on the pavilion one-armed bandit and went home £60 better off plus a generous share of the gate.

The ground was kept in superb condition by Harold Shallcross and later Tom Hulme. The good square and fast outfield ensured that Northwich

> 1908 - The *Northwich Chronicle* reporting on the Northwich CC AGM makes a reference to pitch improvements: "The special manure which had been put on had a beneficial effect and a great improvement had been made by having the grass cut to the edge." Later that year the same newspaper quoted Charles Hughes, referring back to his playing days some 45 years earlier: "More matches were lost by bad fielding than bowling or batting, a department neglected by many clubs."

The Northwich team outside the 'new' pavilion, 1959.
On the front row are John Pickup (extreme right) and Mike Talbot-Butler (fourth left).

was a regular choice for Cheshire's Minor Counties matches for 25 years. Cheshire also hosted the national touring teams of Canada and Kenya at Vicarage Road.

Members of the Manchester Association from 1951 until 1974, Northwich's best season was in 1967, when they won the coveted Stockton Trophy under the captaincy of Terry Melia, an ICI chemist who later became HM Chief Inspector of Schools. Meanwhile, with Tom Cadwallender and Jack Buckley in joint charge, the 2nd XI completed a hat-trick of Burrows Trophy successes in 1976-77-78.

Northwich went on to become founder members of the Cheshire County League in 1975 under the captaincy of local solicitor, Geoff Culey. They did well for a period, especially in 1980, when, inspired by the superb batsmanship of David Bailey, they finished close runners-up to Cheadle Hulme in a final day drama.

Secretary John Pickup, who went on to become Cheshire, Minor Counties and ECB Recreational cricket chairman, helped to organise the club's 150th Anniversary Dinner at the Smoker Inn, Plumley in October, 1976. Every other club in the league was represented and the guest speaker was the legendary Freddie Trueman, who earned himself a standing ovation which seemed to last well into the night.

As the most influential members passed away and replacements could not be found, the club began to fall on hard times again. Junior cricket had been neglected and there was little opportunity for younger members to make their way into the senior sides. In one brief spell, Northwich won the Mid-Cheshire Youth Association Under 15s title in 1983 and repeated the success two years later at Under 17 level. Led by Roger Stubbs, meanwhile, a somewhat semi-detached 3rd XI also did well for a time, but were unable to promote players to senior cricket and the end seemed nigh.

1997 - Northwich Cricket Club faced bankruptcy, repayments on a loan secured by a previous administration could not be met, the club had been forced out of the County League because the ground and pavilion were both in a sorry state of repair and the end seemed near. However, the membership, which consisted mostly of the players from the junior sides of the previous ten years, were determined not to lose the club, and they were accepted into the Cheshire Alliance League, at the bottom of the Cheshire cricket ladder. With all possibilities explored, the only recourse was to sell the club's only asset, its ground, relocate and make a fresh start. A deal was secured just before the threatened closure, which ensured the existence of the club and provided the opportunity to rebuild the structure and reputation of the historic and proud name of Northwich CC.

In 1999, with the invaluable assistance of Vale Royal Borough Council, the club relocated to the Moss Farm Leisure Complex. For two seasons matches were staged on a temporary ground with a single Portakabin as a pavilion, but by 2001 a county standard facility was completed and the process of improving the pitch began. With the valued contribution of committee members and volunteers the last decade or more has been a period of improvement and strengthening. There is now a full set of junior sides, girls' cricket and three senior sides. After that fateful expulsion the club regained its place in the senior competition in 2014.

> In partial fulfilment of his 1982 M.Ed degree, S. Joseph wrote a paper entitled *The development of physical recreation in Northwich in the late 19th and early 20th Centuries*. He rather superficially discusses the early cricketing days at Winnington Park, Northwich, Davenham, Hartford, Barnton and Lostock, but goes on to make an interesting reference to Charles J Hughes. A one-time cricketer at the Northwich club, he became their Secretary, Chairman and then President. More significantly, he was instrumental in the formation of the County Cricket Club and became their first Chairman in 1908. An auctioneer by profession, Hughes (b 1853, d 1916) was an enthusiastic rifleman and Secretary of the Northwich Rowing Club, but his first passion was football and it was in that sport he made a very notable mark. He played for Northwich, was joint founder of Cheshire Football Association and then served as its Secretary for 30 years. He was a top referee and officiated in three FA Cup Finals: 1891 (Blackburn Rovers v Notts County), 1893 (Wolves v Everton) and 1894 (Bolton v Notts County).

Oakmere

Overdale Lane, Oakmere, Northwich CW8 2EL

IN THE EARLY 1950s, while many clubs were celebrating their centenary, plans were being made by Bert Houghton to establish a new village team in Mid-Cheshire. Bert had bought a television set and when he switched it on, as fate would have it, cricket was being shown. This was the seed and the architect turned farmer soon began to prepare a field within his farm on Laundry Lane. Would it be called Oakmere or Cuddington?

From that humble beginning, the exceptionally well-appointed existing facility has developed. Laundry Lane later became Overdale Lane.

1959 - The ground was grazed when not in use for cricket. The tiny square was protected by an electric fence which had to be dismantled prior to each match. Before the mowing could start the most offending cow pats were removed from the outfield. Older members can recall with glee the occasion

---

1960/70s Mark Bevan recalls... The actual playing of cricket was to me rather secondary. Of far more consequence was the serious business of Thursday three-card brag. The home dressing room would be lit by a flickering old oil-lamp and you could hardly see the end of your nose, let alone a hand of cards. Yet somehow we managed and often late into the night, as piles of pennies and tanners crossed from one side of the dimly-lit table to another. I never learned much about cricket, but I became an expert on betting blind! We reckoned Colin Woodward ran his car on the winnings. Indeed, if Woodward was in, it was wise to be out!

> Oxford tours...1970s/80s/90s... on one occasion 15 players arrived at the Lincoln College ground in just two cars – four in Tony Newall's and 11 in Peter Jones's, including three in the boot. There was a marathon card school playing through until breakfast, golf until lunch and cricket all afternoon! Stefan Kazmierczak stepped through the bottom of a punt on the river and Val Sellars gave us a demonstration of his athleticism when climbing a street light outside Balliol College, only to find it painted with an anti-vandal substance.

when one visiting bowler actually stuffed his trouser bottoms into his socks to assist his run-up through the long grass!

The first captain was Denis Gore and he skippered the team for the first nineteen seasons. In his formative years, Denis had been a prisoner of war and this had endowed him with a steely determination and real strength of character. He never shirked responsibility, demanded maximum effort from all who played under him and led by example. He had his critics, including some opposition captains, but he was worshipped by those who played under him and a good many players owe much of their development to his guidance and advice. "Denis was always there, a cross between a benign headmaster and a hungry rottweiler and woe betide anyone who dropped a catch or missed heeding one of his field placings." At one time or another he held the office of Chairman, Secretary, Treasurer, Fixture Secretary and chief fundraiser. Undoubtedly, 'Mr Oakmere Cricket', he was made a Life Member in 1976.

1978 - The year of the new pavilion and a jump in standard from the Cheshire Association to the Cheshire Cricket League, but steady progress was made and in 1981 the club was promoted to Division 1 after ending as runners-up to Sandbach. Only friendly cricket had been played between 1954 and 1969.

1984 - An injection of new talent! Manchester United and England star Steve Coppell, made his first team debut. He was living locally and was keen for a game and, as with most sportsmen, he had an excellent eye for a ball. His first away game, at Sandbach, attracted probably the largest crowd the team had ever played before and his athleticism and enthusiasm certainly encouraged other team members to work harder. Unfortunately for the club, Steve was appointed manager of Crystal Palace and his cricketing talents were soon lost to the club.

1986 - Ladies' cricket got underway. Captain Helen Newall takes up the story. "This was no means of fighting the flab, or keeping in shape, this was my dream! Instead of bowling at the dustbin in a game with my brothers and being out if I managed to hit a six over the vegetable patch, here was my chance to actually produce that beautiful sound of leather on willow, to run between those creases, basically to participate in the sport which had been so central in my life and yet a sport which has kept me as its spectator." To this very day Ladies' cricket thrives at Oakmere.

Do pay a visit and observe the efforts of Pat Hutchinson, who has kept the ground in fine order for many a year.

From the Oakmere scorebooks

1956 Dan Lennon scores the first century made by an Oakmere player - 101 not out against Barnton.

1957 Oakmere dismissed for 16 against Greenall Whitley, but the opposition were made to struggle. They eventually achieved 18-7! (Brian Crawford 6-8).

1958 Denis Gore (106) and Brian Crawford (102) both take over a 100 wickets during the season.

1960 Crewe Vagrants are bowled out for 5. Denis Gore 5-0, Gilly Jones 5-4.

1967 Arley all out for 7. Denis Gore 5-2. John Birtwistle 5-4.

Offerton

The Paddock, Woodlands Drive, Offerton SK2 5AP

OFFERTON CRICKET Club was formed in 1921 by players originally connected with the local church team, St Albans.

Plans to build a new housing estate led the club to approach Joseph Ramsden, a local landowner, with a proposal to create a new cricket ground in an area close to the Goyt river which had originally been used to train racehorses. The ground was officially opened by Mr Ramsden on 27 May 1937 and it was formally named the Paddock to reflect the nature of its original use. When the landowner eventually died, he generously left the ground to the cricket club.

When cricket resumed after WW2 the club joined the High Peak League. They also had the foresight to form a junior section, one of the first clubs in the area to do so.

The 1955 handbook *Club & League Cricket in Lancashire & District* included an article about Geoff Edrich (b 1918, d 2004), who was the Lancashire CCC beneficiary that year, and reported that Offerton would be hosting a match for him on 7 August. This was a good time for the club as they had won the top division of the High Peak League the season before. The handbook documents that at the end of August, Marple appeared to be the favourites for the championship, but after they suffered two unexpected defeats Offerton grabbed their opportunity and overtook them.

In 1963 Ray Gallian, the father of Lancashire, Nottinghamshire and England star Jason, and Gordon Potter both scored centuries against Stockport Georgians. A demoralised opposition were then skittled by Richard Day, who ironically later joined Georgians.

After spells in the North Western League, the Saddleworth League and the Glossop League, Offerton moved to the Cheshire League in 1993. Promotion from the second division was achieved at the first attempt and in 1995 the 1st XI finished runners-up to Prestbury. By 2015 they had joined the Derbyshire & Cheshire set-up.

At the far end of Woodlands Road, just when you think you must have missed the entrance, you will notice a gate identifying the cricket club. Follow the steep road down through the trees and, hey presto, at the bottom of the bowl is the ground, totally secluded and totally unexpected. Follow the track behind the pavilion down to the river Goyt.

Old Parkonians

HM Curphey Memorial Ground, Holm Lane, Oxton CH43 2HU

OLD PARKONIANS Rugby Club was formed in 1928 by the old boys of Birkenhead Park High School and they moved to their current home in Holm Lane, Oxton in 1948. The cricket club was established in 1950 by the late, once met never forgotten, Ronnie Caton. Initially the cricketers played at Holm Lane on a coconut matting pitch, but they subsequently moved to a ground-share arrangement with Victory Kidder CC in Arrowe Park. When the Holm Lane ground was re-developed in 1970-71, a cricket square was made between the two new rugby pitches.

Friendly cricket was played up to and including 1986, when many of the then Liverpool and Merseyside Competition clubs provided the opposition. In 1987 the club joined the Wirral League, finishing the 1988 season as champions. In 1990 a 2nd XI was formed. Since then the club has always had a minimum of two Saturday league teams as well as a Sunday friendly XI. From 1992-96 the club played in the North Cheshire League, from 1997-99 in the Merseyside Competition and from 2000 in the Cheshire pyramid. In 2001 the club introduced a junior section.

Beckett, Hitchell and Westwater are familiar names in the history of 'Old Parks'. One of these three names has captained the club in 28 of the last 30 years. Chris Hitchell was skipper for 15 of the seasons, including an unbroken spell of 11 (1996-2006). Twice there has been father and son leadership: Colin Westwater, chairman, and son Adam as captain; Richie Beckett and his son Chris, the captain, are the present pairing.

The Hitchell family has provided four brothers to the 1st XI for the past 30 seasons with all four regularly in the team at the same time. In age order they are Mike (wicketkeeper), Chris, Nick and Tim. There is a fifth brother, Sean, the eldest, who has helped out on occasions. Mike Beckett (brother of Richie) captained the 1st XI for six seasons and was Club Secretary (1989-2010). Richie Beckett captained the 1st XI for two seasons and is Fixture Secretary (1987- to the present day), 1st XI scorer (2007- to the present), club historian and President of Old Parkonians Association (2013- to the present). His son, Chris, is the current 1st XI captain (2009, 2015- to the present). Dave Westwater captained the 1st XI for three seasons, was Club Chairman (1991-2009) and has been ground manager of the club for more years than he cares to remember. He is also currently Chairman of Old Parkonians Association (2007- to the present).

In 2016 the 1st XI won both the Cheshire Cricket Alliance Division 2 league title and the Division 2 league cup under the captaincy of Chris Beckett and the 2nd XI won the CCA 2nd XI West Division under the captaincy of David Buey. All this is persuasive evidence that the club continues to prosper and they are justifiably proud of the fact that they have won the CCA Umpires' Panel Trophy for the past three seasons, emphasising the spirit in which Old Parkonians CC play their cricket.

Oulton Park

Pinfold Lane, Little Budworth CW6 9BS

A WELCOME MAT at the pavilion entrance suggests that Oulton Park CC was founded in 1820 and a wall plaque quaintly announces 'from parish pump to premiership'. The origins of the club, more realistically in the 1850/60s, revolved around the Egerton family-owned Oulton Estate in Little Budworth. It was founded as a recreational activity for the farmworkers and tenants of the Oulton Estate, with Sir John Grey Egerton, 9th Baronet, as its President. The link continues to this day with the position now held by Sir William Egerton, 17th Baronet.

Originally matches were played in front of the old hall, which was badly damaged by fire in 1926 but remained until World War Two when a German bomber returning from an aborted raid on Liverpool dropped its load and destroyed what was left.

When the park was finally established as a racing circuit conflicts with cricket became patently obvious and the then Sir John leased the present ground to the club in 1968. The old wooden pavilion was originally the Nat West bank in Northwich and was bought from them for £200 and transported by club members on a flatbed truck. The framework was erected but blew down on the first night as it hadn't been properly secured! It was quickly re-assembled and survived until the splendid new pavilion was opened in 1993.

The tranquillity of the lovely setting, with its tight boundaries, tree in the field of play and the distant village church of St Peter's, is sometimes interrupted by the noise of motorbikes at the nearby racing circuit, but there is always a warm welcome for visitors and the boundary-edge Egerton Arms offers an unrivalled watering-hole view of the cricket.

It would be impossible to write about Oulton Park without making a reference to the late Roy Ramsbottom. It was under his influence that the club enjoyed a meteoric rise through the Cheshire pyramid. He brought a string of well-known former professionals to the club and was instrumental in its rise from the comparative obscurity of the South Cheshire Alliance in the mid 1980s to become the Cheshire County League Premier Division champions by 2005. Roy was an avid collector of cricket memorabilia and had a prized collection. An accountant by profession, he was the senior partner at Murray Smith, who sponsored the Cheshire County League for an extended period.

**ROY F. RAMSBOTTOM
PLAYER, MEMBER AND CHAIRMAN
1960 - 2006
FROM PARISH PUMP TO PREMIERSHIP**

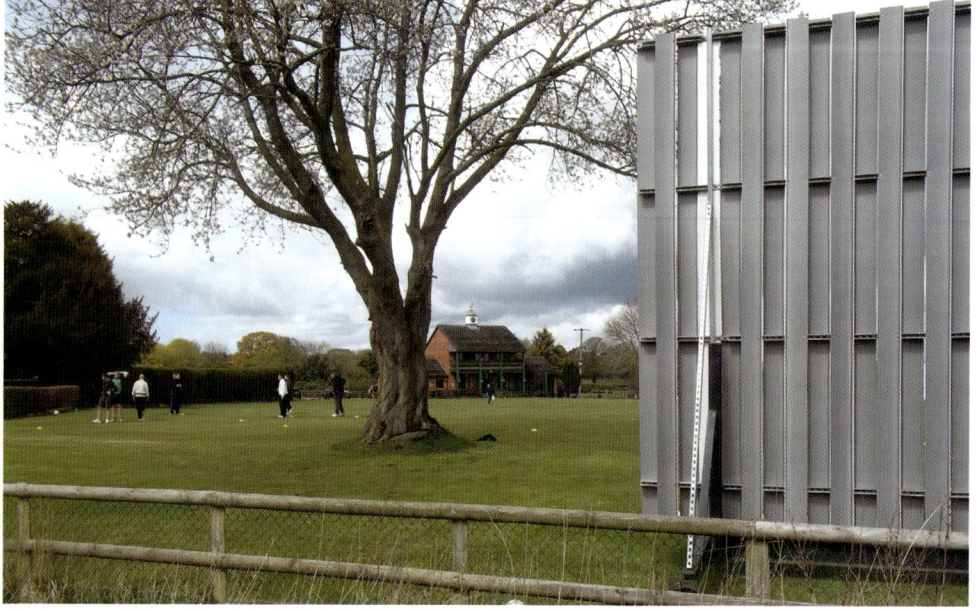

The ultimate dream of winning the Cheshire Premier League was achieved in 2005. For good measure they won it again in 2006 and 2007. Their domination of cricket across the county was also demonstrated by winning the Cheshire Cup in each of those three years - the ultimate hat-trick.

Over Peover

Wellbank Lane, Over Peover, WA16 8TZ

THE FIRST cricket club in Over Peover was founded in the Edwardian age and played on Parkgate Field. The president at that time was Mr Peel of Colshaw Hall. This club ceased to play in 1932, was reformed in 1938 and finally went out of existence in 1939 at the outbreak of war.

After WW2 there was a strong feeling in the village community for cricket to be re-established, although the original cricket pitch had been put to the plough. Mr Frank Groves, a member of the Parish Council, convened a public meeting of residents of Over Peover on 21 January 1947. The purpose of the meeting was to establish a club for the "charitable purposes of organising and encouraging games, sports, entertainments, amusements and other recreation, and to absorb, when desirable and take over the funds of any other club, association or society having similar objectives and wishing to hand over its affairs to this club."

This meeting was chaired by Mr William Tully and the new club, initially formed as Over Peover Sports Club, held its inaugural meeting in the Chapel Schoolroom, Cinder Lane on 4 February 1947. There were separate committees for cricket, football and tennis.

After several anxious months of meetings to find a suitable ground, Mr Wainwright "kindly offered a field near his house which was to be known as a temporary measure". At that time Mr George Reed rented the field but he agreed to 1600 square yards being turned into a cricket square. Mr Reed was given permission to graze young stock on the outfield in the winter as long as they did not stray onto the square. This field is still used by Over Peover Cricket Club today thanks to Mr Peter Wainwright and his sister, Margaret, who inherited the ground from their father. The first match was played on 2 July 1947.

Committee meetings were initially held free of charge in the Methodist Hall, but when a fee of 7 shillings 6d was proposed the club moved to St Michael's vestry where the fee was 2 shillings 6d, although no smoking was allowed.

Enquiries had to be made to the Food Office for a ration of tea and sugar for home matches – various foodstuffs were still rationed for several years after the war.

The football section of the club eventually broke away and tennis never became an active part of the club's activities due to a lack of courts. On 17

January, 1950 the constitution was amended and the name of the club changed to Over Peover Cricket Club.

Between 1947 and 1949 the club had a temporary shelter for use as a tea tent plus an adequate shed until the club managed to acquire an ex-army hut from Toft Camp in 1950. A volunteer working party took one weekend to take the hut down and on the following weekend re-erected it at Over Peover. Local farmers and vice presidents loaned tractors and trailers and gave valuable assistance as well as materials. A changing room was constructed with extra timber and together with the electricity connection fee and other manual work the total cost to the club was £81-15s-4d. The first AGM to be held in the new pavilion took place on 15 January 1952. Over 60 years later the pavilion is still there, although much has been replaced and repaired.

The verandah was built shortly after erection of the main pavilion. In 1953 the ladies were provided with an Elsan closet behind the practice nets. Seven months later a second-hand hut with a wooden floor was acquired. This facility lasted 20 years until it was vandalised. Eventually a new ladies' toilet was constructed at the rear of the pavilion with access from within, but it took two years to complete. No record remains of how the ladies coped during this period!

A bar facility was added to the main pavilion in 1979. In 1987, assisted by a Council grant of £350, showers were installed and the changing rooms improved. The last few years have seen the creation of an umpires' changing room.

For the first twenty or so years Over Peover CC played friendly cricket against neighbouring clubs. Matches started at 2.30pm with a tea interval two hours later and games finishing at 7.00pm. However, in the 1970s they joined the South Cheshire Cricket Alliance with some fixtures now being played in Shropshire and Staffordshire. In 2003 Over Peover was promoted into the Cheshire League, where they have remained ever since.

OPCC 1st XI won the League's Knock-Out Cup in 2006, whilst in 2004 the Under 15s won their Knock Out Cup.

A six-a-side competition became a popular local tournament from 1955 until the turn of the century. Teams such as Bukta, including Fran Cotton and Steve Smith, participated. OPCC finally won this trophy in 1973.

Local names such as Baskerville, Brandrath, Carr, Groves, Mullineux, Newton, Perks, Slater, Street, Tully, Walton and Wood feature in the early scorebooks, together with Peter Wainwright, who topped the 1st XI batting averages fifteen times, and Levi Jervis, who won the 1st XI bowling averages on ten occasions.

I'm extremely grateful to David Young, who kindly extracted the above from *A history of Over Peover Cricket Club* by Jill McKeown.

From Alvanley CC to England - Sophie Ecclestone

Born in Chester (6 May 1999) and educated in Helsby, Sophie Ecclestone, a talented slow left-arm bowler, made her England bow in a T20 match against Pakistan on 3 July 2016. She recorded bowling figures of 1-21 from her allocation of four overs. In October of the same year she made her ODI debut when England defeated the West Indies in Jamaica. Sophie dismissed both openers (9-3-28-2). Her first Test match appearance was in November 2017 against Australia at North Sydney CC (37-7-107-3). By the end of November 2017, and more than six months before her nineteenth birthday, she had represented her country on ten occasions. She capped off 2017 with another success when the England Women's World Cup-winning team walked off with the *BBC Sports Personality of the Year Team Award*. Sophie was up on stage at the Liverpool Arena on 17 December as a member of the attending England squad.

Oxton

Townfield Lane, Oxton, Wirral CH43 2LH

AN EXTRACT FROM the minute book refers to a meeting held on 27 September 1875 at the Queen's Arms Hotel to 'consider the advisability of forming a cricket club in Oxton'. The motion was passed and the Committee were authorised to negotiate with Mr Caregan for a lease of his land for five years. The field was inspected but the offer to pay £7 per acre was declined. At the October general meeting the Committee were made aware of a new proposal from the Earl of Shrewsbury, who was offering a piece of land lying below the Chairman's house for a rent of £5 per acre. However, Mr Caregan's field must have been preferred as a further offer at £10 per acre for ten years was made. When that bid was rejected, the Committee accepted the Earl of Shrewsbury's offer. The rent was eventually fixed at three guineas per acre for ten years. Work on the ground started in early 1876 and included a plot suitable for croquet and lawn tennis. Plans for a pavilion to cost £320 were approved, but in the first season Major Horner's cottage and a tent were used. Shortly afterwards a quoits rink was added. Lacrosse was also played from a very early date. By 1883 the pavilion had been enlarged. Hockey came along in 1906. The ground was eventually purchased in 1928 for £4000. Subsequently additional land was procured.

The minute book makes a number of references to the club 'tractor(s)'. In 1886 the Secretary advised that a horse had been bought for £3, the one belonging to the club having died during the winter. In April 1910 permission was granted to

Extracts from the minutes

20 April 1885. It was decided that the pavilion would not be open upon any consideration on Sundays.

19 May 1924. Sunday play. No alteration should be made to the decision reached at the Extraordinary General Meeting held on 16 June 1922.

18 April 1933. The Hon. Secretary reported the following figures as a result of the ballot of the members for or against Sunday games:

For	85	40%
Against	46	21%
Not voted	83	39%

Mr Stratton pointed out that from these figures it was obvious the club was in favour of Sunday play. It was finally agreed that a notice should appear in the pavilion informing members that the club would be open on Sunday afternoons from 2pm to 6pm.

buy a new set of boots for the horse. By June the horse had died and another was taken on trial at five shillings per week. Perhaps it was not found to be satisfactory or maybe the boots did not fit as another was bought in July for £10. In 1935 another reference to the horse, which was now too old to work, appeared. A year earlier it was decided a rat-catcher needed to be employed owing to the damage done to members' belongings. Staying with the agriculture theme, no cricket was played on the ground between 1915 and 1918 but a hay crop and garden produce helped to generate some income.

The club employed a string of professionals from the very early days as both a groundsman and a player. The list includes a good number who had played first-class cricket. Among them were Percy Mason, who turned out for Nottinghamshire on 43 occasions between 1896 and 1901. He was said to be an excellent coach and bowled off-spinners. He served the club between 1906 and 1914 and played for Cheshire between 1909 and 1912.

When Harry Tyldesley, brother of RK, JD and WK, came to Townfield Lane in 1924, he was employed for his cricketing talent and his work on the ground was regarded as secondary. He had played for Lancashire and went on the MCC tour to Australia and New Zealand in 1922-23 under the captaincy of AC MacLaren. His coming to Oxton brought about a big change in the fortunes of the club. Between 1924 and the end of the 1930 season he contributed 822 wickets, with a seasonal bowling average hovering around 10. In that golden period Oxton won the Liverpool Competition outright on four occasions, shared one championship and also secured a second and third place.

> There is a long history of Oxton 'on tour' and the 1875-1975 centenary handbook gives an outline of some of the highlights over an extended period. A tourist's quiz is included. Here is a sub-set of the questions:
>
> 1. Which Oxton fast bowler, on being told by the captain to "cut out the histrionics", left the field to consult a dictionary?
> 2. Describe – in 'four letter' words only – Raymond Short's opinion of Cyril Higby's ability as a convoy leader.
> 3. In what year was the then club Hon. Secretary, later to become President, found late at night half way up an obelisk in the heart of Worcestershire?

Some years later (1931-3), Bernie Flint joined the club, taking 95, 87 and 79 wickets during his three-year stay. He played 13 matches for Nottinghamshire in 1919-20. If his name is not a familiar one, his daughter-in-law will be better known to you as Rachael Heyhoe Flint. When Flint moved on, he was replaced by Len Hutton's brother-in-law, Frank Dennis, who was good enough to be awarded his Yorkshire cap (1929). He played with distinction between 1934 and 1939.

Much more recently the current club chairman, David Varey, played for both Cambridge University and Lancashire. His 66 first-class appearances resulted in a highest score of 156 not out and a career aggregate of 2723 runs. Gayan Fernando (14 first-class matches in Sri Lanka) has been a familiar face at the club in recent years. He first appeared in 2011. Gareth Andrew (Somerset, Worcestershire and Hampshire) and Shaaiq Choudhry (Warwickshire and Worcestershire) are other recent players with first-class experience. Paul Horton (Lancashire and now Leicestershire) also played very briefly in 2007.

The Danson Gates (see Birkenhead Park entry)

Parkfield Liscard

Pembertons Meadow, Central Park, Liscard, Wallasey CH44 5UP

BY 1902 FOUR clubs were playing in compact Central Park. Shared boundaries were the norm.

Liscard CC was founded in November 1901, but by 1922 they had moved to Harrison Park and subsequently merged with New Brighton in 1935.

Egremont, so long considered the best team in Central Park, played here until 1973 when their pavilion was destroyed and they moved to Prenton Dell Road, Prenton where they merged with Old Rockferrians.

The third club, founded in 1892, was Liscard St Mary's. In 1934, after a dispute over the sale of Irish sweepstake tickets, they severed all links with the church and hereon played under the name of Liscard Central.

The fourth team was Seacombe Wesleyans, but by 1907 they appeared to have disbanded or moved to another ground and were replaced by St John's, Egremont. A parish magazine reported that an 'enthusiastic meeting' agreed

> **Snippets taken from *One hundred Not Out - The History of Liscard Central CC (1892-1992)*... The Merseyside CA competition was won in 1970, 1976 and 1980 and Oxton were defeated in the Liverpool Echo Cup in 1976... It relates an amusing story about jovial member George Jones and an umpire, Robin Sutton, who was a man of the cloth. George got a faint touch to a rising delivery and was comfortably caught by the wicketkeeper. In true Corinthian fashion, George immediately headed off for the pavilion. As he reached the steps he was stopped in his tracks by Robin shouting, "George, I haven't given you out!" Not wishing to offend a churchman, George, by nature a mild-mannered man, returned to the crease and started to prepare for the next delivery. In astonishment he looked up to see the regimented finger of the umpire pointing to the heavens. "You can go now," he uttered in his characteristically haughty manner as a poor, demoralised George walked back to the pavilion for a second time within a minute!... Skipper Phil Gallagher recalled Phil Gwatkin hitting one of the highest sixes he could remember and the ball landing unbelievably in his own child's mercifully empty pram... The booklet finishes with the sentence 'Long may the club flourish', but twelve years later it merged with Parkfield CC.**

to form a cricket team for the 1907 season. By the 1930s they were fielding three sides and were very fortunate to have a cricket fanatic as their clergyman. The Reverend CR Montgomery was the brother of Viscount Montgomery of El Alamein. It was said he always asked one thing of his curates, and that was they played cricket! There is evidence to support the story as the Reverend Simmons topped both the batting and bowling averages in 1937 and the Reverend Tarleton went on to play for the Gentlemen of Ireland.

WW2 - Prior to the war the standard of cricket played in the park was high, but little did the players realise it would be ten long years before cricket was played again as the Home Guard used the ground during the conflict and all three pavilions had been destroyed. Intriguingly, in early 1939 the *Wallasey News* questioned whether a party of German schoolchildren should be allowed to visit Wallasey and repay a visit that a group of Wallasey Grammar School boys had made to Berlin the previous summer.

1962 - St John's Church, Egremont, was, of course, a church-based team and at this point disputes over the playing of Sunday cricket caused those links to be severed. The club adopted the name Parkfield CC, taken from Parkfield Drive, the approach road.

> Along with his father and his brother, Simon Renshaw (b 1974) played for Liscard Central. He moved on to Oxton and played for Cheshire (1994–2004) either side of a six-year spell with Hampshire (1995-2000). He played 39 first-class matches, taking 93 wickets and recording a best score of 56.

1970-2000s - After Egremont moved on in 1973 only Liscard Central and Parkfield remained. Both had setbacks (both had pavilion fires) and periods of significant success, but eventually, after two aborted efforts, they decided to join forces and did so in 2004. The histories of Parkfield and Liscard Central were intertwined by their joint presence at Central Park, but that coming together more than a decade ago as Parkfield Liscard CC was a sensible step which secured a firm cricketing presence in this corner of the Wirral peninsular.

It is an indisputable fact that the Costain family have made a tremendous contribution to the club over the years. Five brothers, Dave, Norman, Alan (574 appearances and 1104 wickets), John and Andy, (well over four decades of continuous service on the Management Committee), have helped the family clock up aggregated service of close to two hundred years.

> Snippets taken from *Parkfield Liscard CC Centenary brochure 1907-2007*... The facilities in the old wooden pavilion (burnt down in 1977, replaced in 1982 and extended in 1997) were very basic. Pre-match, water had to be carried from the tap outside the public toilets some distance away and there was no gents loo in the pavilion. Using the 'jug' saved time!... Some notable success in the Cheshire Cup in 1978 when they defeated Irby and then Cheadle before succumbing to Bowdon. The following year they beat Hyde in the same competition.... On 24 August 1986 Parkfield entertained St Mary's College Old Boys in a Sunday friendly match and spectators witnessed a second wicket partnership of 317 between Dave Hadden (200 not out) and Mark Wilkie (132). For the record Parkfield declared at 386-2 and dismissed SMCOBs for 140.... Amongst the most memorable and enjoyable episodes in Parkfield's history were the cricket matches against Everton FC played in the 1980s through until 1991. The fixtures gave the club tremendous publicity in the local press and radio and were always well attended. In 1987 the club entertained Joe Mercer as a guest and persuaded Granada TV to report on the match as part of their local evening news coverage. Over the period Kevin Ratcliffe, Peter Reid, Adrian Heath, Gary Stevens, Trevor Steven, John Bailey, Alan Harper, Dave Watson, Mick Lyons and Terry Darracott all played, as did local hero Derek Mountfield, who had played for Parkfield for a couple of seasons as a teenager. A classic half century by manager Howard Kendall, a talented cricketer, plus a hostile fast bowling spell from goalkeeper Martin Hodge and a superb century from Ian Snodin linger in the memory of those Evertonians standing beyond the boundary. And finally a question – Against which team did Gary Lineker make his Everton debut? No, not Manchester United, Arsenal or Chelsea but Parkfield CC! Lineker played in the annual fixture on 17 July 1985 within days of signing for Everton! For the players' protection from well-meaning fans and autograph hunters the matches were played at New Brighton and Wallasey CC.

Port Sunlight

Leverhulme Fields, Green Lane, Bromborough CH62 3PU

THE NINETEENTH century Port Sunlight village created in 1888 by William Hesketh Lever for his soap factory workers is, arguably, the finest surviving example of early urban planning in the UK. It remains today much as it was a hundred years ago and it was within this very village that the roots of the cricket club were laid. In 1924 Port Sunlight CC was founded out of their previous inter-departmental factory and office teams.

Tucked away in the pavilion is a lovely old cup revealing the early winners of the Port Sunlight Recreations Association Cup.

    1920 Engineering
    1921 Planters
    1922 Head Office
    1923 Soaperies
    1924 Planters
    1925 Soaperies
    1926 Time & Wages

Cricket was originally played within the village at Poolbank, but from the very early days they regarded home as the Bebington Oval (see Merseyside Sports & Cultural CC) where, at the time, the pitch was regarded as one of the best on Wirral.

The club became founder members of the Merseyside Competition in 1937. They were a very strong outfit and in 1939 both the 1st and 2nd XIs won their respective divisions. Their strength can be demonstrated by the fact that Cheshire selected one of their number. David Leonard 'Len' Hughes made five appearances for the County team in 1939 and in seven innings scored 197 runs with a top score of 84. Born in Rhos-on-Sea and educated at Rydal School, he also represented Wales as an amateur footballer. In that 1939 season he scored 658 runs in only seven completed innings for an average of 94 and a top score of 165. Surviving records show C Colwell averaged over 50 and also collected 30 wickets, RE Cash also averaged more than 50 and H Taylor took 51 wickets at 10.49.

In 1947 another factory player turned out for the County team. Ernie Richards was selected for two matches. He scored 12 runs in two innings, claimed two wickets and two catches and although his stay at this level was brief he continued to play for Port Sunlight CC for many years and is generally recognised as their greatest all-rounder ever. In 1952 he helped them win the very strong Merseyside Competition again, with other valuable contributions from Roy Rowlands and Brian Harris under the captaincy of Jack Bewley.

In 1965 the club moved to their current home at the Leverhulme sports field, but within five years Lever's had severed their link with the club. It was now an open club, but at one time it was a condition that 80% of their players worked for the company and many Lever pensioners used to pay a shilling a year to receive a fixture card and become an honorary member. In 1983 the Council assumed responsibility for the maintenance of the ground, but don't be fooled into thinking the playing surface is sub-standard.

Former player and long-serving groundsman Gary Bland is very proud of his pitches and rightly so.

Coming right up to date Port Sunlight has had a remarkable rise up the Cheshire pyramid. Starting in 2012 they have been runaway champions of their respective division for five consecutive years and in 2017 they performed creditably in Division 1 of the Cheshire League.

When you are in the area it would be very remiss of you not to see the splendid housing in the Port Sunlight Village. A walk around the acreage along with a visit to the Lever Art Gallery and the Sunlight Museum is a very rewarding experience.

The Port Sunlight sports field foundation stone

Pott Shrigley

Shrigley Road, Pott Shrigley SK10 5RT

WITH SOME very liberal interpretation 'Shrigley' derives from two Old English words: 'Scric', a mistle thrush, and 'leah', a woodland glade. 'Pott' was the name given to a hollow formed by streams of the steep sided valleys tumbling off the moors.

When the club was celebrating its 75th Anniversary in 1994 little did it appreciate the difficulties immediately ahead. Access to the ground had been challenged by the new owners of the adjoining farm and a gate was erected across the entrance. In a 190 page book entitled *Gone to Pott*, long-standing club member Derrick Brooke tells the full story about how the 'right of way' was subsequently, and painfully, secured. The story made the national headlines and was covered for *Sky Sports* by Paul Allott.

1919 - Pott Shrigley was founded when there was a post-war upsurge in forming and reforming clubs and societies. Colonel Lowther was approached with a view to occupying part of his estate. One shilling a year was paid for the use of an area rather smaller than the existing site which had originally been part of an old golf course.

1928 - Against Adlington, Pott recorded their highest ever score of 129 and Walter Hough hit the club's first individual score of

> The *Macclesfield Courier & Herald* of 24 July 1920 reported – Pott Shrigley met the Manchester Ramblers last Saturday. The score was Pott Shrigley 53 and Manchester Ramblers 42. The weather was favourable and there was a good gathering of spectators. There will be no cricket today (Saturday) being the Wakes.

over 50. He actually contributed 54 and then took 5-26, sending the opposition back for 62. In 1931 he bowled six Higher Poynton batsmen with six consecutive deliveries. All told he took 9-4. Pott Shrigley won the league for the third consecutive year.

1936 - Minor clubs were struggling to survive in the 1930s and the 'Hillmen' issued a press release - 'Rumours that Pott Shrigley CC had approached Bollington CC to be absorbed into their club and become a Bollington 3rd XI are officially denied. More efforts will be made to raise money to put the club on a more secure basis. Meanwhile, work to improve the ground will continue in the hope

> In the 1950s one of the first jobs that Joe Higginbotham did was to extend and improve the square. He killed off the worms on the square by spreading one hundredweight of lead arsenic. "If we chuck this in the 'Trentabank' we'll kill half the population of Macclesfield!" "When there was unresolved debate about upgrading the pavilion, ten of us went up to the ground, put a rope around it, pulled the thing down and burned it!"

10 years. The amusing article recounted a 2nd XI fixture with Lindow and pictured the Pott XI as muscle-rippling 'Hillmen' trooping onto the turf. The game see-sawed back and forth and eventually Lindow won off the final ball of the match, the descriptive report making the point that as long as cricket was played in such a way the game had nothing to fear.

1968 - Joined the Cheshire Club Conference.

1971 - The Parish Council purchased the ground.

1995 - The *Macclesfield Express* reported that Blackburn Rovers and England footballer Graham Le Saux and Lancashire and England cricketer Graham Fowler were among the stars lined up to appear in the 75th anniversary match.

2015 - With an ECB grant of £50000 the pavilion frontage was given a stylish facelift. A delightful little ground, but be sure to visit on a sunny day. It gets cold in these parts!

that the Adlington & District League will be reformed.'

1949 - Joined the North Cheshire Cricket Division.

1958 - A new pavilion was opened (but it was not until 1976 that flush toilets and electric lighting arrived). By 1959 a 2nd XI had been formed. An offer to buy the ground was rejected.

1966 - The figure of a 'Hillman' was adopted on the club crest following an article in the *Daily Express* claiming cricket would be dead within

> When Pott played Styal, the opposition needed a six off the final ball to win the match. The ball was hit to deep mid-off, which should only have resulted in a single being scored when the fielder sensibly under-armed the ball back towards the bowler. In the event it was intercepted by the mid-off fielder and recklessly thrown to the wicketkeeper, who, anticipating victory, was removing his gloves. Fine leg managed to stop it going to the boundary, but his wild return throw only added to the confusion. While all this was going on five runs were acquired and the match tied!

Poynton

London Road North, Poynton SK12 1AG

IT IS DIFFICULT to imagine the days when Poynton was a small village with a thriving coal mine. In the nineteenth century mining provided a living for a good number of its residents. Agriculture was also important and many ladies and girls were employed in local cotton and silk mills. The coal mine closed in 1935.

The origins of the cricket club go back to the support that Lord Vernon, the owner of Poynton Colliery, gave the game. There is evidence of cricket being played in 1872, when Lord Vernon made part of his grounds available for matches, but the exact date of change from a colliery team (originally known as Poynton Vernon) to a club team is uncertain but taken to be 1885. In the early days the cricketers played on a rota basis due to the underground shift patterns. In 1873 thirty-one different men played in three consecutive matches. In 1879 the *Stockport Advertiser* printed the first Poynton scorecard. The home team scored 108 and Marple were dismissed for 57.

1889 - A local appeal for a pavilion raised £80. St George's Church magazine promoted the appeal, 'The building will be an ornament to the village, and a great encouragement to those striving to provide innocent amusement for the villagers in their leisure hours'.

By the start of the 20th century the club was firmly established as a part of Poynton village life and other sports were being offered. The bowling green was completed in 1907 and in the same year lacrosse was demonstrated on the cricket outfield. By 1912 some of the cricketers decided to try their hand at tennis and two grass courts were laid.

1914-18 - Cricket virtually ceased during WW1 although one or two matches were arranged, including one in 1916 for the benefit of wounded soldiers who were at nearby Barlow Fold (a fine house built in 1844 by Lord Vernon for his Estate Manager) which had been converted to a war hospital.

1924 - Some of the cricketers formed a hockey section, but within two years a sombre mood was brought about by the miners' long strike of 1926, which hit the village particularly hard. The club found itself in severe difficulties in maintaining both its facilities and its membership.

1926 - Although he was playing for Bramhall at the time of his selection for Cheshire, Ernest

Frosch was a Poynton boy who had played for his local club along with his brother, Bernard. Unfortunately his Minor County career was short-lived. Playing against Staffordshire in 1926 at the Oval, Wallasey he was twice out for a duck and in a return match at Wolstanton a week later he made 0 and 9. The legendary Sydney Barnes snared him three times. He never played again. He died in Poynton in 1971, aged 73.

1939-45 - During the war the club facilities were made available to the RAF based at Handforth and, latterly, to the Americans who caused mild consternation by playing baseball on the cricket pitch. In 1943 the club pony, which was used for pulling the roller, was sold, never to be replaced.

1948 - The Annual General Meeting, much to the consternation of the local clergy, voted for Sunday play by 18 to 16 votes. The Revd JGS Winstanley resigned from his long-standing membership.

1956 - The ground was secured for a bargain price of £2000.

1962 - Poynton played in the Derbyshire & Cheshire league between 1953 and 1966* and a high point was achieved in this particular season when both the 1st and 2nd XIs won their respective competitions. The 1st XI were led by Donald J Smith, a former Cambridge Blue (1955-57) and Cheshire player (1952-71), who caused some consternation by using just three bowlers for virtually the whole season - himself, Mike Eyre and Ian Brookes. The following year the 1st XI title was retained and the JA Thompson Knock-Out trophy won. (*Poynton played in the Manchester Association 1923-1952 and the Lancashire & Cheshire League 1967-1980 before joining the Cheshire County League in 1981).

1978-80 - Celebratory cricketers abound. A David 'Bumble' Lloyd benefit match attracted a crowd of 2000, and then in 1979 Sri Lankan, Siddath Wettimuny (23 Test appearances between 1982-87) was enlisted as a professional and helped the club secure the coveted Walkden Cup. In 1980 Duleep Mendis (subsequently a Sri Lankan captain) was signed up. Hereabouts, Steve Smith, later to become the England Rugby Union captain, played 1st XI cricket and was a very useful batsman.

1980s - The early 1980s saw four teenagers break into the first team and Brian Kingham, Steve Douglas, Ian Middlehurst and David Watkins went on to dominate Poynton cricket for the next quarter century. All are now retired, in Brian's case after 32 seasons in the 1st XI, where he amassed over 17000 runs. He was nominated as the Cheshire County League, Division 1 Player of the Year in 2008.

1995 - Unquestionably the most successful season in this club's history as Poynton headed the Cheshire County League top division as well as lifting the Cheshire Cup and, for good measure, the Stockport KO Cup. Andy Greasley won the League's Player of the Year award when he captured 76 wickets in the season. The U17 team were also very strong at this time. They won the John North Cup in 1994 and 1996.

Ladies' cricket has had an important place in Poynton cricket and a number of Cheshire players have emerged, but none have done better than Jenny Halstead, who at the age of 19 was called up to the England A squad. The Ladies XI were Cheshire West Division 1 champions in 2009.

Over the years the large clubhouse has undergone significant change and continues to offer a wide range of social events and sporting opportunities.

Brian Kingham

Prestbury

The Village, Prestbury SK10 4DG

MENTION PRESTBURY CC and I immediately think of Julian Cheetham, who, in the 1990s, crashed the ball around that charming ground, tucked behind the butcher's shop in the High Street, with fierce regularity. There will be plenty of other local cricketers who with stinging fingers will have a similar recollection. He could play alright!

Vital club history is often displayed on clubhouse walls and a framed scorecard and an account of a particular match against Irby reveals a surprising outcome. It reads… On 22 July 2000 the Prestbury 1st XI were scheduled to travel to Irby, already runaway leaders of that year's Division 1. A combination of circumstances that weekend meant that Prestbury were only able to raise a team of eight, of whom only four could be described as regular first team players. Dismissing the possible offer of a forfeit, Irby insisted that the fixture be fulfilled regardless (no doubt expecting the near certain collection of maximum points). And so, like lambs to the slaughter, the eight men of Prestbury duly set off across the plains of Cheshire for what would surely be a mismatch of epic proportions.

Wary of chasing leather for 45 overs, (additional fielders were rightly not offered), Prestbury were delighted when stand-in skipper Hope won the toss and duly elected to bat, with openers Ganguly and Hope both grafting hard to make fifties, well supported by Leigh with a battling 28 at number four. They scrambled to a semi-respectable score of 141-3 and secured three batting bonus points. Prestbury enjoyed their tea safe in the knowledge that whatever happened thereafter they had avoided the anticipated humiliation.

Taking to the field with a bowler, a wicketkeeper and a ring of six, Prestbury looked to bowl a tight line and length and build whatever pressure they could on the Irby openers. Before long a wicket fell, and then another. With every man fielding like two (or three in Roberts' case) wickets continued to tumble with only Irby's captain (Mike Newman) seeming to offer notable resistance. Delighted they had picked up some unexpected bowling points, and seeing that the opposition were perhaps vulnerable, the intensity gradually increased, with Leigh and then Murray bowling with both control and penetration.

The Irby batsmen were now playing nervously – fielders were taking their catches cleanly, stumps were being splayed on a regular basis, and worthy leg before appeals were duly being given. Panic in the Irby ranks even led to a run out as the pressure steadily grew. Seven down (no, surely not), eight down (well, just maybe), nine down (game on!)…

The rest, as they say, is glorious history, with Irby all out for 93 and Prestbury winning by 48 runs. Leigh finished with 6-30 from 15 overs and Murray 3-7 from 3.2. To put this truly incredible victory into context, Irby ended the season as champions of the League, winning 15 of the 21 matches they played and losing only this one fixture. Full marks for their sportsmanship in defeat, with the enduring image being of the Irby skipper arriving in the Prestbury dressing room with a tray of Budweisers, eight, naturally!

The 'Irby Eight' were Mark Hope, Deep Ganguly, Ben Roberts, Rick Leigh, Kevin Murray, Jonathan Davies, Joe Brough and Joe Wells.

Another framed newspaper clipping, this time from the *Macclesfield Express* of 23 July 2014, reports the success of the Prestbury U17s in the County Cup final. After notable wins against Heaton Mersey, Hyde, Marple and Cheadle, they entertained Neston in the final. After their allocation of 18 overs Prestbury had put a total of 137 on the board, but at 52-0 after 8 overs Neston looked to be certain winners. But there is no such thing as a certainty in cricket and Neston found themselves needing 14 runs off the last over. They scored a mere four and finished up 128-9 and Prestbury were crowned as champions, the first team from outside the top section of the Cheshire pyramid to do so for 35 years.

A claimed foundation date of 1872 could justifiably be dragged forward by a year given the existence of an 1871 fixture list. The opening matches were -

> May 13 Bollington (H)
> May 20 Wilmslow (A)
> May 27 Olympic Macclesfield (H)
> June 3 Alderley Edge (A)
> June 10 St Stephens (H)

Can you resist the temptation to wander through this lovely village, perhaps spot the odd celebrity resident, and then nip in to watch the cricket for an hour? Note the electric gates at the entrance to the ground. Now there is another first.

Cheshire's finest

Q: Who has scored the most runs for Cheshire CCC? Who has taken more wickets for Cheshire CCC than anyone else?

A: Those of a certain age will think it's a simple question. The answer is JA (Arthur) Sutton. He played 236 championship matches for the county between 1959 and 1986 and scored 10545 runs and pocketed 435 wickets. Additionally, along with Gerry Hardstaff, he still holds the county record fifth wicket stand. In 1969 at Northwich they shared a partnership of 271 against Shropshire, Sutton 147 not out and Hardstaff undefeated on 143.

Rode Park & Lawton

Knutsford Road, Rode Heath ST7 3QT

TONY LOFFILL'S delightful book *Fifty Years On* (celebrating the 50th anniversary of the North Staffordshire & South Cheshire Premier Cricket League) reveals there are rumours of a document referring to a match between the Gentlemen of Cholmondeley Castle and the Gentlemen of Rode Park in the 1700s. If such unsubstantiated rumours are true, this would set the date of foundation of Rode Park alongside some of the distinguished Surrey and Hampshire clubs who were, undoubtedly, the cradle of the modern game. We shall never know.

What is clear is that Rode Park and Lawton amalgamated after WW2 with Rode Park chosen as the home ground. In 1963 the club was playing in the Cheshire Conference, a haphazard sort of league where clubs arranged their own fixtures at mutually convenient times. In 1977 they joined a breakaway Cheshire Competition (1st Division winners 1982-4) and they subsequently played in the North Staffs & District League (Senior 'A' winners in 1999 and 2001) before progressing into the NS&SC competition.

Back in the 1970s the accommodation was said to consist of three 'chicken' sheds – home, away and teas! Eventually that rudimentary housing was replaced with an old site office, but all this is a far cry from the modern pavilion which now adorns the beautifully picturesque ground within the Rode Hall Estate, the home of the Baker Wilbraham family.

When I visited the ground I was fortunate enough to meet up with Tony Chadwick. He is a former first team captain and a previous chairman of twenty years standing. He joined the club as a 13-year-old and 57 years later is the club President. He introduced me to the bleeding wolf story. The wolf is featured on the club badge. Legend tells how a local forester by the name of Lawton saved King John from being killed by a wolf. As a reward the King promised the forester all the land he could walk over in a week starting at the wolf's body. Lawton took the King at his word and founded his own estate! Tony also told me about club member, Brian Crump, who played county cricket for Northants (1960-72) and made 321 first-class appearances. He was a one-time first team captain and later the groundsman. His daughter, Julie, also played and coached here and represented England Women on two occasions in One Day Internationals. A plaque in the pavilion confirms Brian's cousin, England player David Steele, formally opened the pavilion in 1996.

Despite the superbly upgraded facilities, the lovely setting helps to retain a sense of yesteryear and a dreamy recall of its patrician history. There is a very substantial tree within the boundary at the pavilion end of the ground which adds to the lovely rural scene.

Romiley

Birchvale Drive, Romiley SK6 4LD

THE FOUNDING fathers must be peering down from their celestial vantage point with pride and sheer amazement at today's splendid facilities.

The club was formed in 1898 on the very site it occupies today, but it was a stuttering beginning with an early winding-up and a subsequent re-forming in nearby Sandy Lane. However, by 1912 possession of the land at Birchvale had been secured and the ground was eventually purchased in the 1920s. A pavilion was bought for £6 (surely a snip even a century ago) and a roller for £2 15 shillings. Early pitches were cut with hand shears.

The club was very fortunate to have a Cheshire cricketer within their midst. John Fallows (b 1876, d 1948) was a Romiley resident (he lived at 5 Birchvale Drive) and became club President in 1918 and through his connections he was regularly able to bring a good number of top-class cricketers to his home town club. His son, John Armstrong 'Jack' Fallows (b 1907, d 1974), played for the club as well as representing Cheshire (1929-32). Subsequently he captained Lancashire as an amateur in 1946. At the time his father became the Lancashire Treasurer (1946-48).

> In the late 1940s Stansfield Smith (b 1900, d 1958), having played lots of Lancashire League cricket, came to live in Romiley with his two sons Don (b 1929, d 2004) and Colin (b 1932, d 2013). All three played for Cheshire. During the late forties and early fifties the family were the backbone of the Romiley team. Colin went off to Cambridge University and then played with Lancashire before retiring from the game in 1957 to concentrate on his career as an architect. He was later knighted for his work in the field of architecture. He advised on the development at Lord's Cricket Ground. Colin Smith played 106 first-class matches, scoring 2339 runs. He had a highest score of 103 not out and best bowling figures of 6-35. He took 293 wickets. Don Smith played only three matches for Lancashire. He came back and played at Romiley in the mid-1970s when the club were in the Lancashire and Cheshire League.

In the 1920s and 1930s, Lancashire County Cricket Club would regularly visit Romiley. The Lancashire stars at the time that graced the ground included AC MacLaren, the Tyldesley brothers and George Duckworth, all England cricketers. Four-figure crowds were the norm. On one occasion when Learie Constantine came to the wicket he was bowled first ball. An alert umpire quickly called no ball (!) and he then proceeded to score a century!

1924 - Myles Kenyon, the Lancashire captain (1919-22) and later High Sheriff of Lancashire (1934), was a guest at a social evening and Neville Cardus was appointed a patron of the club. The club decided to run a third team and a ladies' hockey team started to use the ground. In September, after much discussion, the square was re-laid on a bed of ashes. Eleven horse chestnut trees were planted.

1926 - A Bazaar raised a staggering £1424, which was used to pay off loans and invest in the new pavilion.

1972+ - The club resigned from the Derbyshire & Cheshire League and became members of the Lancashire & Cheshire League. There were further moves into the South Lancashire League, the Glossop & District League and then a return to the Derbyshire & Cheshire set up before settling in the Cheshire pyramid in 2010.

Learie Constantine signs autographs at Romiley in 1932

The club has some great facilities, the centrepiece of which is a modern two-level pavilion. There is a splendid collection of photographs and memorabilia displayed to maximum advantage on the stairs and the upper level. The ambitions at this go-ahead club match the facilities, so watch out for further progression.

Neville Cardus was the Cricket Correspondent for the *Manchester Guardian* between the 1920s and the 1960s. In April 1966 he wrote a piece for *Cheshire Life*. He reported that each September the Romiley President hosted a match . "No one could decline an invitation from this perfect gentleman; consequently many a world-renowned player was seen on early autumn Saturdays watched by an attentive crowd." The famous JT Tyldesley was often captain of the challenging team. Cardus continued... "Round about 1920 I was becoming well-known as a writer and JT asked me to join his team. The honour of the invitation overwhelmed me. I bought a new outfit of flannels for the occasion. Alas, when the great day arrived, I awakened in my Fallowfield home to see a sky of inky and torrential rain. It ceased not for a minute. At noon the sky was unbroken, Manchester gloom, and there was no abatement of the rain's downfall. Not for a moment did I think of journeying to Romiley. But on the following Monday, according to custom, I went in the morning to meet Tyldesley for coffee. He was in his usual seat, and when I sat down to join him he abruptly asked 'And where were you on Saturday afternoon?' 'Why, good heavens Johnny,' I said, 'in all that rain? It never entered my head.' He interrupted me, saying with a quite awe-inspiring deliberation, 'You of all people should know that the first duty of a cricketer is to turn up.' I have never forgotten this pronouncement of Tyldesley's (for pronouncement it was, and nothing less). It was a moral injunction, applying not only to undertakings at cricket, but to every intention, promise and activity in the world and life itself."

The following year Cardus was asked to play again... "To my amazement and embarrassment JT asked me to open the bowling. My first five balls were hit for fours, but from the last one the batsman was caught on the boundary. JT then came up to me and said, 'I think I'd best take you off now, before you finish off the game too soon.' He had a pretty irony."

Rostherne

Rostherne Lane, Rostherne WA16 6RY

CRICKET HAS been played in delightful Rostherne for more than a century. The pavilion is quite charming. Not quite a dolls' house but those familiar with the quaint little construction will readily appreciate the comparison. An outsize bat within the pavilion carries a brass plate confirming local resident, the former Lancashire and India wicketkeeper Farokh Engineer, re-opened the pavilion in June 2006. It was not until that refurbishment that water and electricity were added to the facility list.

Chris Bone, who played for the club back in the 1980s, recalled the weekly job of emptying the 'bucket' and shaking the mice droppings out of the tea-cups! He was recruited into a working party that re-painted the pavilion. Green paint was a pre-requisite to comply with the terms of the peppercorn rent agreement.

To appreciate the full beauty of the ground, complete a circuit beyond the boundary rope. Peer over the fence at the opposite end of the ground from the pavilion and admire the magnificent church of St Marys. Listen out for the bells. Parts of the building date back to 1188. It provides a splendid backdrop to the cricket. The impressive Rostherne Mere, away to the right, does likewise. At midwicket is an impressive horse chestnut tree and next to it a lovely strawberry tree (*arbutus unedo*). You'll see plenty of evidence of the resident moles who make regular unwanted appearances in the outfield.

My good friend and umpiring colleague John Bone (no relation to Chris) recalls playing for Hale Barns in the 1980s at Rostherne and classified the changing rooms as 'cosy to intimate'! He has no recall of the match scores, but he vividly remembers there was no bar and the after-match drinking session was in the Swan at Bucklow Hill. At much about the same time he also fondly remembers playing at the same ground in a Sunday friendly match between the Hale Conservative Club and the Hale Wine Bar. Surely this match was not a dry one and a return to the Swan was a near certainty.

The Economists CC now use the ground in midweek. Their origins date from the 1970s when members of the Department of Economics at Manchester University first decided to form a team to play evening friendly games, which they now do in the South Manchester Casual League.

Ken Williams, the understated groundsman, is central to the day-to-day running of the club, Rostherne's Mr Indispensable.

Above: St Mary's church – Below: Rostherne Mere

Runcorn

Moughland Lane, Runcorn WA7 4SD

> The Runcorn website pays tribute to Charlie Bilsborrow for his work as the Runcorn groundsman, but I found another reference to him in the *History of Elworth* when Charlie was keeping wicket for Runcorn, aged 76. The author of the book, Allan Littlemore, was opening the batting with Roy Trewin and the latter told his opening partner in a mid-wicket conference that however he was dismissed he had no intention of being stumped by a septuagenarian! Charlie died aged 88 in December 1979. At one time he was qualifying for Northants, but WW1 put an end to that opportunity and he moved to Warrington to join the police force. I also came across another reference to him in Alan Bolton's *Warrington Cricket 1851-2001*. That document reports he was the Warrington wicketkeeper from the late twenties until almost the end of the Arpley era. It adds that after leaving the police force he became the club's groundsman and coach and that many juniors benefitted from his schooling. It further records even in his late seventies he was still standing up to every bowler, and when he eventually left Warrington it was only to join Runcorn, for whom he played and was still playing when he was eighty!

SANDWICHED BETWEEN a report about the reduction in the number of local vagrants and an advertisement for a hatter, the long-defunct *Runcorn and Widnes Examiner* reported the results of the first known match for Runcorn CC. The year was 1873 and the game was against Everton CC, probably played in Stanley Park, Liverpool. The visitors lost 154 to 29.

Club records include correspondence on a Runcorn CC letterhead dated 1914, but the club did not continue after WW1. Between the Great Wars and beyond, Brunswick, a Sunday School side formed in the 1920s, and St Michael's were the two main sides in the town and it was not until December 1952 that a motion was unanimously carried by the Brunswick Institute & Recreational Club that the team should be renamed Runcorn CC. The reformed club played their first game at Moughland Lane on 25 May 1953 against Winsford. Brunswick had played at that venue since the 1930s and the club are indebted for the kind patronage of the Posnett family, who have been keen supporters of local cricket for many decades.

On the final Saturday of the 2017 season Runcorn secured top spot in their division and in 2018 will proudly take their place as one of the top 36 clubs in the Cheshire pyramid. It was a tense and exciting conclusion to the season at Moughland Lane as they defended a declared total of 158 -8. In reply, at one time the Disley score was 140-1, but they subsided to 151 all out. Runcorn's Sam Rowlands was having his first league bowl of the season and returned figures of 4.3-3-14-6! Saturday night celebrations ensued and Sunday morning sore heads resulted!

> Runcorn golden oldies... Brian Pendlebury, Les Yates, Peter Redican, Frank Pierce, Clive Hooper, Brian Rawlinson, Steve Foster, Robbie Roan, Mike Best, Norman Barton, Rob Beech, David Batty, Andy Bennett, Roy Darlington, Alan Richards, Phil Bennett, Paul Tyrrell, Tony White, Mark Cahill, Andy Booth, Iain Williams, Steve Ollerenshaw and Matt Shaw.

Rylands

Gorsey Lane, Warrington WA2 7RZ

HAVE YOU ever wondered why the official Warrington Wolves Rugby League club badge has the words 'The Wire' incorporated into its design? Warrington residents will consider this to be a very simple question given the town's association with wire-making which lasted for just about two centuries. Rylands was a major employer in the town specialising in the production of chain-link fencing. The factory gates closed for the very last time in 2005.

The existing site was once the Rylands factory sports and social centre. It remains an impressive multi-sports facility. In addition to the cricket it offers excellent football and rugby league surfaces and a range of indoor recreational activities.

Having finished bottom of the Cheshire Alliance Division 1 in 2013, the 1st XI were relegated, but in Division 2 in 2014-15-16 they improved from tenth to third to the runners-up spot. It came as a surprise in early 2017 when the cricket section folded.

By my own 'active club' rule this entry should not be included, but they did exist in the early part of 2017 and the clubhouse is a gem and, surely, deserves to be recorded as a part of the county's cricketing heritage?

Sale

Rookwood, Clarendon Crescent, off Dane Road, Sale M33 2DE

SALE CRICKET Club is recorded as being founded in 1854. The pavilion was a thatched cottage close to the edge of the present square. The ground was expanded to its present size in the late 1940s.

In the early years the club employed a good number of professionals, including William Wotherspoon and John Fullalove who both played for Cheshire in the 1880s. The latter once took 10 wickets, nine bowled, in 1897 for his club. James Cookson (b 1867, d 1956) not only played cricket for Cheshire but also tennis, rugby and hockey.

Sir Edwin Stockton and his brother Albert dominated the club for 40 years from both a cricketing and organisational perspective. Leg spinner Edwin headed the club bowling averages for many years and Albert was a forceful batsman. Albert played for Cheshire while Edwin was the Lancashire CCC Treasurer from 1918 to 1924, President for 1925-26 and then Chairman from 1928 to 1931. He was the MP for Manchester Exchange for one year in 1922-23 and in 1923 he played in a match at the Oval for the House of Commons North against House of Commons South. He opened the batting for the North with future Prime Minister Clement Attlee. Stockton managed a single but Attlee failed to trouble the scorers. When Sale were the first winners of the Manchester Association's Stockton Trophy in 1920, Sir Edwin presented the cup to his brother who was the Sale captain.

Other notable Sale players have included Charles Hartley (b 1873, d 1927), who joined Sale after retiring from first-class cricket with Lancashire. He made 106 first-class appearances for the Red Rose County, scoring four centuries with a highest score of 139. Fred Beattie (b 1909, d 1989) played seven first-class matches for Minor Counties and Lancashire and was captain of Sale in the 1930s, leading the side to a second Stockton Trophy in 1938.

Battle of Britain pilot Alan Gilbert returned to captain the 1st XI with style and success from 1946-51 and again in 1954. Under his leadership Sale won the Stockton Trophy once more in

1947. He was a magnificent wicketkeeper, prolific batsman and respected captain who played for Cheshire from 1951 to 1956. Slightly more recently Sale won the Manchester Association HC Smith Cup at Old Trafford in 1974 under the astute captaincy of Neil Fitton (b 1937, d 2016).

Other notable ex-players include Derek Peaker, Keith Peet, Gordon Cooper and Mike Newton. In 1975 Duncan Smith matched Fullalove's performance when he took all 10 wickets against Ashton-on-Mersey. Glyn Roberts, Sale's longest-serving member, scored no fewer than 6651 runs and took 432 wickets. He joined in 1968 and remains an active member. After his playing days finished Glyn took up umpiring and is now the Cheshire County League Umpires' Secretary. Leigh Burns, a Western Australian, scored a club record 1064 league runs in 1996.

After being founder members of the Manchester Association in 1892, Sale joined the Cheshire County League in 1996, but found itself at a low ebb in the early 2000s. They had no junior section and were relegated to the 4th tier of the pyramid.

The turnaround in fortunes since then, initially under the guidance of Cricket Chairman Rob Moore, has been commendable. In recent years the improvement has continued and there have been substantial contributions from leg-spinner Rick Halkon (610 wickets), brother Dan (3450 runs), Hasan Khan (1972 runs in 2009-10) and Wihan Lubbe (1011 runs in 2012). The last decade has also seen major developments at the club, including the addition of a 4-bay net facility in 2006 and the relaying of the entire cricket square between 2007 and 2008.

Plans are now in train to replace the elderly existing clubhouse and the pavilion with a combined building and improved facilities for all sports played at the club.

From Heswall to Hollywood

It's a long way from Heswall to Hollywood and the journey was never quite the spectacular success envisaged.

The front cover of the December 1985 edition of *The Cricketer* featured, Wirral-born Ian Botham. He was wearing a yellow, red, green and black hooped shirt and a pair of bright yellow joggers embroidered 'Tim Hudson's Hollywood XI'.

Inside the magazine Bridgette Lawrence described her visit to Birtles Hall and the adjoining cricket ground where she interviewed both Ian Botham and 'Lord' Tim Hudson. Earlier in 1985 the man with the self-appointed title had hosted a good number of celebrity matches on his 'field of dreams'. At the time of the writer's visit Botham was sitting for John Bellany's portrait of him, which subsequently hung in the National Portrait Gallery. Presented as 'a folk hero of our times' it contrasts vividly from the formal painting of WG Grace, the only other cricketer honoured by the National Portrait Gallery.

Botham's new pig-tailed colourful agent had great plans to market the leading all-rounder and a late 1985 trip to Hollywood was planned with Viv Richards where he would present them as Ebony and Ivory. He said that Botham had already been offered a starring film role opposite Oliver Reed. Hudson added, 'We realise he's not going to be Lord Olivier but perhaps King of the 'B' movies?' And then President of the United States!

The whole thing quickly fell apart and Botham went off in another direction. Hudson sold up and returned to the USA. The ground was neglected, eventually sold and no longer hosts cricket.

Sandbach

Hind Heath Road, Sandbach CW11 3LZ

ON 18 SEPTEMBER 1886 a Lancashire side played 22 of Sandbach & District. The county team amassed 274-6 and in reply the home team chalked up 73-20 (one absentee and 12 ducks!). This auspicious event might have helped to determine the foundation date of the club even though there are earlier references to matches in the town. One such match was played in July 1879 when Sandbach hosted Crewe Alexandra at the Belle View Terrace ground. The owner of that land entrusted it in his will to William Latham of 'Sandbach Gentlemen'. This was the original name of the club and clearly taken from its private membership of the middle and upper classes. Of course, this elevated status would not preclude the employment of a club professional! The first paid player was P Dannatt and the *Crewe Guardian* records: 'A benefit match was played on 25 August 1894 for the professional. There was a good gate and the proceedings were enlivened by the brass band.'

1932 - Finances were reported to be a serious concern and members were asked to sign guarantees for £10 each as a security on the club's overdraft.

1934 - Previously rented, the club bought the ground for £750. At the time the Secretary, EA Faulkner, regarded the purchase as the most momentous step in the history of the club as it preserved the land as a cricket ground forever. Little did he realise how things might unfold fifty years later.

1937 - Admission charges at the ground increased from 2d to 3d. The Secretary was concerned about the large bank overdraft.

1939 - Ernest Shaw recorded a maiden century against Trentham but found himself batting at number eleven the following week. The captain, H

Harper, was determined to keep the young ones in their place! Discipline was very strict, with a pecking order that had to be observed. The captain's word was law. Heaven help any player who turned up with dirty flannels or boots.

WW2 - Some cricket continued to be played but the pavilion was requisitioned by the military for use as a sergeant's mess, for which the club received a rent of £15. The highlight of the 1945 season was the visit of the Jack Iddon XI to play an augmented club side in aid of the 'Welcome Home' fund. Nineteen well-known cricketers of the day, including Eddie Paynter, George Duckworth, Bill Farrimond and George Pope, all played. Over two thousand spectators watched the match and two hundred guineas was sent to the fund.

1951 - An EGM agreed 'by a considerable majority' to open a licensed bar. Jack Ikin, Lancashire and England, was the annual dinner guest. In the same year the question of Sunday cricket was raised. There was strong opposition and it was not until some 13 years later that the club voted for Sunday cricket 'at the discretion of the committee' and not until 1973 that an official Sunday captain was elected.

1976 - At the annual meeting the chairman mentioned the possibility of the Sandbach inner relief road being built, which would impact on plans to build a new pavilion. However, as government cut-backs had put the highway scheme in jeopardy it was decided to proceed with the building of the new pavilion with loans provided by the Sports Council and Marsden's Brewery.

1980 - A new pavilion was built and the official opening ceremony took place in May against Elworth. Within two years a momentous change was forced upon the club when it became known that a new inner relief road would, after all, be constructed and the club would need to find another home. Negotiations took place to sell the Belle View ground to the council and for Sandbach CC to purchase the Welles Street ground, which in the past had been used by Fodens CC. A sub-committee was formed and after protracted dialogue the deal was finally done in 1982.

Into the new millennium an opportunity to sell the Welles Street ground arose and a new green field site at Hind Heath Road was acquired and a splendid new clubhouse developed. No doubt Mr Faulkner, from his high vantage point, peered down with incredulity?

The Cricketers Arms, Crewe Road, Sandbach

Saughall

Golden Jubilee Park, Fiddlers Lane, Saughall CH1 6DH

RESEARCH BY local historian Ann Stuart reveals that Saughall Cricket Club was formed in 1893. The following summer on 23 June 1894 Saughall played their first ever fixture against a Stoak & Stanney team that included a player called Grace. Surely not a relative of the great doctor? For the record W Bennion was Saughall's hero that day, taking 6 for 14, including a hat-trick, as Saughall opened their long history with a victory. Ann Stuart wrote in her book *Saughall - A Social History* that 'Cricket was always high priority in Saughall and the only sport that has gone uninterrupted through the century'.

For many years Saughall CC played at Sea Hill, a ground which was very close to the border between England and Wales. Some liked to say they hit the ball from one country to another! The Greyhound pub was the club HQ. On Sunday 24 August 2008 Saughall moved to their new ground in the village, Golden Jubilee Park, largely thanks to the tireless efforts of club stalwart Brian Huxley, who fittingly stroked the first run at the new ground. The move to the new ground was delayed by a few years when environmental researchers discovered that the great crested newt resided within a hedgerow at the new site, so a pond was landscaped and 160 new trees planted in order not to affect the habitat of the local wildlife.

Saughall's geographical location has meant that from the 1970s Saughall have played in the Flintshire League and the Wirral League before joining the Cheshire structure.

Star player was former Leicestershire batsman Martin Schepens, who scored 964 runs in 1996 at an average of 74.1 when Saughall were in the Wirral League. Memorably, he once received a delivery from a medium-pacer, which bounced erratically and flew past his nose. He joked, "I didn't wear a helmet against Hadlee or Holding and I'm not starting now". He played his initial first-class match in 1973 and his final one in 1980.

Twins James and Martin Huxley made newspaper headlines in June 2000 when both scored their first centuries in the same match, sharing in a partnership of 213 at home against Prescot. It was featured as a full-page story in the *Daily Mail* on Friday 23 June under the headline 'A one-day record for two-ton twins'. James Huxley also made front-page news in 2005, when in an away fixture at Mossley a bull escaped from a nearby field and chased him around the outfield. The story, 'The day the bull stopped play', made the front page of the *Chester Evening Leader*.

Saughall's long-term plans include a new pavilion.

Proposed pavilion design for Saughall CC

Stalybridge St Paul's

Gorse Hall Road, Dukinfield SK16 5HN

THE ACTION-PACKED final of the 1987 Cheshire Cup kept the sizeable Stalybridge crowd on their toes until the very last ball of the match. Visitors, Birkenhead Park, needed two runs off the final delivery, but managed only a single and ended up on 152-9 (40 overs). The Man of the Match adjudicator was former Cheshire player and the one-time President of the Cheshire County League, Pat Kelly (1958-1977). He nominated Stalybridge's Peter Hemmings for the award, he having contributed 54 with the bat and then snatched two key wickets. Opening the batting for Stalybridge, and a strong contender for the award, was current Cheshire panel and former Minor County umpire John Lofthouse, who made 61 and ran out two of the Birkenhead batters.

> Was George Radcliffe (b 1877, d 1951) the most distinguished of all Stalybridge cricketers? He served the club for 38 years and scored a total of 15326 runs. In 1915 in the Central Lancashire League he scored 1000 runs before the end of July. He was captain for 18 seasons. He played for Cheshire in 1895 and subsequently joined Lancashire CCC. He played seven first-class matches between 1903-06. In 1922, in recognition of his service to the club, he was presented with a smoker's cabinet.

subsequently played in the Denton & District League, the Ashton League and the Glossop League. By 1985 they were based in Mottram, some distance from their original roots, and so when the merger with Stalybridge became an option it was a dream come true for the smaller club, who up until this point could only dream about playing regularly on a senior ground which had hosted Minor County cricket. As Ian Hodgson, the club Secretary at the time, so descriptively put it: "They were three clouds above us".

This match was one of many peaks in the long and distinguished history of Stalybridge CC - they were founded in 1879 - and it is hard to believe that within another dozen years of this fine victory their proud name would no longer stand alone. By 1999 the club had suffered a series of 'irreconcilable issues', and a merger with the St Paul's club proved to be a neat and effective outcome.

Staley St Paul's CC had a rather more modest pedigree, having emerged in 1904 as a summer sporting activity for the Young Men's Institute where in the winter the members played football and various table sports. Having started off in the Stalybridge & District Sunday School League they

The pavilion 1935-style

The newly merged club continued in the Cheshire Cricket League, where Stalybridge had played latterly, but they were subsequently relegated to the Cheshire Alliance. Of course, their easterly location committed them to some long away trips and they eventually decided to join the Derbyshire & Cheshire League, re-joining old friends from the former Glossop competition from 2016. As one travel-weary 2nd XI member said: "Audlem, I don't go that far for me 'olidays!"

The club has now resurrected a junior section and can look forward to a successful future building on the grand past of the former town club. St Paul's church in Staley is a good step away and, ironically and perhaps surprisingly to all but the locals, their Gorse Hall Road base is actually in Dukinfield (just) rather than Stalybridge, but what's in a name?

> The lasses who wait... 'We women provide cheerful, voluntary help for any occasion requiring our special skills and our men welcome such help. It appears this may not have always been the case as there is no mention of ladies in the records until 1906. What were they doing in the first 27 years? It is my belief that the Emily Pankhursts and Keir Hardies of this world finally influenced our cricketing fraternity to accept us as a force to be reckoned with. The realisation dawned on them that the ladies might make valuable allies in the organisation of our club'...
> Cyndy M Stokes, 1979

Stayley

Oxford Road, Millbrook, Stalybridge SK15 3JJ

OVER THE Hill by way of Highmoor, written by Phil Taylor, tells the story of the history of the Saddleworth League. It was published in 1998 to coincide with the centenary of the League's formation. The author suggests there is evidence to indicate that Stayley Mills, which had its origins in the 1860s, was the predecessor of what became Stayley CC. Conclusively, the last mention of Stayley Mills CC was on 1 June 1878 and the first record of Stayley CC on 8 June of the same year.

1892 - The North Derbyshire and Stockport League was formed and Stayley had their first taste of league cricket by becoming founder members. A mere seven years later they were founder members of the Saddleworth League and in their first season of the competition in 1899 they finished eighth out of nine. For reasons which I have not been able to establish Stayley were the first Saddleworth League team to resign at the end of the 1902 season, but re-joined for the 1904 season.

1936 - The *Oldham Evening Chronicle* reported on a match played between Mr Tanner's XI, which was a League representative team, and the 'Yorkshire County team' played at Greenfield CC. The star-studded visitors included, under the captaincy of Brian Sellers, Wilfred Rhodes, Herbert Sutcliffe, Cecil Parkin and Len Hutton. J Goulder of Stayley would have been thrilled to have been selected for such a prestigious match and the scorebook records he held two catches, but he is a 'no show' in a list of thirteen batsmen.

1962 - A new batting record was established when Harry Pilling (b 1943, d 2012) scored 1034 runs in the season. In the front of Phil Taylor's book he wrote a congratulatory piece on the league reaching its centenary and fondly recalled being brought through the ranks at Stayley along with his good friend, Stalybridge-born John Sullivan (b 1945, d 2006). They both went on to have successful Lancashire careers.

1963 - Syd Baker was one of the best all-rounder cricketers in the area. He had a spell at Stayley but he was best associated with Flowery Field, and he certainly had no sympathy for his former team in the Tanner Cup final. He finished with match figures of 60 and 7-64, but still ended up on the losing side! Stayley 173, Flowery Field 168. This was a good year for Stayley as they also won the top division of the Saddleworth League.

1978 - A remarkable coincidence occurred in the home and away matches between Stayley and Newton Heath. In May, Stayley were dismissed for 39 and in August they recorded the same meagre score in the away fixture!

Some might be surprised to see Stayley CC included, but Millbrook, where the ground is located, was part of Stalybridge Municipal Borough

Stayley's unusual ornate clock

until the 1974 boundary changes. In the first year of the new Pennine League (2016), formed by the merger of the Saddleworth League and the Central Lancashire League, Stayley won promotion to the Premier Division, a position they consolidated in 2017.

FIRST CLASS CAREERS							
	Matches	Runs	HS	100/50	Ct	Wkts	B/B
Harry Pilling	333	15279	149no	25/81	89	1	1-42
John Sullivan	154	4286	81no	-/18	85	76	4-19

Stockport

Beech Road, Cale Green, Stockport SK3 8HD

OVER THE years all clubs suffer peaks and troughs, but perhaps Stockport have experienced the extremes more than most?

One source suggests that the club played the Gentlemen of Stockport in 1852. No matter, by 1869 it seems likely there were three clubs in the town – Stockport, Charlestown and Cheadle Mosley. It is said that the then Stockport President suspected his club sent out 'quislings' to infiltrate the others in order to bring them down! There may well be some truth in that statement as before long they all amalgamated and played on a ground in Charles Street, High Hillgate and later in Greek Street.

Displayed in the pavilion are the 1855 'Rules'

Rule 9 That naval and Military Officers quartered in Stockport be considered Honorary members.

Rule 12 That members appointed to play in a match appear in the recognised costume of the club, viz, white flannels, trousers and shirt and blue cap.

Rule 13 That the eleven elect their captain at the commencement of the game and regard obedience to him throughout it.

In 1876 and 1877 a Stockport and District side, including AN 'Monkey' Hornby, entertained a South of England team, who counted WG Grace amongst its number, and only a year later the touring Australians formed the opposition. In 1880 they returned with a team which included Murdoch, Bannerman and Bonner. Stockport 132 & 156, Australia 70 & 118. To this day the ball used in that match sits in a case in the Committee Room.

All this was before the club moved to its present home at Cale Green in 1883. The detail of its acquisition is hazy, but some say it was donated by a former mayor of the town whose only condition was that the club should contribute towards the cost of laying out the ground.

Having been founder members of the Manchester Association it was not an easy decision to join the Central Lancashire League in 1937. Any regrets soon faded as they won that competition in 1941 and retained it the following year. Although the 2nd XI won their division 13 times between 1937 and 1971, the senior team had a lean time from

Stockport CC 1904

1942 until the 1960s. Although the club did not win any honours, in 1955 they employed the great Australian all-rounder Colin McCool (1024 runs & 107 wickets) and in 1956 the charismatic Indian Test player Vinoo Mankad joined and stayed for four seasons.

> Writing in *The Cricketer* in 1970 Rachael Heyhoe described the National Club Knockout final between Stockport and Cheltenham at Lord's as... 'a thriller worthy of Agatha Christie's pen. Cheltenham, the underdogs, were chasing Stockport's 169-4, of which the Indian Test batsman Ashok Mankad hit 83 not out, needed a four to win off the last ball of the match. Locke, Cheltenham's number eight, unleashed a mighty hook and scattered the voluble Tavern crowd with a thunderous six. Once his shot had soared Tavernwards he hurled his bat to the heavens and Chris Coley, his batting partner, emulating a footballer's amorous intentions, swept him off his feet!'

> 1989 - An amazing transformation. At 45-years-old Bob Cooke, one time of Essex CCC, decided to part company with Bramhall and join Stockport as captain. With financial help available from Jungheinrich Fork Lift Trucks, he persuaded Steve Wundke to move from Bacup and then pulled off the *coup de grace* signing of Ian Tansley, who had taken the captaincy at Cheadle. With the strong side he had put together the rest is history. As Rex Pogson wrote in *The Cricketer* magazine... 'It is unfair to blame a side for being too strong but the truth remains that Stockport's obvious superiority took a lot of the interest out of the season.'

Success came in 1966 when Stockport swept all before them and lifted both the Central Lancashire League title as well as the Wood Cup.

The Cenotaph at Stockport CC was erected after the First World War to honour those 16 club members who gave their lives between 1914 and 1918, and a further inscription was added to commemorate the two members who died in the Second World War. The memorial is a stone pillar sited at the north east corner of the ground. The memorial includes the following verse as well as the names of all the members who gave their lives in combat.

SONS OF THIS PLACE LET THIS OF YOU BE SAID
THAT YOU WHO LIVE ARE WORTHY OF YOUR DEAD
THESE GAVE THEIR LIVES THAT YOU WHO LIVE MAY REAP
A RICHER HARVEST ERE YOU FALL ASLEEP

Reverend T E Royde

Before the first game of each season a wreath is laid on the steps of a cenotaph by the club chairman and the home captain and thereafter a one-minute silence is observed in memory of those who gave their lives for their country.

Stockport Georgians

Cromley Road, Woodsmoor, Stockport SK2 7DT

THE CLUB quotes 1923 as the year in which it was founded. The actual date is likely to be a little earlier but remains unknown as all pre-war cricket club records were lost when the secretary of the time, AM Findley, was killed by an enemy bombing raid while in barracks at HMS Raleigh, Plymouth.

The club originates from St George's church in Heaviley, which was built in 1897. It would seem that over the next 20 years or so various sporting clubs and groups, including cricket, were set up by the parishioners. At a meeting held at the church in 1923 there began a series of meetings which led to the formation of St George's Athletic Club, which was to incorporate the cricket, football, tennis, hockey, scouts and guides sections. It would seem that the purpose of the Athletic Club was to provide a single structure and to seek out and purchase some land on which the various sections could settle. This was achieved in 1924 when the current ground, or as it was then 'Field 73', was purchased for £981 with loans secured from parishioners.

The cricket club clearly predates 1923 as it was first mentioned in Athletic Club minutes in that year as having a committee and a debt! It also seems likely that the club played occasional friendlies against other church or workplace teams on the playing fields adjacent to the current ground or actually on the current ground, which may have been used on a rental basis prior to purchase.

Before the war, all matches were classified as friendly games and played against local companies or other religious groups. It was a condition of membership that players were affiliated to the St George's Church Men's Society. That clause was relaxed in 1955.

Straight after the war the club entered a competitive league for the first time and a new square was laid in its current position. Also at this time, current Treasurer and President Gerald Bailey began his unbroken association with the club. He recalls going along to the ground with his father, Charlie, a member of the side who at that time played in the Stockport & District League. Facilities were sparse and he remembers water having to be wheeled to the ground in a water cart from the nearest house 200 metres away and the pavilion being made up of a series of oddly-shaped wooden huts connected end to end. The outfield was usually cut a couple of times a season!

A 'new' pavilion was procured and built in 1962. Post-war Ministry of Defence pre-fabricated houses were being sold off locally and a sealed bid of £35 secured one. Members rallied to lay a concrete base and re-construct the building in readiness for admission into the High Peak League. The club has been extended and refurbished many times, but a number of concrete panels and the original roof trusses still remain, although now shrouded in latter-day progress.

1963 - The club achieved independence from the church and St George's CC became Stockport Georgians.

1969 - In the days when footballers were mere mortals, the Stockport County centre forward, Jim Fryatt, played for the club during the summer. He was profoundly deaf but was an excellent cricketer and records showed he won the Single Wicket crown.

> **In 1964 Jim Fryatt, playing for Bradford Park Avenue against Tranmere Rovers, scored a goal after four seconds. It remains a Football League record.**

1973 - The club left the High Peak League and joined the Lancashire and Cheshire League. More significantly the club began its proud tradition of junior cricket in earnest.

1979 - The investment in junior cricket really started to show dividends as the U13s came third in the National finals at Sherborne School having won the Cheshire competition and the regional final at Old Trafford. Ex-FA Cup semi-finalist and League Cup finalist, goalkeeper Jon Hallworth (Oldham and Ipswich), was part of that very talented side.

The Stockport Georgians' gates

1986 - Mike Atherton, who had already made his Lancashire 2nd XI debut, played at Georgians for Woodhouses but didn't get a bat or bowl! In 1995 ex-Pakistan all-rounder Mudassar Nazar (Cheshire 1980-88) graced the ground and scored 150* in the Bolton total of 233-3 (40 overs). This chanceless knock has widely been recognised as the best-ever innings seen on the ground. A good Georgians side replied with 214, narrowly missing out on the Lancashire Cup final which was to be played at Old Trafford.

1991 - The club escaped an arson attack on the pavilion. Happily the fire was extinguished before it took hold and the frontage and the roof were repaired.

1994 - An acrimonious split with the Lancashire & Cheshire League. A move to the Manchester Association resulted and there they stayed until they joined the Cheshire pyramid in 1999.

1999 - A successful season as the club proudly opened its new pavilion and gained promotion to Division 1 of the Cheshire County League in its first season. The construction of the new pavilion enabled the space in the old pavilion to be re-worked and extended into the excellent social space it is now.

Stockport Georgians have always been a forward-looking club and it continues to develop year by year. At the forefront of this has been its commitment to and growth in junior cricket. The club currently boasts over 180 juniors and ten teams, including two girls' teams, playing in thirteen competitions. There is a conveyor belt of good players heading through to the Cheshire youth system and into the club's senior teams.

2015 saw the club self-fund an excellent new extension to the bar area, which in turn has greatly increased revenues. Most recently the club was able to overhaul and upgrade its scorebox to a fully electronic one and on the field to form its first Women's senior team in 2016. Playing on Sundays it successfully negotiated its first season, further strengthening the club's place in the community whilst adding further depth and members to what is already a vibrant, hard-working club.

The Bailey family

There has been a thread running through the club's post-war history and it is the name 'Bailey'. There have been four generations playing in the senior sides at the club. It is fair to say that Stockport Georgians would not be where it is today, and maybe not in existence, without a lifetime contribution from Gerald Bailey. He was the second Bailey at the club following his father, Charlie, around 1954.

He is now better known as President and Treasurer, but in his day he was an excellent opening bat who scored many runs over a long career. He would have scored more too but his cricket season was often foreshortened by his appearances as a Football League official.

His eldest son, Trevor, is now the club chairman and junior organiser. His youngest son, Hayden, coaches the Under 9s as well as maintaining and developing the excellent playing surface at the ground.

Between them they have scored comfortably in excess of 35000 senior runs, Hayden being the most prolific with 14500 1st XI runs... and still counting.

Stockport Trinity

Highfield Road, off Grange Road, Stockport SK7 3BE

TRINITY CRICKET Club was formed in 1923. It took its name from the nearby Trinity Methodist church which owned the land. In 2012, the club prefixed its original name with 'Stockport' to identify more closely with its locality.

On the original tithe map of North East Bramhall, drawn in 1842, you will find two adjacent plots appropriately named 'Nearer Priest Field' and 'Great Marlfield'. Appropriately named because it is there that Trinity Methodist Church Cricket and Tennis Club was built and, in the north end corner of Great Marlfield, is a pond which was originally a marl pit. The cricket club has suffered with drainage difficulties due to the depth of clay for its whole existence.

The plot was purchased by the Trustees of the Church in 1923 and a cricket pitch and tennis courts were erected together with a wooden pavilion. The cricket club competed in the High Peak Cricket League while the tennis section played only socially and ceased in the late 1950s as the state of the courts gradually declined.

The wooden pavilion was rudimentary in the extreme, although nobody seemed bothered by the primitive facilities in those days. The building provided two small changing rooms, a tea area and kitchen. There was no electricity and gas powered the small stove in the kitchen and provided light via

1923-75	High Peak League
1976-77	Cheshire Conference
1978-85	South Lancashire
1986-99	Glossop League
2000 >	Cheshire League or Alliance

gas mantles. Toilet facilities were of the chemical variety. Stewart Coates, the current Chairman, can vividly recall his job of emptying the two of them and at the end of the season having to dig a hole deep enough to take the contents. The ladies' loo was housed in a converted garden shed with windows, some very old net curtains and a large population of spiders. However, the windows faced away from the playing area so ladies could not keep up with the progress of the game while seated even if the spiders did not scare them away! The gents' toilet was in an area of the pavilion reached by an outside door and with sufficient room for only the slimmest of players! There was a urinal at the rear of the club which drained to a soakaway and which, in the hot dry days of summer, gave off a distinctly unpleasant smell! The pavilion remained largely unaltered throughout its sixty-seven year life.

It was only in 1990 that a new pavilion was built, but for a club with only two male teams and one junior side, grant aid was limited and the present clubhouse was built with a grant of £5000 from the Sports Council and a gift of £3000 from Trinity Methodist Church, which provided for almost 50% of the cost of materials, the rest being raised, gifted or loaned by members. The herculean efforts of Barry Ashton, with support from Derek Hatt, Stewart Coates and other members, enabled the new pavilion to be erected at a cost of a little over £16000, complete with electricity, running water and modern loos.

Like all other clubs they have had their fair share of characters and Bernard 'Sunny Boy' Selby was one such member. Bernard was one of four Selbys to play for Trinity, along with brothers George and Bill and nephew Paul. He gained the nickname of 'Sunny Boy' as he was regularly brought on to bowl his very slow right-arm spin from the Highfield Road end as the sun went down behind his arm. Bernard would bowl his 'moon ball', to which he gave plenty of air, as the

Current chairman Stewart Coates

batsman, blinded by the light, groped for the ball. The more discerning umpires would halt play until the sun had slipped below the rooftops, but most did not and Bernard captured many a wicket in the latter stages of the game while Reg Hardie captured plenty at the other end as batsmen tried to blink away the spots before their eyes. The local newspaper, *The Green Final*, in a match round-up, accused 'Sunny Boy' of sharp practice and the following week published a letter from him in which he denied the allegation. He, indignantly, pointed out that unless three of his victims had some magical radar interception apparatus they must have seen the ball well enough given they whacked it to the boundary where they were caught, and a fourth batter was clearly untroubled as he asked the umpire to hold his cap!

BATTING AND BOWLING RECORDS

Best batting (Men)	166	Brian Cheetham	v Newton Hurst	1979
Best batting (Ladies)	155*	Hannah Gradwell	v Hyde	2012
Best bowling (Men)	10-43	Reg Hardie	v Moorfield	1974

Stretton

Pewterspeare Green, Beamish Close, Stretton WA4 5RL

THE CRICKET ground is alongside the A49 and clearly visible from that busy road, but the main entrance is through the executive houses that make up the Pewterspeare estate. The route is a bit like one of those maze puzzles in a children's fun book – avoid all the cul-de-sacs and you'll eventually arrive in the well-appointed car park. Probably!

The land was handed over to the Pewterspeare Trust in 1995, who now ensure the substantial acreage is sensitively managed right across the housing development, the sporting facilities and the woodland areas.

The ground was laid out in the mid-1990s and the first matches were played in 1997. The team was built around one that had previously played in the grounds of Arley Hall, but recruitment of new players burgeoned as the new houses began to be occupied. A portakabin was quickly replaced by a pavilion built with the support of national lottery funding through Sport England. A flourishing junior section was soon established and Rob Jones, now of Lancashire CCC, was a member of the U9 team in the early 2000s. Dave Hill, now known to many as an excellent contracting groundsman, was a driving force behind the club at the outset and, indeed, for many years and in 2005 Tim Mullins won the Warrington Guardian Unsung Hero award for his efforts. Latterly, hard-working Iain Hill has been at the helm.

The church of St Matthew's inquisitively peers over the trees. The church tower has a clock on two elevations and those spectators wandering the boundary, and with 20/20 vision, will notice there are not numbers but letters on its face. The elevation facing the cricket green spells out 'Forget Not God' and the other one 'Time is not all'.

Stretton is less than two miles from Appleton CC, so when the two clubs play each other there is plenty of opportunity to establish the current dominant force. Both played in Division 3 of the Cheshire League in 2017. Stretton were the runaway champions and so hold the crowing rights for at least the next year.

The Stretton clock tower

Styal

Altrincham Road, Styal SK9 4JE

THOSE OF A certain age (and now in receipt of a state retirement pension!) might recall a smaller playing area to that which is available today. Away to the left of the pavilion the outfield is rather deeper than in the 1960s and over by the Ship Inn car park there has been some boundary expansion. Do you recall the bowling green which was located in an area which is now the pub car park? There were also three trees within the field of play, one remains but the other two were removed in the 1970s and 2009.

In those heady days of the 1960s and 70s three particular names stand-out. Tony (William Anthony Davenport) Riley, known to everybody as 'WAD', made an enormous contribution over more than 50 years. He was Chairman and President for a lengthy period and is still a strong supporter of the club. Whenever machinery or general repairs needed attention Tony was the 'go to' man. Mr Fixer extraordinaire! He was a key figure when the pavilion was extended and an important negotiator when the provision of a bar was a contentious issue. The Greg family left the land for the use of local sports back in the 1880s and in late 1950s a descendant, Harry Greg, funded the building of a pavilion, but he was very insistent there would be no bar. He was eventually persuaded by Tony and others that beer and wine (but not spirits) could be sold through a serving hatch. In 1975 Tony built the current bar, but his contribution was not just confined to off-field activity. In his day he was a pugnacious hitter, once hitting a young, fast bowler for two sixes in the opening over of a match. Tony's father and grandfather were previous chairmen of the club.

Another star personality was John North. His contribution to cricket, of course, extended way beyond Styal. A much-loved character, he had a long playing career which culminated in a match at Bramhall in 2007 to coincide with his 75th birthday celebration. In 1983 he was the founder of the very successful Cheshire Over 40s competition, which continues to this day. He was also an inspirational manager to the CCCL Under 18 side, which won the North West Trophy thirteen times between 1980 and 1999. His charges will readily recall, with much affection, his often hilarious team talks. After his death it transpired that his Will generously bequeathed money to the League for the benefit of the 'forties' and Youth cricket. WAD kindly sent me a note with a couple of personal memories of John. He writes: 'Back in the days when the Mobberley ground was somewhat smaller, opening the bowling from the Church end, John dropped one short. The ball passed over the wicketkeeper and hit the site screen half way up. Yes, he was quick in his day. On another occasion playing on a Sunday at Cheadle I opened the batting with John's brother, David North. He was out in the first over and John arrived at the crease. His comment to me was, "you stay in while I get a few". The partnership was broken when the score was something like 150. I had scored 30 and John had done the rest!'

Another real character was Frank Houston, he who never wore a box and when asked about it would say 'never been hit there'. He got through his medium pace overs faster than any spinner. He has been a generous contributor to the club over the years.

The Cheshire County League President, Ian Brown, (2013-14), has given me some lovely reflections of his happy days at Styal as a young scorer and player. He recalls the wooden floor in the old pavilion and the resulting splinters, each player having to bring sandwiches for two, John Kenyon being a

> Brothers Arthur (b 1835, d 1899) and Henry Russell Greg (b 1832, d 1894) both played a single match for Cheshire in 1863. Both were born at Norcliffe Hall, Styal. They both had a single innings and both scored 7 runs. Arthur played against Knutsford and Stockport provided the opposition when Henry played. Both matches were played at Chelford.

star player – he played for Cheshire (1956-57) while a Styal player – and John North (8-2) and Eric Newton (2-4) bowling out Mobberley for 6 on Cup Final day 1954. West Bromwich Albion beat Preston 3 -2. It was the first time he had seen TV. He is aware of a photograph of the first cricket hut in the Norcliffe Chapel archives (c 1860), the Sunday School being fundamental to the club's nativity.

In 1990 Division 1 of the Cheshire League was won. Steve 'Chalky' Shawcross was the opening bowler then and is still playing in the 1st XI today.

2016 - South Manchester CC joined forces after using Styal as their home ground for some years and now play as Styal Souths on Sundays. Together the Greater Manchester Cricket League Division 3 Cup was won in 2016.

The Styal tree

Tattenhall

Flacca Field, Field Lane, off Burwardsley Road, Tattenhall CH3 9QF

APPRECIATING THE attractive, peaceful village setting of today, it is difficult to imagine the scene at Flacca Field in 1940; surrounded by heavy ack-ack enplacements and searchlight units, and with the military using the ground to the full, it reflected the scars of war. The field was being used as a landing-strip for an artillery spotter plane and the wooden pavilion was being utilised as a lock-up for army defaulters.

All that wartime activity was a far cry from the joyous scenes of 1897 when Tattenhall defeated Mold to win the Chester & District League.

> By 1911 the Tattenhall playing strength, largely due to the prestigious Jones family (LN, W and WE), was beyond most of their local rivals' resources, but increasingly they had to share the Jones boys with both Boughton Hall and Cheshire. The family served the club in various capacities for more than six decades.

The team proceeded to Tattenhall Road by the next train and there a sight presented itself the like of which had probably never been seen before in the district. Directly they moved out of the station the Drum & Fife Band from the Tattenhall Home, led by Mr Hicks, the popular superintendent, together with children carrying flags, welcomed the team with 'See the Conquering Hero Comes'. A procession, headed by the band, marched to the residence of Mr W Jones.

The roadsides were literally lined with people, whose excitement and enthusiasm knew no bounds. When they arrived at the Aldersley Arms, the League Cup was filled with champagne. The health of the team was drunk over and over again. After a few more toasts, the procession proceeded to Tattenhall village, the team leading the way in traps, the rest following as best they might. The Cup was held on high at which the shouts of the crowd were almost deafening. En route through the village the householders and their families appeared at their doors, waving handkerchiefs and shouting in a most excited manner. The health of the team was drunk again, anyone who cared having a drink from the Cup.

> George Harper always showed the sort of humour which members like to feel is typical of the Tattenhall spirit. On one occasion Mike Reece was having the outside of his house pointed and the building was surrounded by scaffolding. George, of course, had the local milk round and the scaffolding was too good an opportunity to miss. Arriving at Church Bank at six in the morning, he filled his crate, climbed the scaffold, knocked at the bedroom window and enquired, "Was it three or four!" George died in 1988.

The first newspaper reference to cricket in the village was recorded in 1864. The *Chester Chronicle* included a very brief mention of a match played against The Albert (Chester): 'This match was played on Saturday and terminated in favour of the Albert with three wickets to go down'. Alongside was an advertisement for Holloway's ointment (guaranteed to cure elephantiasis, bad breasts, gout, cancers, bunions, scurvy, tumours, ulcers, yaws, sore nipples and burns). An elixir indeed!

During the Wakes Week of 1888 the Tattenhall Road XI defeated Tarvin and until a merger occurred around 1900 there were two clubs in the village.

Amid some amusement, and not a little ribaldry, the Chairman, Dave Wilson, launched a most unlikely fund-raising project - a sponsored walk to Lord's. The walk took place in February 1986 and £2000 was raised.

The club badge features three castles. Stand on the square and see if you can pick out them out; Beeston, Bolesworth and Peckforton. Even with 20/20 vision you'll do well to do so in summer when the trees are in full leaf.

> **Garry Sobers makes his debut for Tattenhall**
>
> In 1961 Chester Boughton Hall invited 'stars' to participate in a local clubs' knock-out competition and Tattenhall might have considered themselves fortunate to have drawn Sobers. Capenhurst scored 84, with Sobers bagging 3-32, but when batting he soon holed out for 19 and Tattenhall were dismissed for 76.

Timperley

Stockport Road, Timperley WA15 7LU

THE LANCASHIRE CCC library at Old Trafford has amongst its stock an attractive, small, green hardback book entitled *Timperley Cricket, Hockey & Lawn Tennis 75th anniversary (1877-1952)*. A mere 20 pages, it is an extraordinary odd mix of photographs of unrelated sports people – an action shot of Manchester City goalkeeper Bert Trautmann, one of cyclist Reg Harris and others of Karel Istaz, a Belgian wrestler, and Jean Westwood and Lawrence Demmy, international ice-dance champions! Its middle pages provide a scorecard of a match to be played between E Hodkinson's XI and G Ranft's Cheshire XI. Hodkinson included three Australian players with first-class experience – George Tribe, Len Livingston and Bill Cockburn. It also includes an extract from an official handbook of the floral bazaar held in 1896 to raise funds for alterations and improvements to the grounds and buildings.

On 8 April 1877 a dozen or more enterprising young men met in the Infants School, Four Lane Ends to discuss the formation of a cricket team for Timperley. The first ground was situated off Moss Lane, but when the lease expired in 1883 the club was compelled to seek new territory and the present ground was acquired.

1925 - Following his release by Lancashire CCC, Lol Cook signed up. He took 10-30 against Manchester Clifford but still ended up on the losing side. He took 85 wickets in his first season and over 200 in three seasons with the club.

> The club's first 'star' was James Cookson, who excelled at virtually any sport he turned his hand to, being a scratch golfer, 1st XV captain of Sale RUFC and a County hockey player. Between 1883 and 1894 he scored over 4000 runs and took more than 700 wickets (including two ten-wicket hauls) before moving to Sale CC.

1935 - Jack Abel joined the club. A nephew of the great Bobby Abel, of England and Surrey, he continued playing into the 1960s and is one of the club's greatest run accumulators, scoring over 10000 runs. He was noted for wearing a cravat when batting.

1939 - War declared. Some matches were played throughout the hostilities. The clubhouse was used by the Home Guard.

1946 - Sixty-nine years after its formation Timperley win their first ever silverware – the Burrows Trophy for the Manchester Association 2nd XI Championship.

1948 - Former Luftwaffe POW Billy Feick becomes groundsman. 4000+ watch Timperley play a George Tribe XI in support of Cyril Washbrook's testimonial season.

1951 - 4000+ watch E Hodkinson's XI (he was the Timperley captain) in support of the Lord Mayor's Appeal for the National Playing Fields Association.

1960 - The 2nd XI bowl out Newton for 8. This is the lowest recorded score by a team playing against Timperley.

1963 - The clubhouse is seriously damaged by fire.

1972 - 1st XI win the Lancashire Cup and the Manchester Association Cup at Old Trafford on successive weekends.

Above and below: Timperley in the 1950s

1987 - Wilf Laidlar retires from playing. He took over 3000 wickets in a career of over 60 years. In 1935 he took 10-53 against Knutsford. When he retired from full-time work in 1969 he dedicated even more time to junior coaching and groundwork.

1988-89 - A Manchester Association trophy is won in both years. The side included Nigel Wood, who remains one of the club's leading wicket-takers. He holds the club's record bowling performance with figures of 10-14 against Cheetham Hill in 1985. Martin Ward was also in that team and he is the current aggregate highest run-scorer for the club with over 13000 runs to his name in a 30-year playing career.

1992 - Timperley left the Manchester Association and joined the Cheshire County League.

2002 - A £1.2 million clubhouse was opened by club patron Stan Moore.

2010 - Oliver Byrne scored a century in a Sunday friendly. He became the youngest ever recorded club centurion (aged 12).

2015 - In July the club played host to the PCA Masters. A crowd of over 500, with another 150 in the hospitality tent, were entertained by a star-studded side which included Mark Ramprakash, Simon Jones and Steve Harmison. Notably, the 1st XI were runaway winners of Division 1 of the Cheshire County League and achieved premiership status.

2016 - The former Manchester United and Arsenal striker David Herd died aged 82. The Scottish international scored twice for United in the 3-1 defeat of Leicester City in the 1963 FA Cup final. He played for Timperley either side of managing Lincoln City from 1971-73. He was chairman when Timperley won the Manchester Association Stockton Trophy in 1977.

Tintwistle

Speedwell, Tintwistle SK13 1LU

IF IT IS NOW classified as Derbyshire, it was certainly a part of Cheshire until the 1974 boundary changes. At your peril pronounce it 'Tintwistle'. Try 'Tinsel'.

Cricket was first played in Tintwistle around 1835-36 on a ground which now lies beneath Arnfield Reservoir. In those days the highlight of the season was the annual fixture between the Arnfield farmers and Tintwistle CC, who then played under the name of 'Tintwistle Unicorns'. In 1850 a meeting of members was held at the Waggon and Horses public house at the corner of Chapel Lane when the club was reconstituted under the new title of 'Tintwistle Royal CC'.

At the outset matches were played on a number of different fields, including one on Conduit Street, but a more permanent headquarters was needed and one of the original members, John Roberts, agreed to rent a field on Speedwell to the club. In August 1854 the ground was ready and the first match played on the new ground was against Gorton Mechanical Institute and was won by the home club. Matches have been played continuously on this ground from then until the present day (except during WW1/2). The current site, which is slightly larger than the original, was purchased in the 1980s.

From 1854 to 1893 the club played friendly matches. Visits were made to Salford, Penistone, Oldham and Tideswell. When the train could not be used, horse-drawn waggonettes were pressed into use. Some players suffered injury whilst travelling by this method. Abel Harrop, a Tintwistle player, fell out of a waggonette travelling up Mottram Moor and broke his arm. On another occasion, a visiting team from Penistone were returning home after a match and on the road above Woodhead Tunnel a player fell under the wheels and was tragically killed. The Tintwistle club was quick to react, organising a charity match which raised £12 for the player's family.

1870 - The Club President and Treasurer was James Sidebottom, who owned Waterside Mills. It was due to his generosity that the club was able to pay for the services of a professional player when a match merited it.

1873 - The local newspaper described Tintwistle supporters as a 'drunken, loud mouthed rabble'. In those days it was not uncommon for a crowd of 300-400 spectators to shout the team on, sometimes accompanied by the Tintwistle Brass Band. The annual expenditure in the 1870s was between £12 and £13. In those days, cricket bats cost 2/6d and balls were 6d.

1880s - The club engaged a full-time professional named Jimmy Robinson from Hollingworth. The club had 153 members at this time, 58 of whom were playing members.

1893 - Tintwistle helped to form the Glossop & District League. It was during the early days of the new league that the club obtained the services of one of its best players, Sam Cadman, who later went on to play for Glossop CC before moving to Derbyshire CCC, where he enjoyed a long first-class cricketing career. Tintwistle's first major success in the Glossop & District League was in the 1903 season when they won the First Division title. William Lees Marshall, a schoolmaster at the Independent Day School, was the captain. He also became the first player to take 1000 wickets for the club.

1920s - Tintwistle enjoyed great success, winning the First Division title for five successive years. It was during this era that a young player was to make his mark by re-writing all the club records. He was Bill Senior, one of Tintwistle's most gifted players. The introduction of the Rhodes Bowl competition saw Tintwistle win the trophy for three successive years. The league presented them with a special trophy, the 'Boak Cup' in 1933 to commemorate this achievement.

1953 - The club had one of its finest years, winning the First Division title, the Rhodes Bowl and the Second Division title – a first for the Glossop & District League.

1963 - A new pavilion, the third on the present site, was built. The club's 2nd XI skipper, Graham Wood, sprang into action and within weeks he had obtained a building which had formerly been used by the workmen at the Woodhead tunnel construction site in 1952. The club members and players supplied the necessary manpower and some can recall the sight of Enus Woodward carrying a section of the pavilion single-handed – a task normally requiring eight people! The finished pavilion was officially opened in 1964 by Les Jackson, the Derbyshire and England fast bowler.

For his efforts, Graham Wood was elected Life President of the club, a title he held until his death in 1996.

1970s - A period of sustained success. The 1st XI won honours time and time again, including the Cheshire section of the Haig Village Cup. (In the 1980s they won the Derbyshire Area final, then sponsored by Whitbread). Charismatic Billy Cropper led the 2nd XI to league and cup victories in the same year. Billy was supported by one of Tintwistle's most successful bowlers, Harry Goddard, who took 1300 wickets.

1990s - Andrew 'AJ' Harris left Tintwistle CC for Ashton CC prior to joining Derbyshire CCC. Later he played for Nottinghamshire CCC and briefly with Gloucestershire and Worcestershire. He is one of several Tintwistle players who progressed to play first-class cricket, but he is the only one to win a Division One County Championship medal, which he did with Nottinghamshire in 2005. In 2008 Andrew was awarded a benefit year, which was supported by Tintwistle CC. As part of the celebrations a T20 match was played at Tintwistle between Notts CCC and a Tintwistle XI. He retired from County cricket in 2010.

2000s - There has been continued success for the club both on and off the pitch. More competition wins, a new netting facility and some personal milestones, with Jimmy Blackwell taking his 1000th wicket and Martin Harris becoming the leading run-scorer in the club's history. The club continues to look to the future and maintain its position as a community cricket club at the centre of village life.

> Sam Cadman played 377 first-class matches for Derbyshire between 1900 and 1926. He scored 14078 runs, took 807 wickets and held 278 catches.

Toft

Booth's Park, Chelford Road, Knutsford WA16 8QP

THE ROEBUCK, the Toft CC emblem, is taken from the landowning Leycester Roxby family coat of arms and it was that family that presided over the cricket on a farmer's field on Toft Road (now the A50) in the 1920s. When, in 1938, the tenant farmer gave notice to quit and ploughed the sacred turf, another local family came to the rescue. The Cowburns offered the club their current splendid setting on the Booth's Park estate. Not only did Mr Cowburn offer the land, he also built a pavilion at his own expense.

1964 - To celebrate 25 years at Booth's Park a dinner was held at Mere Country Club. Yorkshire's Arthur Booth was the after-dinner speaker. In a first-class career spanning the period 1931-47 he captured 131 wickets, of which, remarkably, 111 came in the 1946 season.

> The 'old' Toft Club was made up of the local farming community, and the membership of 15 was restricted by a club rule to residents of Toft and Bexton. In the very early days replying to a mere total of 12, 'batting like Kamikaze pilots', Toft were soon 12-9 but eventually won with the help of a bye!

> Although 1928 is accepted as the founding date of the existing club, Jeff Tenner, the dedicated club historian, has unearthed, within the Ashley CC records, a match played in 1888. That early side disbanded in 1914.

1978 - To celebrate their Golden Jubilee year Toft entertained a Geoff Pullar XI on 9 July. In the team of the England opener were Peter Parfitt, (Middlesex), David Allen, (Gloucestershire), Peter Lever and Bob Barber (Lancashire), Harold Rhodes (Derbyshire) and Freddie Millett (Cheshire and Minor Counties). A programme was produced and a centre-page note suggested it should be retained for guaranteed free entry to the centenary match in 2028!

When the Jubilee match took place it could not have been expected that a mere two months later Toft would be playing at Lord's in the final of the Village Cup. They lost to Linton Park, but they only had to wait another eleven years for eventual glory. The current groundsman and club steward, Bernard Manning, was in that 1978 side.

1989 - Victory in the National Village Cup, but not (quite) at Lord's. On Sunday 26 August, when Hambledon were struggling at 72-5, it rained and the match was abandoned and re-scheduled for the following day at Beckenham. Hambledon again batted first and were dismissed for 104. Toft knocked them off for the loss of only 4 wickets having been 5-2. Ronnie Locke had bowling figures of 9-5-11-3 and then contributed 19 not out with the bat. A great day for the club was nicely rounded off when the team returned to the clubhouse at midnight to find it decorated in appropriate style and their faithful supporters waiting to crack open the champagne. Current members and Cheshire Over

Village Cup winners 1989

to mention that Ewan McCray made a great contribution in the qualifying rounds; 50 against Marchwiel, 72 and 5-6 against Woore, and then 139 and 3-21 in the defeat of Belvoir. At that point he was selected for Cheshire and disqualified from further participation in the Village competition. Toft suffered a blow soon after their return home when the magnificent silver trophy was stolen while on display in the *Knutsford Guardian* shop window in the town.

> Bernard Manning has spent a lifetime at Toft. He first played in 1967 after university. Now, more than fifty years later, he has served the club as a player, committee member, groundsman and club steward. He scored six hundreds for the club and once captured over 50 wickets in a season. He was regarded as a very fine cover fieldsman. Recognition came when he was selected to play for the Haig National Village Representative XI against Surrey at Charterhouse in 1976. He scored 36 not out. In 2016 he was Cheshire's nomination for Outstanding Service to Cricket Award 'get the game on' and received an invitation to attend the annual OSCA ceremony at Lord's.

1991 - Toft did the double by winning both the League and the Cheshire Cup. In cup games Paul Bertenshaw played in seven matches and recorded aggregate figures of 52-17-100-12. In the game against Cheadle his match analysis was 8-4-4-4.

1993 - Toft won the Cheshire Cup again, defeating Grappenhall on this occasion. Brian Coutts took 22 from the final over. Overall he scored 32 from just 13 balls.

50 players, Bob Ashley and Brian Coutts (both played in the 1978 side) were in that winning team and so was Paul Bertenshaw. His involvement provided a neat family double as his elder brother David had played in the 1978 final. It is fair to say it might have all been rather different. The semi-final against Bomarsund at Toft was washed out when the home team were in a very commanding position and the replay was played in Northumberland. On this occasion Toft carved out a score of 155-5 and in reply Bomarsund got to 131-3 with five overs remaining when the batsmen complained about the deteriorating light. The umpires took them off without returning and Toft won on run-rate by 0.02 of a run! It is proper

> Ronnie Locke retired from cricket in 1999 having taken the most ever Cheshire County Criket League wickets, 1262 between 1977 and 1999. He topped the table for the most wickets in a season on twelve occasions, three times with Cheadle Hulme (1979-81) and nine times with Toft (1985-90 and 1992-94). He held the record for most wickets in a season, 90 in 1989. He also had 12 five-wicket hauls in that year – eleven in the League and one in the cup.

2015 - Henry Hughes, the Uppingham captain in 2011, played two first-class matches for Oxford against Worcestershire and Middlesex.

2016 - Barely a year after his young teammate made his first-class debut, Rob Jones repeated the deed for Lancashire against Surrey at the Oval. The former England U19 player started off with 25 and 10, but in only his third match, against Middlesex, the eventual champions, he sensationally carried his bat for 106 not out and added another 25 not out in the second innings. In the same year, Jake Hancock, his former Toft teammate (2012-15), made his first-class debut for Tasmania against Victoria in Hobart. He scored 4 and 10. During his four-year stay at Booth's Park he chalked up fourteen centuries, of which eleven were undefeated.

We are privileged to have so many lovely grounds within the County but Toft is most certainly in the top bracket and undoubtedly fits the colourful descriptor of 'rural idyll'. Nigel Muirhead is the energetic, enterprising and enthusiastic Chairman.

Rob Jones going out to bat on his first-class debut at the Oval.

Cheshire CCC
– last four captains

Andrew Hall (2002-11)

James Duffy (2012-14)

Danny Woods (2015)

Lee Dixon (2016 -2017)

Trafford MV

Macpherson Park, Finneybank Road, Sale M33 6LR

PRIOR TO BECOMING fully independent, Trafford MV was originally formed on 2 May 1923 by a group of 17 apprentices at an engineering company called Metropolitan Vickers (later becoming AEI Ltd and eventually becoming GEC Ltd) in Trafford Park to provide a sports facility and the opportunity to play rugby against other companies around the region under the name of Metrovick RFC.

Twenty-five years after the rugby section came into existence, by very popular demand, a cricket section was founded in 1948 and the club became Metrovick Rugby Football and Cricket Club. The cricket also prospered and within two years of forming, three regular sides were playing friendly matches against other company sides in the area.

In 1960 the cricket section made a formal application to join the Cheshire Cricket Association and were accepted. The 1st and 2nd XI won the 2nd Division titles in 1980, the 1st XI were 1st Division runners-up in 1982 and won the league knock-out competition on three occasions.

In 1989 the cricket section joined the South Lancashire League and, over the following nine seasons, the 1st XI were placed in the top three on four occasions and won the Wilkinson Sword Knock-Out in 1995 and were runners-up on two further occasions. The 2nd XI won their championship in 1990.

With league cricket in the North West facing a complete shake-up in the mid to late 1990s the club saw that it was time to join a more organised structure with the possibility of upward mobility. In this respect it was decided that an application be made to the Cheshire Cricket Alliance, a new alliance between clubs of the old Cheshire Competition and South Cheshire Alliance, and return the club to its Cheshire roots. In 1998, the club was placed in the 2nd Division of the Cheshire Cricket Alliance, effectively the bottom rung of the Cheshire Pyramid, but were immediately successful. The championship was won at a canter and the following years saw the 1st XI reach the top division of the Cheshire Cricket League by 2006.

The final most important development in MV's history happened when the club changed its name. As the decline in the engineering function at the company (now GEC Ltd) became more and more significant, the close ties of the early days between club and company were becoming less and less. In 1993, as the club had no further ties with Metrovick, and along with the desire to promote the club within its more regional surroundings, it changed its name to Trafford MV RFCC. This was the end of a long association with Metrovicks, and as a mark of its past history, the MV was kept in its name.

With the help of grants from both the Rugby Football Union and the England & Wales Cricket Board, a £600000 changing facility was opened in 2009, which, together with significant clubhouse improvements in recent years, have given Trafford MV some of the best off-field facilities in the county.

Tranmere Victoria

Victoria Park, Bebington Road, Tranmere CH42 6PX

MENTION OF Tranmere probably conjures up a picture in the mind of the footballing Rovers rather than the cricketing Vics. The respective sporting venues are less than half a mile apart.

Victoria Park opened in 1901 and was originally the garden of a very large property called Arudy House. The French-style chateau was demolished in the 1960s. It was originally owned by Victor Poutz, a French cotton merchant. A large block of flats now stands on the site of the old house. From the top of the park on Bebington Road there are fine views towards the River Mersey and across the water to Liverpool.

The club evolved from the local Methodist Church and claims a founding year date of 1922, but good evidence suggests it existed before WW1. I found a clip from the *Liverpool Courier* dated 27 May 1918 which reported that… 'Private Robert F Edwards (36), who has died from wounds, leaves a widow at 30 Crofton Road, Tranmere. He was a member of the Tranmere Victoria Cricket Club, and at one time Secretary'.

Arthur Plimley, who started playing for the club in 1946 and has followed their fortunes ever since, told me about the succession of pavilions during his association. He could recall when the pavilion was on the other side of the park and other subsequent rudimentary facilities, so he is delighted with the existing building which in 2008 replaced the old RAF huts. Arthur could recall the original dismantling of them at RAF West Kirby and the eventual on-site rebuilding of them.

The Vics is a real community club who have played most of their cricket in the lower leagues, but that has not stopped them having some top players. One such talented cricketer was Peter Carlton, who went on to captain Birkenhead Park to the championship of the Liverpool Competition in 1986. He almost led his new team to a great double, but BPCC lost to Cheadle in the final of the Cheshire Cup.

For the last three years the Vics have entertained the Cheshire Cobras, a side made up of blind and visually impaired cricketers. Matches are played with a larger ball with beads inside, which assists the players to best judge the speed and angle of flight of the ball. So that the hosts could experience how visually impaired players cope they wore simulation glasses provided by the Cobras which ranged from tunnel vision to 80% blindness.

Walk around the boundary and imagine you are in the garden of the old house. For those feeling particularly energetic, try a bit of circuit training on the various exercisers located in the park. Those with less energy can pick out the splendid Liverpool buildings which peer through and over the trees. Nip into the pavilion and say hello to Sylvia Walker, who is a tireless worker at the club.

Upton

Old Greasby Road, Upton, Wirral CH49 6LT

WEEKEND DRIVERS using the Upton By-pass get a clear, albeit, fleeting, glimpse of the cricket as they whizz by. This is, of course, a very different highway from that which existed in 1901 when the club was founded. For highway substitute 'a picturesque narrow winding lane'.

In those early days the club was heavily influenced by William 'Buddy' Hannay. In addition to founding the club, he was the Captain (1901-1931) and the Chairman (1901-1912), plus he also acted as the Secretary (1923-1957), Fixture Secretary (1932-1957) and President (1950-1957)! He made 482 appearances, scored 8149 runs, took 338 wickets and claimed 149 catches. He was a wealthy cotton trader and died in 1957.

1904 - Douglas Quentin Steel joined the club from Liverpool CC and made a significant contribution, both on the field, as a player and an influential Chairman (1913-1926). He was educated at Uppingham School and Cambridge University. He played in four Varsity matches (1876/7/8/9). He also gained both a football and a Rugby Union Blue. He played 57 first-class matches, mainly for Cambridge University and Lancashire, with a top score of 158 and a best bowling analysis of 5-65. Needless to say he was a prolific scorer at club level and contributed an aggregate of 4950 runs for Upton. His brother, AG Steel, played for England.

1926 - A Wildgoose achieved the ambition of every bowler by taking all ten wickets in an innings. against Liscard St Mary's. His figures were 12.3-3-43-10, including a hat-trick. He took 109 wickets in 1926 and another 103 the following year. Overall he collected 1238 victims for the club.

1928 - The first club tour took place. Slough, Beaconsfield, Wargrave, Burnham and Hurst provided the Berks/Bucks opposition.

> The away trip to Eaton Hall, the residence of the Duke of Westminster, was a grandiose affair, for the team travelled by steam train to the Eccleston Ferry, lunched at the nearby hotel, and were then transported to the ground in Buddy's car. The sight of a car was rare and the villagers used to turn out to greet their arrival.

1929 - A new lease was signed and extra acreage secured which allowed for the development of the back pitch.

1940s - Cricket was played through the war and in 1941 the club joined the Merseyside Competition. Membership was boosted by the recruitment of servicemen stationed at RAF West Kirby. In 1946 there was a meeting at Victory Hall to discuss the compulsory purchase of the cricket ground for housing. It came to nothing and a new tennis pavilion was erected in 1948 (more courts were added in 1953, but by 1968 the tennis had folded). In 1948, although the war had been over for almost three years, the club found the allocation of coupons for food to be insufficient and were forced to apply to the Food Office for an additional allocation.

1960 - Stanley Lewis, playing for Helsby CC, was inadvertently served a drink containing chloride of lime which was used for cleaning the pumps. A visit to Birkenhead General was necessary, but after a stomach pump session he was allowed home. Twenty years later he played for Christleton against Upton and happily joked about the incident.

1980s - President Bill Bothwell died in 1981 after falling ill during a BBC commentary at Old Trafford. He joined Upton in 1946 and served as Secretary, Fixture Secretary and 1st XI Captain and was instrumental in bringing many celebrity cricketers to the club for charity matches. Ray Lindwall (Australia), Frank Worrell (West Indies) and Gamini Goonesena (Ceylon) were among that number. He was replaced as President by Norman J Halsall, who had joined the club in 1940. As well as being an outstanding player, he served the club well as 1st XI Captain, Treasurer and Grounds Committee member. His three sons all played for Upton and his namesake son (Norman Richard) went on to have a very distinguished career with Oxton, Birkenhead Park, New Brighton and Neston as well as representing his county (1962-80) on more than one hundred occasions. Norman J died in 1988, but in the same year his son 'NR' organised the first in a series of highly successful and profitable Sportsman's Dinners. Footballing World Cup winner, Jackie Charlton was the very popular guest speaker. During a well-attended 1989 Cheshire Cup match against Birkenhead Park a cigarette machine was stolen. It was unscrewed from the wall in the busy bar area and taken away in the back of a van!

1990s - After much speculation in the 1950s the potential ground development came to the fore again in 1995. Leverhulme Estates wanted to build on the present ground and proposed a re-siting of the club at Greenhouse Farm. Things moved forward and by 1997 the club had endorsed the plans and a 'Heads of Agreement' had been signed, only for the Wirral Planning Committee to reject the plans a year later.

2017 - Going into the 2018 season Upton are classified as the nineteenth best team in the county (7th in Division 1), but Jez Lamb, their enterprising and resourceful Chairman, has ambitious plans for this vibrant, well-appointed and homely Wirral club. In 2018 keep your eye on Simon McGowan's ever-lengthening list of victims. He is only 22 wickets adrift of overtaking the legendary Pete Clark, who has clocked-up a staggering 1278. Ian Sharrock should also achieve the remarkable landmark of 20000 club runs. Could they do it on the same day!

Every club needs loyal members and talented players. This table shows the five players who have made the most appearances for the club and highlights their all-round contributions.

	Most appearances	Most runs	Most wickets	Most catches
Brian Shenton	*1221*	16792	695	467
Ian Sharrock	916	*19678*	879	318
Simon McGowan	858	4353	1257	290
Graeme McGowan	772	10193	176	278 (65 st)
Pete Clark	738	6647	*1278*	215

Club records in italics

Urmston

Moorside Road, Urmston M41 5UU

URMSTON IS definitely not in Cheshire and never, ever has been, but they have played in the Cheshire County League since 1993 and thus qualify for inclusion!

In 1996 Urmston celebrated their 150th anniversary with a series of key events throughout the summer. Things kicked off with a pre-season dinner, at which former Lancashire, Durham and England opener Graham 'Foxy' Fowler was the chief speaker. In June a League Representative side provided the opposition; in July Lancashire 2nd XI played Derbyshire 2nds and an MCC side were also entertained. In August it was the turn of the Lord's Taverners to visit, followed by another Lancashire 2nd XI match, this time against Ireland. The final high-profile event was a grand dinner, 'a sumptuous repast' at which Fred Trueman and football referee Neil Midgley were the speakers.

150 years earlier the Urmston & Flixton CC had been formed and had the reputation for being quite a strong side, but interest waned and the club became dormant in 1864. Samuel Reade was a founder member and arranged the original playing area around his house in Newcroft. It was through the

---

FROM THE MINUTES

1902 That H Whitnall be engaged as umpire at two shillings per match.
1912 JH Sutton complained of members trespassing and trampling the oats.
1919 The grazing of sheep had helped to keep the ground in tolerably good order.
From the accounts
1931 A listing of the assets owned by the club included a piano, two ping-pong tables, 140 deck-chairs, 8 dish cloths and 6 teapots!

Reade family that Sir Bosdin Leach became involved with the club. He went on to promote the financing of the Manchester Ship Canal and later became Lord Mayor of Manchester. It revived in 1870, moving to a field off Railway Road before settling at the present ground. A pavilion was erected in 1895 and another in 1925. Land was sold off to finance the existing building, which was erected in 1972. Use of the adjoining Grammar School ground was gained in 1960 and became the home of the 3rd XI.

In 1930 the scene looked rather different. The entrance was in Roseneath Road where the scorebox now stands and there was no busy Moorside Road fringing the club, merely a dirt path and brook.

The Parkinson twins began playing club cricket at Urmston in 2012. Callum Parkinson made his first-class debut for Derbyshire against Leicestershire, 4-7 August 2016. Remarkably he bowled 70 overs in the match, took eight wickets and fell only just shy of a maiden first-class half century: 1st innings 33.4 overs 4 maidens 90 runs 4 wkts, 2nd innings 37 overs 7 maidens 88 runs 4 wkts

In his only innings, batting at No 11, he shared a 10th wicket partnership of 73, of which he scored 48 not out.

Intriguingly, his twin brother, Matt, had made his first-class debut for Lancashire against Warwickshire on 20 June, recording 5-49, so they made their respective debuts within 41 days of each other.

Twins making their first-class debuts so close together - it sounds like a record? But no, research showed the Somerset-based Overton twins, Craig and Jamie, made their debuts on 26 April and 16 May in 2012 - a mere 20 days apart! If that sounds impressive, going back more than seven decades the Bedser twins made their respective first-class debuts in the same match against Oxford University at the Oval on 21 June 1939.

The last ball of the 2015 season... What a game and what a story. If you weren't there you wouldn't believe it and, even if you were there, you can still barely believe it! Urmston needed a win against Weaverham to gain promotion to the Premier Division, BUT only if Sale did not win. In the event the Moorside Road team looked dead and buried as last man, 17 year old James Epsley, walked to the wicket to join Zeeshan Assi with the bowler on a hat-trick. Urmston needed 44 runs to win off 22 balls. The large crowd had given up hope, and when a huge appeal for LBW went up on the hat-trick ball it seemed that the game was over, but the umpire raised his arm and signalled a no-ball. Suddenly things changed.
Cut to the last over – 19 needed off 6.

Ball 1 – Smash! It's a huge 6!
Ball 2 – A single taken. 12 off 4.
Ball 3 – James Epsley facing. The young man drills one down the ground and scrambles back for 2 but there's an overthrow. Three scored. Zee back on strike. 9 needed off 3.
Ball 4 – Zee takes two. Now 7 needed off 2.
Ball 5 – Zee in the zone! He steps away and smacks the ball over cover for four. The crowd erupts! Three needed off the final ball.
Ball 6 – An unforgettable moment. It's a six! Match won. Promotion to the Premier Division secured as Sale were defeated.

Unbelievable match. Unbelievable ending. Fantastic scenes at UCG!

CRICKET CLUB – The Members of the Chester Cricket Club, we learn, will meet on Thursday next, on their play-ground under Blacon Point: and the following day, it is said, the Grand match between Cheshire and Shropshire will take place on the same ground.

A very early reference to cricket in Cheshire. An extract from the Chester Chronicle dated Friday 28 July 1820.

Wallasey

The Kevin McCullagh Oval, Rosclare Drive, Wallasey CH45 6UX

THE WALLASEY CC Centenary Souvenir Brochure 1864-1964 refers to Len Hopwood as being the only Wallasey cricketer to have gained Test status (two Tests for England). This was undoubtedly true at the time it was written, but in more recent years he has been joined by a list of Zimbabwean Test players – Heath Streak (65 Tests) in 1993, Alistair Campbell (60) 1993-95, Grant Flower (67) 1996, Brian Strang (26) 1997 & 2000 (part) and Paul Strang (24) 2002 & 04. That said, all are overshadowed by Australian Ashes winner, wicketkeeper/batsman, Brad Haddin (66) 2000 (part). Having scored 697 runs in a mere 12 innings he was called back to Australia.

1864+ - It is probable the first ground was in Leasowe Road. Other early sites included Claremount Road, Flynn's Piece in Grove Road and then Shepherd's Field in Green Lane, where the field was shared with 200 sheep and a number of young heifers.

1914 - The club moved to Harrison Park and a match was played between the respective Town Councils of Wallasey and Birkenhead. The *Wallasey Chronicle* reported... *The scene was a gay and joyous one. The reserved enclosure presented an animated appearance, and members of the less privileged public sported themselves on the slopes of the surrounding hillocks, whilst the Birkenhead Shore Road Silver Band whiled away the intervening moments by rendering selections'.*

1919 - Joined the Liverpool Competition when Rock Ferry CC ceased to exist.

1921 - The club started to play again at its current home (previously referred to as Claremount Road). An old army hut was used as the pavilion. The Corporation built the current pavilion in 1934.

1926+ - With the help of Len Hopwood, Wallasey became Liverpool Competition champions jointly with Oxton in both 1926 and 1927. A third top-spot was achieved in 1930 and they were runners-up in 1931 and 1932. Cheshire played their first county match at the Oval in 1926 and Hopwood enjoyed the match by taking four wickets in five balls, including an all stumped hat-trick.

1940 - Early in the season a stranger walked into the club and asked if he could become a member. It was not until he had signed an application form that it was realised they had signed a top-class batsman who had a fine record with both Middlesex and Sir Julian Cahn's XI. The newcomer was TB Reddick, who later played for Nottinghamshire and subsequently became Lancashire's coach. In his one season with the club he averaged 57.25.

1941 - No cricket was played. A parachute mine severely damaged surrounding houses and put the club out of action.

The end of cricket at the Oval for a year. This photgraph was taken in 1941, when a parachute mine put the club out of action.

2000 - The Liverpool Competition Premier Division title is secured and then won again in 2002.

2004 - The ground was re-named the Kevin McCullagh Oval as a tribute to the Cheshire wicketkeeper (1979-82) who played more than 600 league matches for Wallasey between 1969 and his premature death in 2003, aged 54. He collapsed during a Liverpool Echo Knockout semi-final at Rake Lane, New Brighton. He appealed for an lbw and turned around to watch the ball as it sped towards fine leg and slumped to the ground. He had a trial for Middlesex, only to be injured in his first match and never getting another opportunity as the county took on another gloveman – Paul Downton, who went on to play for England. Kevin's reputation and popularity were exemplified when over 700 mourners attended his funeral.

Jerry Brace died in February 2017, but only a few months before I had chatted to him about his long association with Wallasey CC. He had been a member since 1947 and was very proud to tell me he was the first one to be elected twice as the club's President. After our conversation he wrote to me as follows... Of all the dynasties, that of the Beaver family must rank as the most influential, certainly the most numerous. Ronnie was a scrupulously fair but popular umpire in the immediate post-war era, a perceptive Treasurer, and a persuasive President in 1983. He had three sons: David - a wicketkeeper/batsman, Mike - an opening batsman whose predominantly leg-side stroke-play defied coaching analysis but became extremely effective, especially during his time as captain from 1994 to 2003 when his 1st XI had more successes than any other side in the long history of the club; and Brian – another wicketkeeper/batsman whose catching ability and all-round agility belied his considerable stature. They were a cricketing credit to Ronnie.

Mike led the club to Premier League titles in 2000 and 2002, Cheshire Cup wins in 1998, 1999 and 2000, a league KO win in 2003, and Echo Cup wins in 1994 and 1997, and saw his progeny help to add a third Echo Cup in 2008. Mike's sons number seven in all – Barrie, Danny, Andy, Greg, Nathan, Ryan and Lewis – and they should ensure the club's cricketing success for decades to come!

Warrington

Walton Lea Road, Higher Walton, Warrington WA4 6SJ

IT WOULD BE about the year 1837 when the first cricket club was formed by the young men of the town to play the now world-wide game. Their uniform was white flannel trousers and a double-breasted Eton jacket, edged with black braid, and ornamented with rows of black buttons, and, as a distinguishing mark of the 'sides' they played on, broad belts of morocco leather, blue on the one side, red on the other, reversible, so that they could be turned as required. In those days of underhand bowling, no pads were wanted – perhaps not known – and the ground was a large field on the south side of and adjoining Sankey Street opposite to Bank Hall... There was not much interest excited, and the club gradually faded away... After I left Rugby School another cricket club was formed in Warrington, which flourished for many years and was the nucleus of the present club. By kind permission of the Colonel Wilson Patten, afterwards Lord Winmarleigh, the club had the use of the plot of land adjoining Bank Hall, now the public park... The then genial Rector of Warrington, the Honourable and Reverend Horace Powys, afterwards a Bishop, frequently played with us – a man of powerful make, and a 'smiter'. When he did hit the ball, it was generally for 'four', but as he was not in training and stoutly built, his 'puff' was not equal to his strength, and he was not seldom run out. In one of our games, after a mighty stroke by the Rector, our captain roared out to him 'run, run' adding an expletive, certainly unclerical, especially so when applied to a bishop in embryo. When the game was over we had a short consultation, our captain wishing to apologise, but it was decided that the rector might not have heard, and that it was better to remain silent.

Extract from an article written by Robert Davies in a Warrington Corporation Jubilee pamphlet dated 3 April 1897

1853 - A very early report of a match appeared in the *Warrington Guardian* on 7 May. The 'May Day' match was played on a field adjoining the St Elphian's Rectory: '...if there was no display of science, still the game was entered into with a hearty goodwill that augurs well for the prospects of cricket in Warrington'.

1854+- There is evidence of fixtures against Chester and Northwich. The fixture list was expanded and by 1860 Manchester and Liverpool were opponents. The status and prestige of the club continued to gain ground and a match was played against a Yorkshire XI in 1862. The Bank Hall ground was considered good enough to stage a match between Lancashire County and a combined team of Birkenhead Park and the Gentlemen of Cheshire.

1869 - There is evidence to suggest that the lower classes were actively discouraged from attending matches. A newspaper commented: 'A charge of 2d is now made to gentlemen entering the field, which has the effect of keeping out the street arabs'.

1873 - Lord Winmarleigh sold Bank Hall and its grounds to Warrington Corporation and the cricketers moved to Arpley Meadows, situated on the north bank of the River Mersey.

1875 - The first Arpley pavilion was erected. It was still in use as a groundsman's hut when the site was vacated in 1968.

1882 - Warrington player Sydney Crosfield was appointed joint captain of Lancashire with AN Hornby. The same arrangement applied in 1883. He was also an excellent shot, twice winning a competition held at the Grand Prix de Casino in Monte Carlo.

1883 - That original hut was replaced by a grand new pavilion, officially opened by the Mayor and the club President and which survived until it was demolished in 1968.

1904 - Clearly the club was now very firmly established and joined the West Lancashire League, where they stayed until they moved to the Manchester Association after WW1.

1920 - Warrington-born George Duckworth (b 1901, d 1966) followed his father as the club's wicketkeeper. Although he played for England he maintained his association with the club throughout his life and was still rolling the pitch the year he died. With the aid of George Duckworth a good number of charity matches were played at Arpley, and such famous names as Learie Constantine, Cyril Washbrook, George Headley, Eddie Paynter, Frank Worrell, Dick Tyldesley and Frank Tyson all played. Five generations of the Duckworth family have now played for the club. His grandson, Hugh De Prez (b 1951, d 2008), played for Cheshire and then served as an umpire on the Cheshire County League panel.

George Duckworth

1930s - Outstanding players in this period were Cliff Lunt, a forceful bat, captain for many years and a member for over 50 years, Tommy Knowles, captain for ten years and also a Rugby Union player for Birkenhead Park, Cheshire and England.

The 1980s saw the arrival of the three Crawley brothers – Mark, Peter and John. Unfortunately they were too good to stay. Peter played some first-class matches for Cambridge University, Mark went on to play for Oxford University, Lancashire and Nottinghamshire and John achieved the most, representing Cambridge University, Lancashire, Hampshire and England. Not a bad trio! John joined Warrington as an eight-year-old and debuted for the 1st XI at the age of 15. When he was only 16 he represented the club when they won the Cheshire U21 Cup, scoring undefeated centuries in both the semi-final and the final. His achievements in the game at the highest level, including a first-class score of 311 not out, were no surprise to his Warrington coaches.

Jimmy Duckworth, younger brother of George, was another who was an outstanding bat and slip fielder. His two sons, Neil and Robert, starred for the club in the 1960s.

1940s-1950s - The club's outstanding member was John Whitley, Managing Director of Greenall Whitley Limited. A useful batsman and bowler, he was 1st team captain from 1946-1953, President from 1951-1964 and a Trustee and Director of the Ground Company. In the mid-1950s he launched a scheme to expand the Arpley pavilion and later he pioneered the move to Walton. Unfortunately he died before the move was completed.

1968 - The move to Walton was completed. Arpley had been sold for £58500, but that sum was soon spent along with grants on significant levelling work and building the new clubhouse.

1978 - The club played host to a Minor Counties match when Cheshire played Lancashire 2nds. In 1993 Nottinghamshire played Cheshire in the NatWest Trophy and in 1995 a Ladies' World Cup match between Holland and Australia was played.

If there were a prize for the clubhouse with the biggest footprint in the county, Warrington would certainly be a front-runner. It has never claimed to be a traditional cricket pavilion and, maybe, is not aesthetically pleasing to the eye, but as a multi-sports facility over two floors it is well-used and highly functional.

Every club needs its stalwart members and for a good number of decades Ian Buttress, Mike Cornelia and Paul Agar, indeed the Agar family, have all rendered splendid service to their club. In 2017 the new scoreboard was dedicated to Paul Agar in recognition of sixty years membership as a player and groundsman.

Octogenerian, Ken Rothwell, still umpiring and the first scorer of a century at Walton in 1970.

Weaverham

Wallerscote Road, Weaverham CW8 3LA

ENGLAND, CAPTAINED by Ivo Bligh, returned from Down-Under with the Ashes a year after that famous RIP notice had been published in *The Times* following the aftermath of England's defeat by the Australians at the Oval. Might we speculate that this momentous event motivated the villagers of Weaverham to start its own cricket team? The year was 1883.

1887 - Initially matches were played in a field belonging to one of the founder members, W Gerrard, off Well Lane, but within four years they had moved to the existing ground in Wallerscote Road.

1897 - Walter Johnson joined the club at the age of 18, one of four cricketing brothers. He was a fine all-rounder and twice won newspaper prizes for his bowling performances. In 1908 he recorded bowling figures of 8-3 against Winsford and the following year 6-1 against Warrington. For the first feat the *Sunday Chronicle* presented him with a WG Grace book and for the second performance he received a bat, autographed by Herbert Sutcliffe, from the *Sunday Express*. He attracted the interest of Lancashire CCC but declined their invitation to join the groundstaff as he only 'played for the love of the game'.

1920s - Jimmy Callan was the wicketkeeper around this period, but after his playing days he became the club umpire and later the first Life Member (1936). A cobbler by profession, on one occasion when umpiring he was standing at square leg when a long hop, travelling like a rocket, hit him on the head and knocked him out cold. When he recovered consciousness, he shakily got to his feet and demonstrated his absolute commitment to the job by immediately signalling a boundary! On another occasion, having turned down an lbw appeal, he called upon the batsman to, "Show us thar navel George, where that ball 'it thee".

Harry Collier was a postman and a key member of the side to the extent that for away matches the team did not travel until he had completed his Saturday morning deliveries. On one particular Saturday he arrived on his bicycle breathless and not best pleased. It transpired the previous day the club Secretary had asked him to deliver a private message to a Crowton resident during his postal round, but Harry declined saying it was rather out of his way and would delay his arrival for the cricket. The Secretary said he quite understood but then posted the letter!!

Ted Ellis played for the club from 1921 until 1976. He was a regular in the 1st XI for almost 40 years. He was a decent batter, but it was as a bowler he was best known. He bagged a hundred wickets in a season on a number of occasions but never achieved 'all 10', although he did take nine wickets on a number of occasions. Once he ran out the last man to deprive himself of the coveted achievement, and another time a nephew dropped a catch off his bowling! During his army service a press cutting reported that while he was playing for 191 HQ Provost Company in Brighton 'he took five wickets in six balls, all clean bowled, the second time he had accomplished a hat-trick in a month'. His enthusiasm for the game was said to be endless and with his fine sense of humour he was regarded as a first class after-dinner speaker.

1931 - A hockey section was started but it disbanded in 1936. It was revived in 1963 but only remained active for another nine years.

1930s - A coach was hired for some away matches. This 'box on wheels' as it was described by the players often required some assistance on hills and the youngest had to jump out and push in order that the 'old hands' could continue their game of cards undisturbed! In earlier times a wagonette was hired and drawn by a pair of high-stepping horses. A trip to Warrington was regarded as quite an event as the players always stayed to watch dog racing at the local track after the match or toured the local clubs.

WW2 - No cricket was played. The AGM minutes of 6 April 1939 record that the Treasurer, Fred Stubbs, tendered his resignation due to his pressure of work for the ARP balloon barrage. His notice was accepted with regret in view of the importance of the work on which he was now engaged. Part of the north-west corner of the ground was used for an air raid shelter and the record book shows an Inland Revenue credit of 2s 7d for 'war damage' to the fence caused by children playing around the shelter. At the end of the war a considerable amount of restoration work was required on the ground, pavilion and fencing before cricket could re-commence in 1946.

1978 - Nigel Wilkinson, playing for the 2nd XI, took 10-29 from 21 overs against Alsager and followed it up the following week with 5-7 off 14 overs. He finished the season with 59 wickets at seven runs each.

1983 - The centenary was celebrated with six days of memorable cricket. A number of Vice-Presidents made presentations to the club, including a new flag, an honours board and a ship's bell.

2013-16 - Antiguan Wilden Cornwall (b 1973), played for the club with significant success. The 2017 league handbook reveals that in his last season with the club he produced three particularly notable all-round performances – 88 & 5-17, including a hat-trick, against Marple, 93 & 4-32 against Bollington and 71 & 4-76 when Grappenhall were the opposition. For good measure he took 133 off the Cheadle Hulme attack. Before coming to Weaverham he had played 53 first-class matches in the Caribbean for the Leeward Islands (1959 runs, including three centuries and 106 wickets). Weaverham officially formed a sistership with Wilden's home club, Liberta Sports Club in Antigua.

The main gates were restored in 2011, funded by donations in memory of Tony Southerton.

Westminster Park

Hough Green, Chester CH4 8JQ

THE CLUB reported they had no plans for an open-top bus tour around the car park, but suggested they might need to invest in a trophy cabinet after their 2013 successes. At the annual Cheshire Alliance League dinner they collected the 1st XI Knock-out trophy, the Division 3 runners-up pot, the Aggregate trophy runners-up award and the 2nd XI were the winners of Division 5 West. Noting that the former Kiwi captain, Jeremy Coney, was the excellent after-dinner speaker, it can be taken for granted that the Wezzy Park contingent had a great night.

The club takes its name from both the park in which they play and the Chester suburb where it is located. The park has been leased to the Council by the Duke of Westminster since 1946 for use by residents and visitors to the borough for a wide range of activities. True to that statement, cricket is by no means the only sport played. The park also offers a nine hole par 3 golf course, a BMX track, bowling and croquet lawns and football pitches. The most recent addition to the facilities was the installation of an outdoor gym and two running circuits, so 'the Parkies' can have no excuse for not being super-fit. Can they?

When 'the Parkies' reformed in 2008 they reported an early objective was to 'offer cricket at dirt cheap prices to a bunch of talentless no-hopers who wanted to play but either couldn't afford it or were too rubbish for other clubs'.

I am reliably informed by the Secretary that the club has a much-loved occasional player who has acquired quite a reputation as a part-time trigger-happy umpire with mannerisms similar to Captain Mainwaring. Known to his colleagues as Lord Gnome when he takes a turn at umpiring, he fires out both his colleagues as well as the opposition with relish and, apparently, with little regard to the Laws! When he is entrusted with the ball he bowls a devastating moon ball.

The Chester suburb of Blacon to the north-west of the city, at one time regarded as just about the largest council estate in Europe, seems an unlikely starting point for a club now playing south of the river, but former Cheshire player, Brian Gresty (1973-74) should know as he played at both sites. In the 1970s he played at Blacon alongside some fine cricketers like Cheshire's Ron Richardson (1963-70), who later became Chairman of the Cheshire County Cricket Club (1984-98). This was at a time when the Cheshire & District Midweek League was very strong and had ten divisions. Eventually they migrated to Westminster Park.

Weston

The Alan Holdcroft Memorial Ground, Main Road, Weston CW2 5NA

SOME MEMBERS might look back with nostalgia at their playing days on a ground set in the middle of a hundred-acre field, protected from the cricket-watching cattle only by a slender electric fence which frequently gave a jolting tingle to the forgetful outfielder. Road improvements put an end to that phase of the club's history and the first match hosted on the current ground was against a Derbyshire XI. There is a plaque in the pavilion which announces that Kim Barnett officially opened the building on 25 August 1992.

Weston celebrated its centenary in 1997, but within a couple of years the late club historian, who gave his name to the present ground, discovered an old newspaper which suggested the club already existed in 1875. No matter, founding dates are often challenged. The earliest matches were played at Toll Bar Cottage (now demolished) and then, by permission of Lord Crewe, in the grounds of the Hall.

The vastly improved facilities at Main Road allowed the club to gain membership of the North Staffs & South Cheshire competition in 2006, and by 2011 they had gained promotion to Division 1. During this period the club were assisted by Rajiv Kumar, who gave five sterling years of service. An experienced cricketer in India with ten first-class centuries to his name, he amassed over a thousand runs each season with Weston. 2010 NS&SC league records disclose that Rajiv Kumar scored a record 1446 runs in Division 2A with an average of 103.28 . The statistics also show that in 2006 the Weston bowlers were whacked for a record 408-7 by Meakins. Ouch!

Notes extracted from the Weston CC archive

1920s The Treasurer was GE Parton. Apparently he lived in Choriton and owned a pony and trap. He liked a drink and his pony would take him to the Crewe Arms and then on to the White Lion. After a heavy session the pony was quite used to getting him home without much assistance from the owner! If the housekeeper had already gone to bed the poor old pony had to stay in its shaft all night!

1965-71 One Saturday each season was set aside for the annual 'Fishing Match'.

1967 Corrugated sheets to be purchased to construct a toilet. A new briefcase purchased for the secretary.

1979 Farokh Engineer played a match at Weston. He bowled spin and batted with panache. He was caught on the boundary for 80 and thoroughly entertained the crowd with his big hitting. Afterwards everybody enjoyed a beer at the White Lion and Farokh generously stood his round.

1987 In two junior games against Betley, Dominic Cork was dismissed cheaply on both occasions-

D Cork c A Wright b M Kinnear 13
D Cork c S Blackledge b M Kinnear 10

Dominic Cork went on to play for Derbyshire and England, but whatever happened to Matthew Kinnear?

Widnes

Beaconsfield Road, Widnes WA8 9LA

THE EXISTING location of the Cricketers' Arms gives a massive clue as to the whereabouts of one of the early homes of Widnes CC (who were originally known as Woodend). Having played on land in Ditton Road and then on fields in Peelhouse Lane and Victoria Road, they moved to Lowerhouse Lane in 1874. That ground was in close proximity to the public house and the Halton Stadium, the current home of the Widnes Vikings.

The formation of the club was the idea of James White, who had moved from Gloucestershire and had been playing for some years in a county that was regarded as a hotbed of the game and home of the famous Grace family. Finding there was no club in the immediate locality, he called a meeting in the George Hotel in Waterloo Road and a committee was formed. All the early addresses are in the southern part of Widnes and it was not until 1933 that they re-located to the more northerly Beaconsfield Road, their current home.

1874 - The minutes record the subscriptions were increased from ten shillings and sixpence to one guinea, a substantial sum when the average annual wage was around £40. Clearly the bulk of the players were from the professions.

1876 - The fixture list included a match against the influential Manchester team, a forerunner of Lancashire CCC, at Old Trafford. The home team only scored 92 but Widnes were bowled out for 82.

1877 - A committee meeting held in the Simms Cross Hotel authorised the engagement of James Briggs as professional at 40 shillings per week. He

> For a number of years Cec Pepper brought a side to Widnes. In 1960 his team included Basil D'Oliveira, who was an unknown at the time. His hitting was phenomenal. He hit one very high into the air and a nervy Robin Faulkner was underneath it at deep square leg. Pepper rang the bell to declare while the ball was still on its way up! An eternity later the relieved fielder caught it, by which time he was the only player left on the field!!

Some Test cricketers who have played for Widnes

	COUNTRY	TESTS	YEARS
Johnny Briggs	England	33	(1884-1899)
Bob Blair	New Zealand	19	(1953-1964)
Craig Evans	Zimbabwe	3	(1996-2003)
Grant Flower	Zimbabwe	67	(1992-2004)
John Rennie	Zimbabwe	4	(1993-1997)
Shahid Mahboob	Pakistan	1	(1989)
Ata ur Rehman	Pakistan	13	(1992-1996)

stayed until 1892 and introduced his three sons – Joseph, John and James - to the club. Joseph went on to play for Nottinghamshire and, more famously, Johnny for Lancashire and England.

1878 - A bat was presented to young Joe Briggs in recognition of his brilliant fielding. In the same year leather shoes were purchased for the horse to limit turf damage and discussions took place with the football club about a possible amalgamation. Over the next few years, in addition to football there are references to lacrosse, tennis and bowls all being played on the site.

1887 - The club declined an invitation to join the Liverpool and District Association. Ironically, in later years their applications to join were consistently rejected.

1894 - JH Smith became captain, a position he held for eight years, but he was more noted as the referee of the first ever Rugby League cup final.

1910-11 - The hockey club were allowed to use the ground and the minutes refer to sheep and ponies being allowed to graze on certain areas. A local farmer paid for the privilege.

1932 - A decade or so before this date the ownership of the ground had changed. Widnes Council purchased the land from Leigh Estates. Confirming fears that had prevailed for quite some time, the club were given notice to quit the Lowerhouse Lane facility in March and effect a removal by September 1932. An offer to buy the ground for £500 was rejected.

1933 - With haste the present Beaconsfield Road ground was acquired. Initially it was rented, but by the time WW2 had started it had been purchased. Previously it had been used by the Co-operative Society as a sports field. The timber from the Lowerhouse Lane pavilion was taken to the new site and rebuilt and the square was lifted and relaid by Jim Briggs.

1950s - During this window a good number of Lancashire players were seen on the ground. Winston Place, Jack Ikin and Geoff Edrich all had benefit matches here, and in 1958 the Cec Pepper All Stars were Sunday visitors. His team included Frank Worrell, Garry Sobers, Sonny Ramadhin, Roy Gilchrist, Chandu Borde and Vijay Manjrekar.

Some first-class cricketers who have played for Widnes

	MAIN CLUB	MATCHES	YEARS
Sam Agarwal	Oxford University	13	(2010-2013)
Joe Briggs	Nottinghamshire	7	(1885-1888)
James Cutmore	Essex	342	(1924-1936)
Kevin Duers	Zimbabwe	30	(1984-1994)
Scott Henry	New South Wales	36	(2011-2015)
Saradindu 'Bappa' Mukherjee	Bengal	30	(1990-1996)
Narender Negi	Delhi	7	(2002-2004)
Daniel Pascoe	Oxford University	8	(2009-2012)
Steve Titchard	Lancashire	107	(1990-2001)
Ben Williams	Oxford University	9	(2011-2013)

1964-5 - In readiness for the centenary a brick extension to the wooden pavilion was added and entry to lady members was permitted. During a week of celebrations the cast of My Fair Lady, appearing at the Empire in Liverpool, played a match and afterwards performed to an enraptured audience.

1973 - Graham Smith took 10 wickets for 5 runs in a Sunday match against Manchester Association visitors Brooklands. Later that year £25000 was spent on rebuilding the pavilion. Membership surged and the annual bar turnover increased from £15000 to £26000.

1980s - In a move that would have a profound impact on the number of juniors playing the game, Bob Blair, a former New Zealand fast bowler still playing as a professional, was engaged as a junior coach. In 1983, having once again been rejected by the Liverpool Competition, the club joined the Manchester Association after 46 years in the Merseyside Competition (Champions on twelve occasions).

1993 - After yet another rejection by the Liverpool Competition, the club joined the Cheshire County League. In their first season they finished as runners-up to Macclesfield, but they became champions a year later.

> In 1994 Shaun Prescott set a Cheshire County league record of 1478 runs, and in 2005 Bappa Mukherjee became the first bowler to take 10 wickets in the Premier League. Against Chester Boughton Hall he recorded figures of 10 for 59.

2000s - Ben Williams, aged 14 years 329 days, scored 109 not out in 2007 against Urmston and became the youngest ever player to score a century in the Cheshire County Premier League. He went on captain Oxford University in the 2012 Varsity match. Remarkably, Widnes also provided the Oxford captain again in the 2013 Varsity match when Sam Agarwal led the side and scored a record 313 not out.

CHESHIRE COUNTY CRICKET CLUB CHAMPIONSHIP RECORDS (1909-2017)

HIGHEST INNINGS TOTALS

476-8 dec	v Herefordshire	Chester	2012
472-6 dec	v Northumberland	Jesmond	2007
460-8	v Oxfordshire	Alderley Edge	2011
455-8 dec	v Shropshire	Nantwich	2013
454-9 dec	v Herefordshire	Nantwich	2009
438-5 dec	v Berkshire	Chester	2006
424-6 dec	v Herefordshire	Alderley Edge	2006
415	v Northumberland	Jesmond	1956
409-6 dec	v Berkshire	Alderley Edge	2003
408-6 dec	v Cornwall	Falmouth	2009
405-9	v Wales MC	Nantwich	2011
404-7 dec	v Wiltshire	Chester	2010
404-7 dec	v Cornwall	Alderley Edge	2002
402-8 dec	v Berkshire	Chester	2009
402-9	v Durham	West Hartlepool	1924

LOWEST INNINGS TOTALS

14	v Staffordshire	Stoke	1909
24	v Yorkshire II	Bridlington	1909
29	v Staffordshire	Stoke	1909
29	v Yorkshire II	Saltaire	1947

HIGHEST INDIVIDUAL SCORES

219	CL Tipper	v Herefordshire	Nantwich	2009
203	JA Duffy	v Shropshire	Nantwich	2013
202	DN Leech	v Northumberland	Jesmond	2007
192	RMO Cooke	v Yorkshire II	Castleford	1971
191	WM Goodwin	v Berkshire	Finchampstead	2013
183	RG Hignett	v Cornwall	Alderley Edge	2002
179	HW Hodgson	v Denbighshire	Wrexham	1930
177*	JJ Hitchmough	v Wales	Neston	1989
175*	RAL Moore	v Cambridgeshire	Wisbech	2013
175	AJ Hall	v Wales	Abergavenny	2003
172	JA Duffy	v Berkshire	Finchampstead	2010
171	MR Currie	v Wiltshire	Salisbury	2000
169	LF Dixon	v Oxfordshire	Banbury	2010
164	K Sawas	v Herefordshire	Chester	2012
163*	FW Millett	v Warwickshire II	Neston	1958
162*	AJ Hall	v Devon	Chester	2007
162	A Vickery	v Staffordshire	Uttoxeter	1950
155*	C Rowe	v Wiltshire	Salisbury	2014

HIGHEST RUN AGGREGATES IN A SEASON

(over 700 runs)

885	SL Wood	12 matches	1971
824	JJ Hitchmough	9 matches	1989
761	ST Crawley	9 matches	1991
755	I Cockbain	9 matches	1992
743	I Cockbain	8 matches	1989
731	B Spendlove	6 matches	2009

MOST RUNS IN A CAREER

10545	JA Sutton	236 matches	(1959-86)
8496	I Cockbain	143 matches	(1984-2001)
8432	FW Millett	212 matches	(1949-73)
7795	NT O'Brien	192 matches	(1970-90)
4898	SL Wood	109 matches	(1965-79)
4897	RMO Cooke	111 matches	(1969-84)
4827	AJ Hall	77 matches	(1993-2011)
4432	RG Hignett	82 matches	(1992-2003)
4285	LN Jones	158 matches	(1910-38)

PARTNERSHIP RECORDS

1st 317 DN Leech (202) and WM Goodwin (154)
v Northumberland at Jesmond 2007
2nd 287* AJ Hall (162*) and DN Leech (119*)
v Devon at Chester 2007
3rd 209 BJ Spendlove (136) and JP Kettle (129*)
v Berkshire at Finchampstead 2010
4th 248 RG Hignett (183) and DN Leech (152*)
v Cornwall at Alderley Edge 2002
5th 271* JA Sutton(147*) and GC Hardstaff (143*)
v Shropshire at Northwich 1969
6th 179 WE Jones (134) and JP Hodgson (89)
v Durham at Oxton 1925
7th 170 LF Dixon (169) and AJ Hall (48)
v Oxfordshire at Banbury 2010
8th 199 JRG Seward (146*) and RJ Digman (92)
v Northumberland at Jesmond 1956
9th 127 G Bull (94) and AD Lord (47*)
v Staffordshire at Oxton 1948
10th 98 LN Jones (158) and TJ Bartley (6*)
v Staffordshire at Crewe Alex 1934

MOST WICKETS IN A SEASON

61	J Cook	10 matches	1921
59	DA Woods	7 matches	2013
55	HG Smoker	6 matches	1914
54	H Dean	10 matches	1922
53	J Cook	8 matches	1922
52	J Cook	8 matches	1920

BEST BOWLING IN A MATCH

15-65	HG Smoker	v Essex II	Birkenhead Pk	1914
14-72	H Wilson	v Lancashire II	New Brighton	1927
14-74	MJ Davis	v Lancashire II	Leigh	1961
14-91	TJ Bartley	v Denbighshire	Bowdon	1933

MOST WICKETS IN A CAREER:

435	JA Sutton	236 matches
341	LN Jones	158 matches
325	H Wilson	78 matches
300	FW Millett	212 matches

MOST DISMISSALS:

202	T Hodson	c 161 st 41	98 matches
197	S Bramhall	c 145 st 52	83 matches
168	JA Sutton		236 matches
162	LN Jones		158 matches
150	KF Holding	c 126 st 24	77 matches
148	NT O'Brien		192 matches
114	JK Pickup	c 83 st 31	55 matches
105	RMO Cooke		111 matches
105	MR Dawson	c 82 st 23	35 matches
101	I Cockbain		146 matches

Cheshire CCC all-time record stand

At Jesmond in 2007 Danny Leech (Oulton Park) and Warren Goodwin (Chester Boughton Hall) put together the best partnership for any wicket in the history of the County club. Opening the batting against Northumberland they accumulated a record stand of 317. Danny scored 202 and Warren 154.

Wilmslow

The Rectory Field, Wilmslow Leisure Centre, Broadway, Wilmslow SK9 1BU

THE LADIES are not quite so keen to follow their partners to the cricket in these more enlightened days, but beware if you are playing away against Wilmslow. The ground is dangerously close to some very nice shops and a trip to the cricket suddenly sounds rather more attractive to the females! While the opening batter toils away to put together a well-earned fifty, his beloved dents the credit card with her own half century with one simple flourishing sweep!

Wilmslow CC was established in 1946 and played its first competitive cricket the following year. Home has almost always been at Rectory Field, although the facilities are rather different from those that were available at the outset. Initially they shared the clubhouse with hockey players and footballers, but plans to develop a Leisure Centre and swimming pool forced the cricketers to find a temporary home. The Oakwood Farm site at Styal was a consideration, but eventually they opted for the rather bland Jim Evison Playing Fields, a council-owned ground with little character and a pitch with variable bounce. To compound the problem a rugby pitch formed part of the outfield. Inevitably this was a difficult time, but a hardcore of senior players and a fledgling youth section kept the club alive.

In recent years they have made steady progress and in 2014 were promoted from the Cheshire Alliance into the Cheshire League. After a consolidating season they were runaway champions of Division 3 in 2016 with a 43-point advantage over second placed Bunbury. In 2017 they finished a commendable fifth in Division 2.

Wilmslow Wayfarers

Oakwood Farm, Styal Road, Wilmslow SK9 4HP

AS THE NAME suggests, the club was originally a 'wayfaring' team, that is to say operating without a home ground, let alone a pavilion. The Wayfarers had a prosaic start in that, during the late summer of 1961, a group of schoolboys who played football and cricket together decided to form a cricket club. To decide what it should be called a match at the Carnival Fields in Wilmslow was arranged - Wanderers v Wayfarers - with the successful team to 'win' the name. In the event Wilmslow Wayfarers was founded. In the subsequent months, a committee was created and among its earliest tasks was to design a club badge. The preferred suggestion was forming a 'W' from three stumps and a bat. To this day the club's logo remains a black 'W' on a scarlet background.

Wayfarers' first season was 1962. To raise funds raffles were held and jumble sales organised. Not having a home ground the club relied on persuading established outfits to play host. The first games were against the David Lewis Colony, Mobberley Boys School, and Birtles CC, where cows were chased from the field before play. Each of these sides was surprisingly strong: David Lewis included former Lancashire League players; Mobberley fielded two sharp bowlers; while Birtles possessed a 'gun' batsman, 'farmer Vic'. Against Birtles the Wayfarers had a trick: win the toss and bat - for after tea Vic had to return home to milk the cows!

After a year's 'wayfaring', it was clear the club's survival depended on a home ground being found. As two of the boys had attended a preparatory school with its own cricket field, it was decided to approach the headmaster. Against expectations he agreed to let the fledgling club use the facilities, providing the players prepared the pitches and tidied the changing rooms afterwards. This was a crucial decision for Wayfarers, and one for which the then headmaster of Pownall Hall School, Oliver Pemberton, deserves eternal credit. Despite only being able to host visitors in the school holidays, the club enjoyed these facilities for several years, during which it was able to expand its membership and fixture list.

The next significant move came in 1969 when the opportunity arose for Wayfarers to secure a more permanent base at Cheadle Royal Hospital, Heald Green, where agreement was reached to

play indefinitely. A striking location, the ground was situated in front of the hospital; a grand grade II listed pile, built in the late 1840s in the Elizabethan style and set in 280 acres of mostly manicured gardens. The cricket field was impressive, with a large, flat surface that had been used for croquet and tennis from Victorian times. Moreover, unlike Pownall Hall, the ground had a pavilion; a charming mock-Tudor structure comprising two changing rooms either side of an arched recess that made it very 'old school'. Indeed, the whole cricketing experience was old school, with the interval seeing sandwiches and 'fancies' served al fresco while tea was served in china cups from a time-honoured urn.

The move to Cheadle Royal was a great success; not only in providing a memorable cricketing experience, but also, and more importantly, in securing a firm base from which to achieve league status. Indeed, not too many years after moving to Cheadle, instead of fielding one 'friendly' XI, Wayfarers boasted two Saturday league teams and a Sunday side that assembled an impressive fixture list, including Bowdon, Bramhall and Cheadle, and an Alderley Edge side skippered by Cheshire captain PAC 'Pat' Kelly. Further, as the club grew in size it also grew in stature, winning several league and cup trophies in the late 1970s.

However, as the decade closed, disaster struck; for in the winter of 1979-80 arsonists razed the Cheadle Royal pavilion. As the hospital declined Wayfarers' offer of help toward the rebuilding of the pavilion, stalemate ensued. The club played on at Cheadle Royal during the summer of 1980, but in straitened circumstances. Indeed, for 'pavilion' facilities the club could offer nothing more than a chestnut tree under whose branches teas as well as shelter could be taken. Cars became the changing rooms and the conveniences were au naturel!

Nevertheless, there was light at the end of the tunnel, for shortly after the fire Wayfarers learned a sports ground was being constructed in nearby Styal, principally for Wilmslow Hockey Club. As a Wayfarers' committee member knew a senior figure at the hockey club, a conversation developed as to whether the clubs might join forces, one benefit being the facilities could be used all year round. After this agreement was reached, Wayfarers joined Wilmslow Hockey Club in taking-up the lease on the Oakwood Farm Ground in 1981. Given that not only Wayfarers' prior pavilion had been destroyed by fire but the hockey club's too, together they formed the 'Phoenix' sports club.

In the decades since moving to Oakwood Farm, Wilmslow Wayfarers, the wider Phoenix club, and the sports grounds have all developed significantly. Wayfarers have continue to be successful, with all sides winning league championships in recent years (even without West Indies pace-man Franklyn Rose, who turned-up at nets one year!). Additionally, the Phoenix clubhouse has been regularly developed through, for example, the changing facilities having been significantly enlarged with the aid of a National Lottery award and major improvements made to the lounge, bar and kitchen areas. In February 2017 an extension to the main structure was completed and the ribbon was cut by Olympic hockey gold medallist Sam Quek. The grounds have also seen much development, particularly with the building of a floodlit all-weather facility. Regular users of this are the Wilmslow Lacrosse Club, which joined the Phoenix some years ago. As a result, the Phoenix now entertains the British National Lacrosse Championships as well as England Lacrosse training sessions. With the recent surfacing of the car park, drainage of the pitches and outlay on other equipment, the Phoenix has invested approaching £1.5 million at Oakwood Farm since 1981.

In sum, Wilmslow Wayfarers has come a long way since taking its first nomadic steps in the early 1960s. Founded by a group of schoolboys, and for some years forced to call a succession of grounds 'home', it has long since been the cricket arm of a large sports and social club.

I'm extremely grateful to John Hassard, one of the original '1961 footballing cricketers', for providing me with the bulk of the above lineage.

> The 1903 edition of Wisden carries Johnny Briggs' (b 1862, d 1902) obituary and reports he died at the hospital (it refers to it as the Cheadle Asylum) from a form of epilepsy. Briggs was the first bowler to take 100 Test wickets.

Winnington Park

Park Road, Winnington, Northwich CW8 4EB

THE STORY of Winnington Park CC is very closely associated with Brunner Mond (ICI). The co-founders, John Brunner, a businessman from Liverpool, and Ludwig Mond, a German Jew and gifted chemist, started their soda ash company in 1881. Housing and recreational facilities for their workforce followed and by 1890 a cricket pitch had been laid, surrounded by a cinder track for athletics and cycling.

The fast cycle track actually cuts in between two hulking oaks, and along the back stretch is sheltered by dense thicket. What could be more delightful than a meeting carried on under such natural advantages?

That description is a very far cry from the 2016 landscape.

In 1898 Sir John and Dr Mond cut the first sod for the construction of the new pavilion, which was to be shared by all the recreational groups. It was subsequently opened in 1901. It was a very grand building, offering excellent amenities and noted for its architectural splendour. The cost of the pavilion and concert hall exceeded £10700, a staggering amount of money at that time.

The pavilion bathing amenities were not only intended for use after sporting activities but were also available to the membership for everyday washing purposes since the company housing did not include bathrooms at the time. A bath at the club cost 2d including soap and a towel, but as the balance sheet reveals the annual income rarely exceeded £3, so perhaps it can be concluded that members retained a preference for the traditional tin-bath in front of the fire in the privacy of their own homes?

> **In the 1890s the club owned a heavy horse-drawn iron roller. So that damage to the pitch would be minimised, the horse's hooves were encased in specially-designed boots. The club often hired out the roller and horse-boots to other local clubs, but it was always a condition of hire that the boots should not be worn by a horse with larger hooves than the one employed at Winnington. On one occasion Northwich fell foul of this stipulation and had to make good the damage.**

The focal point of the pavilion was the billiard hall. Such was the popularity of the game at the time four tables were purchased at a cost of £200 each. (They are still in place today). The day-to-day responsibility of brushing and ironing the tables fell to the 'billiard marker', who also had to collect the table charges and had the unpleasant task of cleaning out the enamel spittoons which were used into the 1940s. The facilities in the billiard room included a bar and the work of the steward was so highly regarded that during WW1 the barman was assigned to munitions work so that he would not be called up for military service and could carry on his cellar duties!

> The inter-war period saw an increase in the employment of women in the general offices of the company and they demanded more recreational facilities. A Ladies' Cricket Section was formed and Kathleen Harrison brought prestige to the club by winning international and county honours at both hockey and cricket. Sadly, the upgraded sporting opportunities did not necessarily bring membership equality as the 1940 constitution was worded in such a way as to classify them as second class. 'Full membership was confined to the MALE employees over the age of 18'.

The excellence of the club's sports amenities gained further recognition in 1909 when the Cheshire County Cricket Club chose the ground as the venue for their match against Northumberland. Further Championship matches followed in 1911, 1913 and 1922.

In 1926 the Winnington workforce received an unsettling jolt with the news of the formation of Imperial Chemical Industries, of which Brunner Mond was to become part. The legacy of WW1, the general economic situation in the country and now the company takeover caused a good number of concerns for the well-being of the recreational club, but it was as ever popular.

The fields were kept in the best possible condition by head groundsman (1928-51) Fred Hyland, who also acted as cricket coach. The extraordinary thing about Fred Hyland was that before he came to Cheshire he had played first-class cricket for Hampshire, but only on one occasion and only

> 1929 The club was at the centre of an occurrence worthy of inclusion in Wisden. A tie is a rare result in cricket but against Bollington in 1929 Winnington Park forced a tie not only in the 1st XI fixture, but also in the 2nd XI match played on the same day at Bollington. As the cricket Secretary AHS Guthrie remarked in his report to the AGM: " This extraordinary coincidence has no parallel in Manchester and District Cricket".

very briefly in that particular match. He made his debut against Northamptonshire at Northampton on 11 June 1924, but after two overs when the home team had put only a single on the scoreboard it rained and no further play was possible in the three-day match. Did Fred field the ball? Was it the shortest first-class appearance in the history of the game!? He was certainly in good company as the Hampshire side was captained by Lord Lionel Tennyson and included Philip Mead, who scored a hundred (actually 153) first-class 100s.

In 1921 Winnington Park joined the Manchester Association, but it was not until 1960 that the competition was won, a feat that was repeated again in 1964 and 1965. This was a period of considerable success as the Northwich Knock-Out Cup was also secured in 1959, 1960, 1961 and 1963. In 1975 the Mid-Cheshire Knock-Out competition was won.

The fortunes of the club have fluctuated over the years, but the lovely old pavilion survives to this very day. If you have not seen cricket played here, add it to your basket of things to do.

> In 1989 the young cricketers of Winnington Park lifted the Harry Secombe Trophy when they won the national Under 15s championship. They defeated South Wiltshire in the final which was played at Basingstoke. A total of 850 clubs entered the competition. The award was made by Minister of Sport Colin Moynihan.

Winsford

Knights Grange Sports Complex, Grange Lane, Winsford CW7 2DL

MEMBERS ARE inclined to think the club was established in 1888 when the team was made up of Brunner Mond workers. They played in Dingle Lane, close to the former drill hall/picture house/bingo club. They, of course, may be right, but a newspaper report demonstrates a cricket team existed in the town some four decades earlier.

What is not in dispute is that Winsford CC moved to the Knights Grange Sports Complex, Grange Lane in 1991 to allow the council to build their new Wyvern House offices. Their current home was once a grange/farm belonging to the Cistercian Abbey of Vale Royal.

Tony Percival's book, *Cheshire Cricketers 1822-1996*, reveals Winsford player James Russell Marsden (b 1911, d 2003) played one game for Cheshire in 1947. The records show he scored 9 and 2 and pouched a catch.

Bell's Life in London and Sporting Chronicle was an English weekly sporting paper published as a pink broadsheet between 1822 and 1886. The edition dated 28 September 1845 reports on a match played when Knutsford Royal Albert entertained Over & Winsford.

These clubs played a game on Tuesday last, on the ground encircled by the racecourse at Knutsford. The day was finer than any that had preceded it for a number of weeks, and could not have been fortunately selected had the prophetic finger of the astrologer pointed to the date in the calendar. The ground was in prime condition, and the playing spirited, scientific, indeed par excellence. At the termination of the game the players and their friends adjourned to Mr Taylor's, the Angel Hotel, where a sumptuous dinner was provided, such a one that would have silenced the complaints of the most fastidious, ably got up under the supervision of Miss Taylor, the daughter of the worthy host, whose ingenuity is invariably restless, on such occasions, to devise new dainties for her epicurean friends. The dessert was such that cannot be obtained in any other county. About forty sat down; Mr James Miller of the Albert Club, presided, supported on his right by Mr Carter of Tatton Park and on his left by Mr Stephenson of Knutsford. Mr vice-chair was ably filled by Mr Blackwell, of Over. The proceedings were characterised by the upmost good feeling unanimity, and throughout considerable cordiality prevailed. Toasts, sentiments, and songs followed each other in quick succession, and the company separated at a timely hour, highly gratified with the unusual good feeling manifested, being something more than is displayed on ordinary occasions. Among the toasts we call the following: - "The Queen," three times three; "The Queen Dowager," three times three; "Prince Albert, the Prince of Wales, and the rest of the royal family," three times three; "Prosperity to the Over & Winsford Club, and success and happiness to its members," three times three, and boisterous cheering; "Lord de Tabley, Wilbraham Egerton Esq, and the other honorary members of the club;" "the magistrates and members for the county;" "the chairman and vice-chairman;" "the clergy," & c., with vivas.

The newspaper provides a full scorecard of the two innings match. Over & Winsford 83 and 23, Knutsford 36 and 73-7. Knutsford winning with three wickets 'to go over'.

Wirral

Thornton Common Road, Clatterbridge CH63 0LT

NO ONE HAS ever suggested that Wirral CC are the strongest side in the county, but in April 2014 they could justifiably claim to be the best known - worldwide! The circumstances which brought about their global fame came about in the second phase of their early-season league match against Haslington. Having dismissed their opponents for a modest 108 and feeling confident of securing a win, they were dismissed for 3! The first ten Wirral batsmen were all dismissed for a duck. The last batsman, Connor Hodson, managed a single and the other two runs were leg byes. Wirral captain Pete Clewes said: "It was just a freak performance. "We bowled well. We fielded well. We bowled them out for 108, and we were feeling perfectly confident when we went into bat, but for some reason we all just batted atrociously. It was extraordinary." The star bowler for Haslington was 17- year-old Sandbach College student Ben Istead, who had bowling figures of 6-1.

The result prompted a global flurry of social media activity and wide coverage in the national press. With their newly-acquired fame the players joined in the tweeting. They asked former England internationals Michael Vaughan, Andrew Flintoff, Phil Tufnell and David Lloyd for some coaching, adding the hashtag #weneedit#3allout. They also asked Piers Morgan whether he would like to play, to which the former talk show host replied: "Sorry lads, my form's too good."

The club was formed in 1957 and played its first game in 1958. Arthur Davis, the current President, was one of the founder members. Games were played at Hooton before the move to Clatterbridge in 1968. The facility is shared with the rugby section.

Wistaston

The Brittles at the Eric Swan Sports Ground, Church Lane, Wistaston CW2 8EZ

LEAFY WISTASTON is situated between Nantwich and Crewe. The cricket club plays its matches at the local sports ground, which is overseen by the 'not-for-profit' Wistaston Sports & Leisure Association.

It was set up in 1997 and is charged by its constitution to provide, develop and maintain recreational facilities for the benefit of the residents and to encourage community-wide participation with a particular emphasis on the youth of the village. The cricket club plays its part by offering matches for all age groups, starting with the Under 9s, and also has both a girls' and ladies' team. The female team were the Division 2 champions in 2017. Alison Smith was the star performer.

The Brittles' pavilion was built in 1999 and extended in 2015. The ribbon cutting for the enlarged building was undertaken by the then MP for Crewe and Nantwich, Edward Timpson, who at the time held the post of Minister of State for Children & Families.

Most Cheshire cricket clubs have been in existence for well over a century, but signage on the front of the scorebox announces Wistaston Village was established as recently as 1980. The tower of St Mary the Virgin peeps over the top of the modern houses behind the car park and the school sits adjacent to the pavilion, otherwise it is surrounded by mature trees and open countryside.

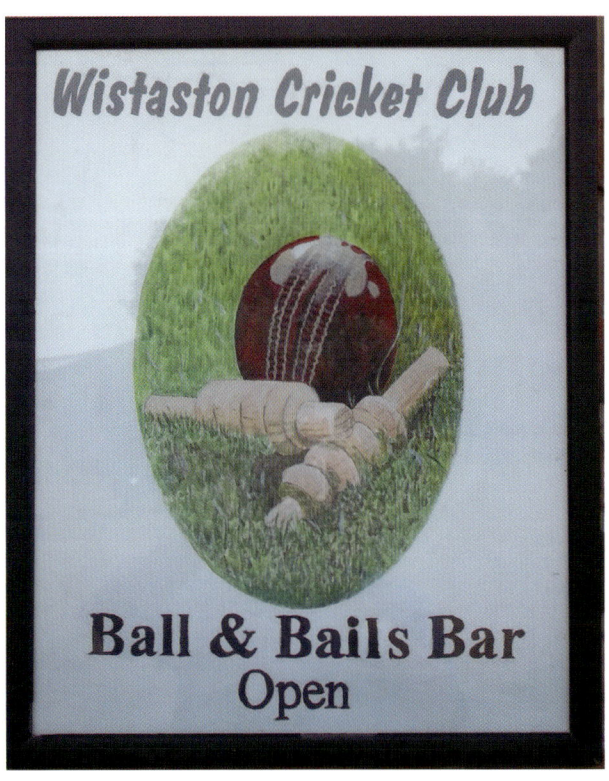

Fundamental to all the cricketing activity here is the Jobbins family. Kevin, a former player, is the hard-working Chairman and groundsman as well as a league panel umpire. His wife Pauline oversees all the excellent catering, and son Chris has been churning out the runs for a good few years.

While the players have their tea an option for the spectators is a pleasant stroll through the woodland trail directly opposite the pavilion.

Woodford

Moor Lane, Woodford SK7 1PW

UNFORTUNATELY, OFFICIAL records prior to 1923 cannot be traced, but a newspaper cutting dated May 1895, mentions the club:

For a powerful eleven in the game of cricket, one would not readily look to the little quiet village of Woodford, between Wilmslow and Poynton, but it is a fact nevertheless.

Another cutting the same year reports a game between Woodford and Prestbury, but its founding year is taken to be 1893. To celebrate their centenary a week of cricket was organised in July 1993. Not unnaturally a Woodford Select XI played in most of the fixtures, but the final one, intriguingly, involved a Piccadilly Radio XI v Rugby League XI.

1935 - A local resident, Mr Elias Holland, very generously leased a field on Moor Lane to the club. The pavilion from the original ground behind the 'Thieves Neck' (Davenport Arms) was uprooted, re-sited and survived until 1971. It is reported that the players regularly walked around the dressing room on the benches and the table to avoid contact with the lethal splintered floor!

1959 - Not many of the 1st XI got the chance to bat, for, in that glorious summer, the opening partnership of Peter Hilmer and Alec Maguire scored over 2450 runs between them in a season which did not start until mid-May and finished at the end of August.

1964 - Steve Smith made his debut as a 13-year-old and topped the first team batting averages when he was 15. A talented all-round sportsman, he went on to captain England at Rugby Union and play for the British Lions.

2017 - Clearly a club with ambition as the experienced Paul Sperring was recruited from Cheadle to lead the side to new pastures.

> Ken Jones contributed massively to the club. He has the distinction of being the longest-serving captain in the club's history; firstly in 1951 and then again from 1953–1961. He was also the Secretary 1952-54 and Chairman 1967-72. He was a very stylish batsman, a friendly and caring man and a true gentleman.

Woodley

High Lane, Woodley SK6 1AZ

DIDSBURY BORN Derek Quinn, a guitarist with the popular Manchester pop group Freddie & the Dreamers, was a Woodley cricketer, and for a good few years raised a Showbiz XI to play the club in the 1970s. He was a very enthusiastic cricketer, indeed a good all-round sportsman. Vitally he also had a good network of contacts. Karl Green, the bass guitarist in Herman's Hermits, and Rick Rothwell, the drummer from Wayne Fontana & the Mindbenders, were in his squad of players and on one occasion comedian Bernard Manning was also in the team. He teased Woodley members that he had heard there were plans to bomb the pavilion but told them he couldn't see the point!

field was acquired by Woodley Cricket & Hockey Club, which formed in 1967. It was not until 1991 that the hockey section moved on and the cricketers became the sole occupants.

A good number of the railway players stayed on, notably Brian Phillipson and Eddie Crompton, and there was some early success for the newly-badged club as the first division of the High Peak League was secured in 1968 under the captaincy of Mike Fielding. By 1974 they had joined the Derbyshire & Cheshire competition.

Every club has its loyal servants and star players and Woodley is no exception. Bert Simpson had been involved from the old railways days, and when

Bernard Manning taking a swipe at Woodley CC

Cricket has been played at High Lane since 1924 and for the first forty-odd years it was the sports ground of railway employees. When the Gorton Tank locomotive works closed in the 1960s the

he died in 2001 he had completed fifty-five years of membership as a player, groundsman and bar steward. Bert's son, Denis, was also a keen member and a talented all-round sportsman. Lloyd and

Sheila Hayes, the parents of Tony Hayes, a former 1st XI skipper, are two other long-serving members. Lloyd, a former player and club umpire, will clock-up his half century with the club in 2018 and is now the President. And how many sandwiches has his renowned tea-lady wife prepared over the decades? Harry Blackhurst was another stalwart. His ashes were buried at the ground and a boundary bench is dedicated to him.

Without doubt father and son, Ernie and Steve Jones, have written themselves into Woodley CC history. Over the years they played together at 1st, 2nd and Over 40s level and on the opening day of the 1993 season as a pair they bowled out Stockport Sunday School. Ernie snapped up 7-15 and Steve 3-26. Woodley 102-8 dec. Stockport SS 83. Steve netted at Old Trafford with the Neville brothers and Ronnie Irani but preferred to enjoy his cricket at his local club rather than try his luck elsewhere. He still holds the club record, set in July 1993, for the best bowling performance, 19-13-14-9, against Compstall.

Gordon Foy, the club secretary for 20 odd years in the 1970-90s, persuaded Ernie to join the club in 1968 and he is still there. Along with Lloyd Hayes and John Northover, he was one of three Woodley members to be honoured by the Derbyshire & Cheshire League in 2002 as one of fifty who had made a meritorious contribution to local cricket. The George Mullaney trophy was engraved with all those names to coincide with the league's golden anniversary celebrations.

Ernie has a vivid recall of tales from the Isle of Man tours and some lovely stories of his playing days at High Lane. He mischievously told me about the day he was persuaded to bowl Bernard Manning a fast bouncer, albeit a wide one. The shell-shocked batsman, fearing for his life, shouted down the pitch: "How would you like a fortnight's holiday at my expense? I'm sure you'd like it in Beirut!"

If you call in at the ground there is a good chance you will meet the secretary, John Yates, and bar chairman Gary Pickin, who both seem to spend as much time at the club as they do at home!

**England hath played at many a game and ever her toy was a ball;
The meadow game with the beautiful name is King and Lord of them all.**

Taken from the Davenham CC Centenary brochure 1885-1985

CHESHIRE PYRAMID

(based on end of 2017 season placing - Cheshire-based clubs playing outside the formal pyramid are excluded)

01 Chester Boughton Hall
02 Nantwich
03 Alderley Edge
04 Toft
05 Neston
06 Timperley
07 Didsbury
08 Bramhall
09 Grappenhall
10 Cheadle
11 Hyde
12 Bowdon
13 Oulton Park
14 Marple
15 Widnes
16 Bollington
17 Macclesfield
18 Davenham
19 Upton
20 Urmston
21 Oxton
22 Sale
23 Warrington
24 Weaverham
25 Barrow
26 Stockport
27 Alvanley
28 Romiley
29 Brooklands
30 Lindow
31 Northwich
32 Mobberley
33 Christleton
34 Tattenhall
35 Bredbury St Marks
36 Cheadle Hulme
37 Runcorn
38 Hale Barns
39 Stockport Georgians
40 Disley
41 Haslington
42 Congleton
43 Port Sunlight
44 Ashton-on-Mersey
45 Lymm Oughtrington Park
46 Barnton
47 Middlewich
48 Irby
49 Kingsley

50 Prestbury
51 Woodford
52 Poynton
53 Wilmslow
54 Oakmere
55 Ashley
56 Winnington Park
57 Stockport Trinity
58 Chelford
59 Heaton Mersey
60 Bunbury
61 Stretton
62 Maritime
63 Langley
64 Wilmslow Wayfarers
65 Cholmondeley
66 Chester County Officers
67 Appleton
68 Cheadle Hulme Ladybridge
69 Aston
70 Wirral
71 Over Peover
72 Wistaston Village
73 Holmes Chapel
74 Old Parkonians
75 Audlem
76 Westminster Park
77 Knutsford
78 Tranmere Victoria
79 Pott Shrigley
80 Winsford
81 Glazebury
82 Trafford MV
83 Frodsham
84 Bowdon Vale
85 Styal
86 Saughall
87 Heaton Mersey Village
88 Malpas
89 Kerridge
90 Mossley
91 Mellor
92 Hartford
93 Rostherne
94 The Groves
95 Bromborough
96 Burton
97 Europa Exiles

The 14 England cricketers born in the historic county of Cheshire are:

	birthplace	died
Agnew, Jonathan P	Macclesfield (4.4.1960)	
Allott, Paul JW	Altrincham (14.9.1956)	
Botham, Ian T	Heswall (24.11.1955)	
Bromley-Davenport, Hugh R	Siddington (18.8.1870)	London (23.5.1954)
Hopwood, John L (Len)	Hyde (30.10.1903)	Denton (15.6.1985)
Howard, Nigel D	Hyde (18.5.1925)	Isle of Man (31.5.1979)
Morris, John E	Crewe (1.4.1964)	
Oldfield, Norman	Dukinfield ((5.5.1911)	Blackpool (19.4.1996)
Ridgway, Fred	Stockport (10.8.1923)	Maidstone (26.9.2015)
Royle, Vernon PFA	Brooklands (29.1.1854)	Stanmore (21.5.1929)
Schultz, Sandford S	Birkenhead (29.8.1857)	London (18.12.1937)
Tremlett, Maurice F	Stockport (5.7.1923)	Southampton (30.7.1984)
Wilkinson, Len L	Northwich (5.11.1916)	Barrow (3.9.2002)
Wood, Reggie	Woodchurch (7.3.1860)	Sydney, Australia (6.1.1915)

Latchford and Warrington, although now within Cheshire, were historically part of Lancashire. Recognising the 1974 boundary changes, arguably the three following entries could now be added to the list:

Dewes, John G	Latchford (11.10.1926)	Bath (12.5.2015)
Duckworth, George	Warrington (9.5.1901)	Warrington (5.1.1966)
Fairbrother, Neil H	Warrington (9.9.1963)	

Grateful thanks

For the sake of factual accuracy and depth of interest I have endeavoured to research as comprehensively as was practical and I have endeavoured to consult as widely as I possibly could. I have spoken with hundreds of people, regrettably, far too many to identify individually, but I am extremely grateful for their energetic oral responses and enthusiastic written contributions; for their patience in tolerating and answering my unending list of questions and my seemingly impossible requests.

When I sometimes found I had the odd bad session batting on a sticky uncovered track, I was extremely grateful for encouraging words of support that re-focussed my concentration.

The material identified in the bibliography is a recommended source of information for those who wish to learn significantly more about a particular club. Again, I am extremely grateful to those who kindly loaned me their treasured books.

I must also thank those friends and acquaintances who kindly sent me some excellent photographs.

Finally, I fear that family and (without doubt) domestic duties have been neglected during this protracted innings, and so I am everlasting indebted to the long-suffering Penny, the million-dollar wife.

Geoff Wellsteed

Although *Pavilions in Splendour* is exclusively about Cheshire, its production has been very much an international effort. When Geoff and I originally spoke about the idea for the book I knew he was someone who was diligent and persistent in his research and would produce a great publication similar to *Inns & Outs* about cricketing pub signs, which he wrote with Anthony Collis. With his meticulous research and encyclopaedic knowledge of Cheshire grounds, not to mention his friends and contacts, there could not have been anyone better to write this book.

I would like to pay tribute to the vast numbers of people who have contributed their thoughts, historical research and pictures. I would also like to thank those who have contributed forewords so willingly: Paul Allott, Neil Fairbrother and Bob Barber, the latter from his home in Geneva! The book has been typeset in Bulgaria by Andy Searle, who has played on many of the grounds and it was a very nostalgic piece of work for him to assemble the pages and artwork. The book was printed in India and thanks go to Hari and all at Parksons Graphics for their help and skill in producing such a tremendous publication. For the design of the cover I can claim some credit for the idea. It was put into graphic form so well by Jane Mantel from Kreativ Ltd in Sale. Ken Grime from Max Books has undertaken the proofreading and thanks go to him for his attention to detail and encouragement. Thanks also to Peter Wynne-Thomas for drawing the map of Cheshire with all the grounds marked on. Also, I would like to thank the 107 people who have had enough faith in the project to be subscribers. I hope you enjoy the book and maybe it will encourage you to visit some of the beautiful cricket grounds in Cheshire.

Rev Malcolm Lorimer, Max Books

Bibliography

Alvanley CC - centenary brochure 1884-1984
Appleton CC - The History of the Lyons Lane Cricket Ground 1908-1976, published 2014
Ashley CC - a history 1888-1988
Barnton CC centenary brochure 1880-1980
Birkenhead Park by Jean McInnes, 1984
Birkenhead Park CC 1846-1996 by Chris Elston
Birkenhead St Marys CC - 125 Not Out (1878-2003)
Bowdon, A fifty years record. Published 1906
Bowdon CC - Paul Allot Benefit brochure 1990
Bramhall CC - 100 Not Out, centenary year 1986
Bramhall CC - 125th Anniversary booklet 1886-2011 by Richard Cragg
Bredbury St Marks CC - A celebration of 100 years 1913-2013 by Steve Amison & Geoff Mountford
Brooklands Sports Club Centenary 1883-1983
Caldy CC - an outline history 1921-81
Cheadle CC centenary 1887-1987
Cheadle CC - 150 Not Out by Andrew Taylor & Paul Sperring. Published 2013
Cheadle Hulme CC - centenary brochure 1881-1981
Cheshire County League handbooks 1975-2015 - Compiled and edited by Mike Talbot-Butler
Chester Boughton Hall - a century at Boughton Hall 1873-1973
Cholmondeley CC - notes prepared by MJ Bourne, 1986
Cricketer magazine - various
Cricketer preferred - estate workers at Lyme Park 1898-1946
Davenham CC - over a century 1885-1985
Davenham CC - a celebration of 125 years of cricket 1885-2010
Dukinfield CC Centenary brochure 1970
Eaton Park CC - notes compiled by Chris Elston, 1999
Elworth CC - the history of by Allan Littlemore, 2001
Flowery Field - sesquicentennial brochure 1838-1988
Grappenhall CC - the history of the club 1881-1981 by TFG Taylor
Grappenhall CC - the first 125 years (1881-2006) by Gerald Hudd
Hale Barns CC - 25th anniversary brochure 1972
Hazel Grove CC - 50th Anniversary dinner brochure in 2008
Heaton Mersey Cricket, Tennis & Lacrosse Club 1879-1979
High Lane CC - centenary cricket festival 1985
Hyde CC - 'Station your fielders down by the shed' by Lee Brown, 2000
Irby CC - scrapbook belonging to Roy Thomas
Lancashire cricket at the top - Vernon Addison & Brian Bearshaw
League Cricket Review magazine - various
Lymm CC - following on, OPCC 1884-1989 by SA McIntosh
Macclesfield CC - the history 1847-1974
Manchester & District Cricket Association Centenary 1892-1992
Mobberley CC - a history 1876-1976 by Peter Chapman
Mobberley CC - 131 Not Out (1876-2007) by Peter Chapman
Nantwich CC - 150th anniversary brochure 1848-1998
Neston CC - fifty years of cricket by JH Gilling, 1947
Neston CC - over 100 years of cricket at Parkgate 1895-1998
New Brighton - Battleground, Rake Lane 1856-2006, Malcolm Barber
Newton CC centenary brochure 1912-2012
North Staffordshire & South Cheshire 50th Anniversary - fifty years on by Tony Loffill, 2014
Northwich - The Development of Aspects of Physical Recreation in the Late 19th & early 20th Centuries by S Joseph, 1982
Northwich CC - copies of minutes 1867-1892

Oakmere CC - 40th anniversary brochure 1954-94
Oughtrington Park CC - 1st XI records 1946-55
Oughtrington Park 1884-1984 recollections and history by HB Whitelegg & CJ Schofield
Oxton CC 1875-1975
Over Peover CC - a history by Jill McKeown
Oxton CC 1875-1975
Parkfield Liscard CC - the club that rose from the ashes 1907-2007
Poynton Sports Club centenary 1885-1985
Pott Shrigley CC - 75th anniversary brochure for 1994
Pott Shrigley CC - Gone To Pott by Derrick Brooke, 2001
Saddleworth League history - Over The Hill By Way Of Highmoor by Phil Taylor
Sandbach CC - centenary year 1986
Stalybridge CC centenary brochure 1979
Stockport Georgians CC - 75th anniversary 1923-1998 by Stephen Barrow
Tattenhall CC - One Hundred Not Out by Dave Wilson, 1989
Timperley Cricket & Lawn Tennis Club 1877 -1952
Toft Jubilee Year 1928-1978
Toft CC - The Road To Lord's, 1989
Upton CC - 100 years of cricket 1901-2001
Urmston Cricket & Lawn Tennis Club 1846-1996
Wallasey CC centenary brochure 1864-1964 by Harold Wolfe, 1964
Wallasey CC 150 years' brochure 1864-2014
Warrington CC - the origins and its development from 1852-1902 - An essay in part-fulfilment of an M.Ed degree by DJ Eccles, 1986
Warrington CC - 150th anniversary 2001 by Alan Bolton
Weaverham CC 1883-1983
Widnes CC - 150 not out (1865-2015)
Winnington Park Sports Club - 100 Years Of Recreation 1890-1990 by Paul Lavell
Woodford CC centenary brochure 1893-1993

The Cricketer magazine cover of August 1970. You'll recognise Brian Close, but the fielder is Richard Cragg (see Bramhall entry) when he was playing for Cambridge University.

Pavilions in Splendour subscribers

The author and publishers would like to gratefully acknowledge the support of the following subscribers to *Pavilions In Splendour*

No.	Subscriber	Town/Cricket Club
1	Robert Sproston	Nantwich C.C.
2	John Bygate	Grappenhall C.C.
3	Gavin Wolfenden	Congleton
4	Tony DeWeever	Didsbury C.C.
5	Bob Floyd	Davenham C.C.
6	Steve Mobley	Hazel Grove
7	Nigel Muirhead	Toft C.C.
8	Mark Turner	Oxton/Birkenhead School
9	John Lofthouse	Hyde C.C.
10	Jez Lamb	Upton C.C.
11	Garry Cash	Marple C.C.
12	Steve Bottomley	Bowdon
13	Brian Boys	Warrington C.C.
14	Nigel Shone	Malpas
15	David Madden	Brooklands C.C.
16	Garry Hambleton	Cheadle Hulme C.C. (formerly Compstall C.C.)
17	Trevor Bailey	Stockport Georgians C.C.
18	Ben Murray	Stockport Georgians C.C.
19	Stuart Anderson	Sale
20	Gary Bland	Port Sunlight C.C.
21	Alan W.R. Smith	Compstall C.C.
22	Richard W. Leng	Compstall C.C.
23	Karl Bamford	Elworth C.C.
24	David Humpage	Heaton Mersey C.C
25	Tony Percival	
26	Stewart Coates	Stockport Trinity C.C.
27	Terry Dandy	Christleton C.C.
28	Roger Ollier	Kingsley
29	Chris Lees	Marple C.C.
30	Peter A. Hall	Heswall
31	Patrick Hutchinson	Oakmere C.C.
32	Neil Kerrison	New Brighton C.C. & Tunbridge Wells C.C.
33	James Law	Chester Boughton Hall C.C.
34	Mike Dunn	Alder C.C.
35	Simon Griffiths	Macclesfield C.C.
36	David W. Sharp	Alderley Edge C.C.
37	Jeremy Scholes	Flowery Field C.C.
38	Jeff Tenner	Toft C.C.
39	Jim Rafferty	Hartford C.C.

40	John Prew	Hartford C.C.
41	P.N.E. Chapman	Mobberley C.C.
42	Ian Buttress	Warrington C.C.
43	Graham Beckett	Davenham C.C.
44	David B. Young	Bowdon C.C.
45	J.F. Williams	President, Lindow C.C.
46	Richard Cragg	Bramhall C.C.
47	Keith Seddon	Heaton Mersey Village C.C.
48	Tony Debenham	Ipswich
49	Malcolm Butcher	Broadbottom C.C.
50	Stuart Hirst	Oxton C.C.
51	Alistair Law	Oxton C.C.
52	Bill Greenwood OBE	Standish, Wigan
53	Tony Hutton	Leeds
54	Brian Gresty	Chester Boughton Hall C.C.
55	John Bone	Hartford
56	Simon Hancock	Barnton Cricket Club
57	Holmes Chapel Cricket Club	
58	John Hassard	Wilmslow Wayfarers C.C.
59	Mrs R.F. Ramsbottom	Oulton Park C.C.
60	John Howarth	Cheadle Hulme C.C.
61	Chris Davies	Parkfield Liscard C.C.
62	Neville Barker	President, Hazel Grove C.C
63	Mike Talbot-Butler BEM & Wyn Talbot-Butler	Northwich C.C.
64	Peter Davies	Holmes Chapel
65	Christopher William Elston	Birkenhead Park C.C.
66	David Buckley	Elworth C.C.
67	Phil Prince	Disley
68	Brian Middleton	Styal C.C.
69	Ged Kinsey	President, Irby C.C.
70	Duncan Anderson	Didsbury C.C.
71	Hesketh Hughes	Neston C.C.
72	James David Lawley	Amblecote C.C.
73	Peter W. Parrish	Chirk C.C.
74	K.G.H. Cooke	Tattenhall, Cholmondeley, Boughton Hall & Cheshire Gents C.C.
75	Simon & Andrew Wilgose	Bunbury C.C.
76	Chris Fleet	Chester Boughton Hall C.C.
77	Ian Brown	Cheadle Hulme C.C.
78	Derrick Hastings	Cheshire C.C.C.
79	George Roberts	New Brighton Cricket and Bowling Club
80	Glyn Roberts	Sale C.C.
81	Neil H Carver	Caldy C.C.
82	Paul Ryan	St. Mary's C.C., Birkenhead Park
83	David Williams	Ruthin
84	Michael Kitton	Congleton C.C.
85	Andy Brow	Berkshire C.C.C.
86	Tony Sheldon	Cheshire C.C.C.
87	Gary Fisher	Timperley C.C.

88	Peter Crutchley	West Kirby
89	Chris & Liz Weston	West Kirby
90	Tony Elwood	Toft C.C.
91	David Smith	Liverpool
92	Jeremy King	Runcorn C.C.
93	Jeff Langham JP	Barnton C.C.
94	Don Hurst	Neston C.C.
95	Stewart Conway	Runcorn C.C.
96	Robin Faulkner	Widnes C.C.
97	Jerry Alderson	League Umpire
98	Steve Amison	Bredbury St Marks C.C.
99	Lancashire C.C.C. Library	
100	Melbourne C.C., Australia	
101	Ralph Trippner	Fleet
102	Chris Bone	Lymm C.C. & Rostherne C.C.
103	Iain Taylor	Old Wimbledonians C.C.
104	Widnes Cricket Club	
105	Gary Zimmer	Middlewich
106	David Kelly	
107	Herbert Wright	Alderley Edge C.C.

By Easter 2018 Gary Dixon (4323) will have completed an incredible 150 marathons. Here he is running the 2011 London Marathon in full cricket gear along with Cheshire umpire, Darrin Clark. Gary has played for Birkenhead Park, Oxton and Cheshire Over 50s, but primarily for Upton. In 642 Upton matches he has scored 13998 runs, taken 971 wickets and pouched 187 catches.

Glorious bygone days

The magnificent board at Stockport CC

Birkenhead Park 1858

Neston CC playing at Parkgate in 1895. The wicketkeeper is Dr Speechly the club founder. (Ian Boumphrey collection)

Bromborough Pool CC (now the home of Maritime CC) in 1905

Tranmere Victoria CC was developed in the garden of splendid Arudy Towers – a 1910 photo (Ian Boumphrey collection)

AN 'Monkey' Hornby's final resting place at St Mary's Church, Acton, Nantwich. Hornby, a true Corinthian, played cricket and rugby for England. He was a fine athlete, an excellent boxer and an outstanding horseman. He played football for Blackburn Rovers. For much of his life he lived in the Nantwich area. He died in 1925.

The attractive black leather-bound 1889 membership card for Crewe CC was heavily embossed in gold lettering. Railway enthusiasts will want to know the locomotive is number 2187 named 'Penrith Beacon'. That year Crewe had fixtures against Runcorn, Wolverhampton, Wistaston, Bunbury, Nantwich, Calveley, Porthill, Audlem, Lawton and Davenham.

Pavilions in Splendour

Lindow CC team photograph taken at the opening of the pavilion in 1929

Cheadle Royal Hospital ground – photo courtesy of Cheadle Civic Society

When football meets cricket – Timperley 1961

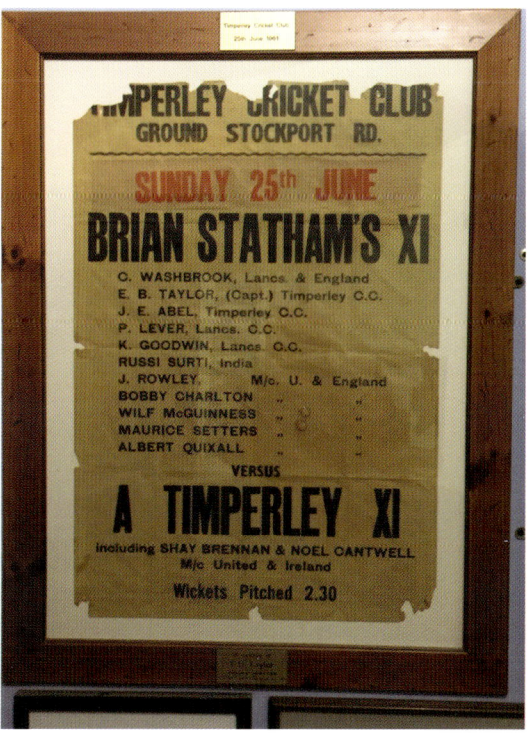

247